LAW FOR SOCIAL WORKERS

Cavendish
Publishing
Limited

London • Sydney

LAW FOR SOCIAL WORKERS

Dr Stephen Hardy, LLB, PhD
Lecturer in Law,
University of Salford

Martin Hannibal, BA, LLM
Barrister-at-Law and Senior Lecturer in Law,
Staffordshire University

Cavendish
Publishing
Limited

London • Sydney

First published in Great Britain 1997 by Cavendish Publishing Limited, The Glass House, Wharton Street, London WC1X 9PX.

Telephone: 0171-278 8000 Facsimile: 0171-278 8080

E-mail: info@cavendishpublishing.com

Visit our Home Page on http://www.cavendishpublishing.com

Hannibal, Martin

Law for social workers

1. Social service – Law and legislation – Great Britain

2. Public welfare – Law and legislation – Great Britain

I. Title II. Hardy, Stephen

344.4'1'031'3

ISBN 1 85941 359 5

Printed and bound in Great Britain by
Biddles Ltd, Guildford and King's Lynn

We dedicate this book to our parents Miriam and Tom (Hardy) and Geoffrey and Joyce (Hannibal).

Preface

We have no doubt that this book will be used in different ways and at different levels depending on the reader. In fact, that was the whole purpose behind writing this text in the manner set out below. However, whilst the contents list will provide some indication about the general structure and vast subject areas herein, let us outline the following, which we hope will assist your usage of this book:

- Each chapter seeks to identify a major area of social work practice.

- It is divided into six parts, in order to group relevant areas of practice together for the convenience of the reader and practitioner alike.

- Within each chapter the reader will find the relevant law and practice in the area being considered.

- The philosophy behind the book seeks to simplify the law and provide a practical approach as to how the law operates in the context of social work law and practice.

- The appropriate legal procedures and skills are highlighted and explained at various points in the book, in order for readers to familiarise themselves with the law in action in the pertinent theme.

- At the end of each chapter we include practice points and further reading to assist the reader should they wish to pursue the issues discussed further.

- This text is written largely for those students seeking to obtain their professional qualification in social work, namely DipSW course students, as well as practising social workers, post-graduate students, lawyers and those with an interest in social policy and issues and social welfare, generally.

Overall it is hoped that this text will not only serve as a useful course companion for those undertaking DipSW and the like courses, but will also become a vital resource post-qualification or at the very least during their placement.

We wish our readers every success in their studies and practice.

Acknowledgments

According to the Central Council for the Education and Training of Social Workers (CCETSW), there are over some 100,000 people employed in the UK as social workers. This book is about the legal knowledge which any competent social worker ought to have, or at least be aware of. Due to both the breadth of the topic and the complex interface between legal and social work practice, many social work and legal practitioners have given advice on various topics in this book. It from these experiences and professional insights which we believe the book has benefited from immensely. Though that will be for our readers to decide.

In particular, we would like to acknowledge the contributions of Micheal Barden, Rhiannon Billingley, Jeff Edwards, Dianne Gibbons, Doug Hearn, Ian Jones, John McCarthy, Peter Robinson and Ian Whitehurst, as well as our other colleagues and students at Salford and Staffordshire respectively and the multitudinous number of social workers and training officers from Social Services Departments across the UK who gave advice on various aspects of this book, or even encouraged us to write it.

We remain indebted to the assistance and patience of our publisher, in particular Jo Reddy and Cathy West. As ever, the support of our families, Louise and Merryn, Matt, Nick and Charlie has allowed both this project to exist and be completed.

The law is as stated at 1 August 1997.

The same law applies to both Scotland and Northern Ireland, unless otherwise stated.

Stephen Hardy, Martin Hannibal
Salford
1 August 1997

Contents

PART III

CRIMINAL PROCEDURE AND JUSTICE IN SOCIAL WORK   141

PART IV

SOCIAL WORKERS IN THE COURTS   225

PART V

SOCIAL WELFARE AND SOCIAL WORK   277

PART VI

THE MODERN SOCIAL WORKER: LEGAL ADVICE AND ACTION 345

Table of Cases

Table of Statutes

Table of Statutory Instruments

Table of European Legislation

PART I

SOCIAL WORKERS
AND THE LEGAL SYSTEM

1   A social worker's legal competence

With more scandals and enactment after enactment now surrounding the daily activities of the social workers, certainly more so now than before does the social worker and student of social work alike need to grasp the nettle and learn the law. Since the late 1980s the role of social workers has never come under such a tide of scrutiny by both the courts, government and not least of all its clients, than in any previous era. That trend of bureaucracy and regulation has increased in the 1990s with further legislation. Furthermore, since the 1997 General Election returned a Labour government to Westminster a deluge of new legislation is expected. Had a Conservative government been re-elected, its White paper entitled: 'Social Services: Achievement and Challenge', of March 1997, highlighted an expectant extension of privatisation within social services departments across the UK. Whether a 'new' Labour government will adopt or modify these ideas will soon be seen.

However, forthcoming proposals on: the reform of the regulation of care services; a Charter of service standards for long-term care; the appointment of independent visitors for children in care; and further rights for carers, as the Labour Party promised in their Election Manifesto, are awaited. Notably, in the May 1997 Queen's Speech the new government has pledged to reform the NHS; opt-in to the EU Social Chapter; assist the homeless in its Local Authority (Capital Receipts) Bill which will amend the Housing Act 1989; lower the age threshold for the capacity for crime and set up a National Youth Justice Board to review the youth justice system, all measures which will impact on the working lives of social workers across the UK. Furthermore, two additional Bills were announced – Social Security Modernisation Bill (seeking to simplify procedures and the appeals adjudications system) and, Immigration Appeals (Amendment) Bill (granting a new right of appeal against deportation on national security grounds).

Whatever, the legislative outcomes are, clearly social services will once more be subjected to reform. In any event, the importance of law is therefore clearly established, if not shown to be even more relevant with the increased dismissal of social services staff due to scandals or breach of statutory duties. For these reasons, the Central Council for the Education and Training of Social Workers' (CCETSW) foresightedness has required since 1988 the improved 'legal competence' of both newly-trained and existing social work practitioners. Social workers must not forget that his or her legal competence could save their client – or even themselves. With this in mind Part I of this text will provide a general introduction to the law as it applies to social work.

An introduction to law and the legal system

The English legal system is a complex web of statutes, case law and procedures. Applying these to social work practise provides an even more complicated situation than one at first might imagine. Since not only do social workers have to grapple with the law and apply it to their client's cases and in the interests of their client, be it a child or adult, but they also have to manage their lawyer and the courts in the process. Coupled with the differences between legal and social work practises, training and the rules of evidence and archaic legal procedures, such a situation is tantamount to many problems and difficulties, particularly for the novice and inexperienced practitioner. Consequently, due to these observations, in this book for very good reasons, we will first and foremost examine the courts and legal system.

Whilst the above gives a general overview, for social workers in Scotland and Northern Ireland both the courts structure and legal system are slightly different. In addition, some of the legislation, albeit either identical or modified for national law purposes, is titled differently. For example, the Children Act 1989 exists in Scottish law as the Children (Scotland) Act 1995. In particular, the Scottish system will be considered briefly in the Chapter 2.

Due to the complex nature of social work law, we have chosen to divide this text into six parts, covering the major legal areas of social work practise, each Part being subdivided into the salient legal provisions:

- **PART I**: deals with the legal system and the social workers in it. Consequently, Chapters 1 and 2 cover a social worker's legal competence; social worker's within the local government structure; the court system and procedures.

- **PART II**: covers children and families in social work practice. In Chapters 3–4, the provisions of the Children Act 1989 and issues of guardianship, fostering and child abuse are discussed. Whilst Chapters 4 and 8 set out the law relating to the family, covering domestic violence, divorce and child support. In Chapters 5 and 9, the duties of the local authority with regard to children and families are considered, discussing community care, costs, carers, mental health, special needs provision and education.

- **PART III**: surveys criminal procedure and justice. This commences in Chapter 10 with a detailed analysis of the criminal justice system, including youth and juvenile justice, offences, prosecution, trial and sentencing, appeals and criminal injuries, and closes in Chapter 16 with an examination of police powers.

- **PART IV**: follows up from Part I by providing social workers with further insights into the courts, by examining in Chapter 17 the social worker's role in investigating, reporting and being a witness. Chapter 22 discusses prisoner's rights, for when social workers and probation officers have to face the inevitable – the conviction of their clients.

- **PART V**: demonstrates the interface between social welfare and social work. Chapter 23 highlights the importance of anti-oppressive practice in examining discrimination law and equal opportunities. It also provides an employment law first aid kit for social work practitioners. Chapter 24 covers the most controversial topic of immigration law, showing social workers the importance of nationality, EU citizenship and asylum. The other daily important issues of most social work clients, in terms of housing, homelessness, poverty, money advice and social security are detailed in Chapter 25.

- **PART VI**: the last of the text, concludes by examining the impact and the importance of the law to modern social work practice. How the modern social worker gives advice and takes action will be critically evaluated. In order to equip the 'legally competent' social worker into the next millennium specimen forms, useful addresses and a select bibliography are also given.

Having taken this journey through law, it is hoped that social workers are not only more legally competent and confident, but are ready to take action, hopefully in a more productive and professional manner.

Law-making in the UK

The British constitutional settlement following the Bill of Rights 1688 gives sovereignty to Parliament to make law. 'Sovereignty' loosely meaning in a constitutional context, the power to make and unmake laws. In modern day parlance, this means that the elected Parliament at Westminster has the power to enact and repeal Acts of Parliament. Hence, the British government of the day, that is the largest party in the House of Commons with a majority forms the Government and with a democratic mandate (that is, it has the highest number of MPs returned after a General Election) can pass the laws it sees fit to pass, or has promised in its election manifesto.

The process for passing Acts of Parliament, or Bills as they are called before reaching the Statute Book, is rooted in Medieval tradition and is a course of debates, known as Readings, followed by scrutiny by a Committee, then a vote and the Queen's assent, as set out below:

The legislative process

PARLIAMENTARY BILL

FIRST READING

The Clerk of the House reads out a short title of the Bill and the sponsoring Minister names a day for the Second Reading. The Bill is printed and published.

SECOND READING

The sponsoring Minister explains the Bill, its purpose and the policy behind it, and moves that the Bill is read for the second time. Amendments can be tabled.

COMMITTEE STAGE

The Bill is scrutinised clause by clause by the committee. Amendments can be tabled.

REPORT STAGE

The Bill is formerly reported to the House by the Chair of the Committee. The House debates the amendments made in the Committee Stage.

THIRD READING

The Bill is debated in its final form. The third reading is usually a formality before the Bill is passed in the House of Lords.

HOUSE OF LORDS

The Bill goes through the legislative stages in the House of Lords.

ROYAL ASSENT

The Bill becomes an Act and is law.

- **First reading**: Here the Bill, that is the proposed legislation, is introduced and a date and time is announced when its first debate will take place.

- **Second reading**: At this stage the Bill is debated and MPs and parties views are expressed.

- **Committee stage**: Following a second reading, the Bill is sent to the appropriate Select (departmental) or Standing (special ones set up for specific issues on an ad hoc basis) Committee, where evidence will be taken from experts on the issue and Civil Servants and Ministers responsible. In Committee the proposed Bill is scrutinised in detail. Also, as this stage amendments can be tabled and voted upon, in order to modify the Bill.

- **Report stage**: Following the requisite Committee's hearings, the MPs who make up the Committee draft and Report, which is tabled to the House in which the legislation began.

- **Third reading**: At last the Bill and the proposed tabled amendments are debated and voted upon in the House.

- **Other House/final vote**: Each Bill then goes to the other House to repeat the above mentioned procedure, before returning to its original House for a final vote.

- **Royal assent**: Having been passed by both Houses of Parliament, every Bill is then sent to the Monarch for Royal Assent. Whilst constitutionally this has become a customary formality of rubber stamping, in fact, the Monarch can withhold her consent to a Bill.

Clearly Parliament is made up of two Houses: the Commons, and the Lords (also known as Peers). The House of Commons is composed of 681 elected Members of Parliament (MPs), who divide to make up the Government, including the Prime Minister, other Ministers of State. And the Opposition, which includes the official Leader of the Opposition and Shadow spokespersons (these are the Minister's counterpart in opposition) and the other opposition parties and their leaders. In contrast, the Lords consists of unelected peers, most of whom are hereditary (that is they have a right to sit in the Lords by right of birth being offspring of a noble family, a so-called Barony, or are members of the Royal family) and the others being life peers (that is given the right to sit in the Lords until their death). The latter group are normally former politicians or senior public figures, such as leaders of industry or trade unionists. Also, in the Lords are the Archbishops (York and Canterbury), 26 Bishops of the Church of England, and the Law Lords, them being the most senior judges in the UK and the highest court in the UK jurisdiction (this will be discussed in detail below). In the absence of the Monarch, the Lord Chancellor chairs the business in the House of Lords, he sits on the Woolsack which is positioned in front of the throne, and the Speaker (the Queen's official representative to the Commoners) governs the debates in the House of Commons. Whilst the Lord Chancellor is appointed by the government, that position being a cabinet post as well as the most senior judge and highest judicial office holder in the UK, the Speaker is selected by the Commoners on a rota basis, with the Speakership alternating between the government and opposition for tenures of office.

In terms of the legislative process outlined above, both Houses of Parliament are involved in the enactment of legislation. Normally, this process commences in the House of Commons, but legislation can be initiated in the House of Lords. However, this usually depends upon the type of Bill concerned. Generally, there are three types of Bills:

- Public Bill

  This is a Bill normally presented, if not supported, by the government.

- Private Bill

  As the title suggests concerns a matter not of huge public concern, but one which requires enactment. For example, the building of a road, or any other form of large planning permission, or the granting of a licence. It is these which usually are commenced in the House of Lords.

- Private Member's Bill

  These are Bills presented by individual MPs on issues which they wish to become law. These are often derived from pressure groups. For example, the Abortion Act 1967 began life as a Private Member's Bill (sponsored by the then Sir David Steel MP).

Apart from enactment of legislation, the courts within the UK also make law. This is known as the common law, or case law. Although the courts cannot challenge Acts of Parliament, they can interpret and enforce them. This will be explored throughout this text, and the courts and the role of the judiciary will be discussed in some detail later in Chapter 2.

Primary and secondary legislation

Statutes, or Acts of Parliament, are sub-divided into two types:

- Primary legislation

  This division refers to Acts of Parliament, as enacted through the process described above.

- Secondary (delegated) legislation

  Delegated legislation alludes to the powers under which a Minister, the

Secretary of State responsible, or his civil servants (acting in *alter ego*) can draft and enact, under the powers given to the relevant Minister under the requisite Act, secondary/delegated legislation (the term 'delegated' best defining what the process as described is, a delegation from the Act to the Minister responsible to make law as she or he sees fit). Secondary or delegated legislation are normally referred to in legal terms as statutory instruments. Of these statutory instruments, the Minister can decide whether they shall be enacted as Regulations (the most common form), Rules, Circulars, Codes of Practice or Guidance.

Even though the Minister holds the power under various Acts of Parliament (ie primary legislation) to enact statutory instruments, all of these have to be published and the persons affected consulted, as well as placed before Parliament, subject to various procedures for discussion (for example, the prayer of annulment procedure), before they become law. The Statutory Instruments Act 1947 makes this extra Parliamentary process very clear, so as to deter Ministers from passing hostile legislation quickly and without public knowledge. Clearly with the context of social work, social workers Circulars, Codes of Practice and Guidance promise to be the most influential and used by them in practice. Due to the enormity of the framework of British government and society the usage of statutory instruments law-making has increasingly become common within the UK.

Social workers in Europe and the pervasive nature of EC Law

With the UK's entry into the then European Economic Community (EEC), now European Union (EU), in 1973 UK law has been superseded by Community law. This means that social workers should be aware of not only domestic laws, but also EU laws. For instance, within the Cecchini Report of 1988 it was noted that a 'social Europe' not only included worker's rights, but also social issues such as unemployment, young people and poverty. Thus, social measures tackling social welfare and other areas of social work practise are expected.

The EU Commission's 1994 White Paper on EU Social Policy, which to all intents and purposes is a policy document establishing a framework for action by the EU in areas of employment, family life, disability, health and old age, sets out as a clear marker that the EU intends to influence the change of social welfare and the respective domestic systems of all the 15 Member States. Such a transnational approach therefore seeks only to inform UK social workers, amongst others, that the character of their practise and the nature of their work is likely to be affected by the legislating of EU-wide minimum standards for social work practise.

Social workers should also be aware that these ambitions could potentially be curtailed by the usage of the subsidiarity principle, whereby social care could be deemed an area which is best dealt with at domestic level rather than the EU. Yet with EU convergence in many related social areas, also with mixed economies in most EU social markets and EU concerns about issues of child care, paedophilia, mental health and disability, then to hold back this tide of interest could be a remarkable task in itself. In any event, a 'new' Labour government is unlikely to deter such ambitions with its pro-EU stance in most other areas.

This has become even more likely since 1988, when the EU Commission sought to recruit four social workers from each of the 15 Member States to consider what social measures could be legislated in these areas. The future therefore not only holds change for UK social workers within Britain, but also at EU level. This ever pervasive EU dimension has in recent years become even more clearer in UK social work practise and is obviously more likely to increase in the near future. So long as social workers are aware of this, then they have nothing to fear in the short term. Given this pervasive force of Community law's, coupled with the Treaty on European Union Preamble's, formerly the Treaty of Rome 1957, commitment to tackling unemployment and achieving equal opportunities in access to education and training in 'new' social dialogues, UK social workers must now also be aware of the EU's regulatory framework in their day-to-day activities.

Relevant statutory bodies

Confidentiality is certainly amongst the most important ethics which a social worker can have. However, ensuring this confidentiality is a hard task when faced by the multi-agencies/organisations nature of social work. Within the daily life of social workers, they can encounter several statutory bodies. For instance and of importance to social workers is the Social Services Inspectorate (the SSI). The SSI is in fact a branch of the Department of Health. It is headed by the Chief Inspector of Social Services, of which there are two, one based in London and the other in Manchester. Its function is to carry out inspections of local authority services, in order to monitor their quality, arrangements and management of services. Whilst the SSI has no legal force itself, following an SSI visit the Secretary of State could order an inquiry from any of the concerns raised by the SSI's inspection visit.

However, more likely contact will be with education authorities, the courts, the Crown Prosecution Service, probation, the benefits agency, housing corporations and other statutory bodies.

Non-statutory bodies

As with statutory bodies, there also exists some relevant non-statutory bodies. These so-called 'non-statutory bodies' refer to bodies whose nature is to provide a service, but one not based under a Statute. Examples of these include many charities and voluntary organisation, such as CABx, the NSPCC or Relate. Within social work, much contact will be had with these non-statutory bodies of various types.

Social workers within the local government structure

In most town halls throughout the UK, commonly the largest department or most expenditure allocated is that of social services. Many statutes, including the Chronically Sick and Disabled Persons Act 1970 and the Children Act 1989, cover the many duties and services which a local authority has and should provide in respect of the persons within its geographical area. Generally, these powers cover services for children, accommodation, day and after care facilities and support for families. Obviously, these powers fall alongside the general duties to educate, house where necessary, public health and consumer issues which a local council holds.

In bygone days, particularly under the NHS Reorganisation Act 1973 and National Health Service Act 1977 and when the Departments of Health and Social Security were a combined government department, social services and health co-run, or at least jointly organised, social services provision in local authorities' areas. Though, the Local Authority Social Services Act 1970 clearly established that the welfare role lay within the remit of social services. Hence, this explains the modern day origin of social services duties. Following the Local Government Act 1972, the coalition between health and social services was simplified with the welfare provision very much in mind. Eventually, after many incremental moves to separate health from social services during the 1980s, especially with the splitting of the joint huge government department into two separate departments, the National Health Service and Community Care Act 1990, effectively split the two functions with social services now formally taking overall control for welfare services. The affects of this and the modern-day role of local authority social services departments is discussed throughout this book, but the general modern-day powers, functions and framework will be addressed in detail in Chapters 4 and 9.

Practice points

All social workers should:

- be aware of the importance of law in relation to their professional responsibilities;

- recognise and uphold the rule of law;

- understand the legislative process;

- understand the difference in process and effect between primary and delegated legislation;

- be aware of the supremacy of Community law and its impact on social work practice within the UK.

Further reading

Munday, B and Ely, P, *Social Care in Europe*, 1996, Hertfordshire: Prentice Hall.

'Social Services: Achievement and Challenge', Department of Health and Welsh Office, March 1997, CM 3588, HMSO.

'The Law Report', Paper 4.1, CCETSW, 1990.

Wadham, J (ed), *Your rights, The Liberty Guide*, 6th edn, 1997, London: Wadham and Munday.

2   Social workers and the courts

In this chapter we examine the UK's courts system. Whilst there are many ways to resolve a dispute, the courts is the most common forum. However, the courts are not the only legal institution for dispute resolution; within the UK there exists a vast framework of tribunals.

The history of the courts is a fascinating one, deeply rooted in the development of British democracy empowering Parliament as the law-maker and making every British citizen equal before the law. Whilst history has played its part in developing the modern courts, for the purposes of this text, we are concerned with the courts system as it exists in the 1990s and how they affect social work.

UK courts

By the term 'UK' courts, we are referring to those which exist in England/Wales, Scotland and Northern Ireland. Hence, we are discussing three separate legal systems which are governed by one Parliament.

In England and Wales, since the Norman Conquest of 1066, the UK legal system and its component courts have undergone radical restructuring from *Curia Regis*, the King's courts, to ecclesiastical courts, to Common Pleas, to the Court of Chancery, to the reforms of the 1970s and 1980s, to the courts today. Divided between civil and criminal jurisdictions, the British courts system makes up a complex web of several rules, jurisdictions and judges. The following diagrams simplify the current system:

The principal courts exercising civil jurisdiction

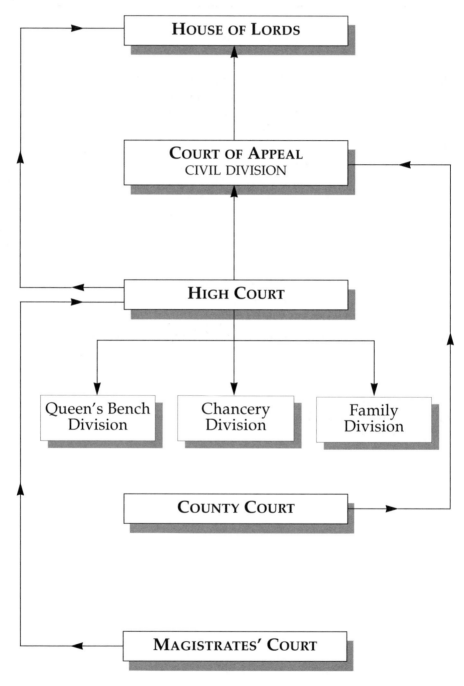

The principal courts exercising criminal jurisdiction

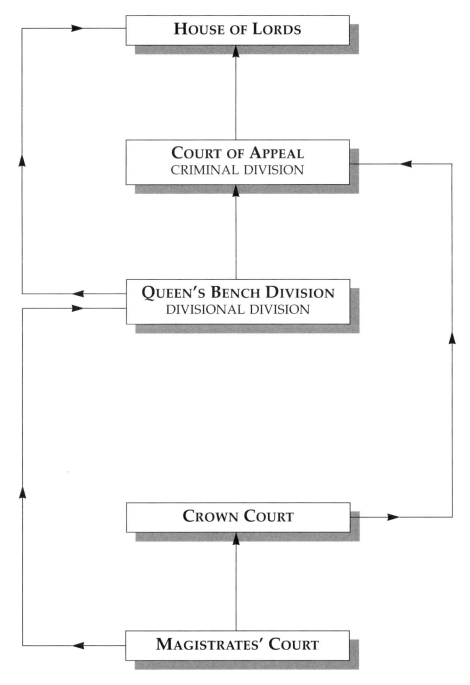

Social work in Scotland is governed by a separate legal regime of courts and procedures. Much influenced by Roman law, the Scottish legal system maintains different courts. For example, at first instance in the criminal courts a District Court or Sheriff's court replaces the English/Welsh magistrates' and Crown courts. As for civil matters, a sheriff's court replaces the Welsh/English counterpart – the county court. Whilst Scotland has its own appeal courts, either the Court of Session in civil matters, or the High Court of Justiciary in criminal proceedings, any further appeals lie to the House of Lords. The higher courts are based in Edinburgh. Consequently, the Scottish judiciary and legal profession are different to those in the Welsh/English jurisdiction. As are the prosecutors, who are known as 'procurators'. As elsewhere, the rule of evidence remain complex and technical. Under the Legal Aid (Scotland) Act 1986, the legal provisions are almost as identical as those in both England and Wales. Having established the basic differences between the systems, readers ought to be aware that such differences also cause some distinctions in certain legal provisions, relating to children and their hearings and in some other social care areas. Thus, is it good practice, as it is in the English and Welsh jurisdiction, for Scottish practitioners to consult each piece of relevant legislation carefully. As a consequence of having a separate legal system Scotland also has its own legislation for social services. For instance, see the Social Work (Scotland) Act 1968, the Mental Health (Scotland) Act 1984, the Local Government (Scotland) Act 1994, the Criminal Justice (Scotland) Act 1995, and the Children (Scotland) Act 1995. As for Northern Ireland, the courts system is the same as in England and Wales, except Northern Ireland has its own Appeal court from which appeal again lies to the House of Lords. Irrespective of these departures from the English/Welsh legal traditions, Community law supersedes their respective domestic laws, as it does in both England and Wales.

Civil and criminal law

Evidently, with the UK courts being divided into both civil and criminal courts, the law must also conveniently be packaged in that manner. In view of this dichotomy it makes sense to explain here the fundamental difference of these distinct paths which affect the whole process of British law:

- criminal law is primarily concerned with disputes between the state and individuals;

- in contrast, civil law relates to matters between individuals in society.

Such an historical distinction has emerged by accident rather than design, due to the various courts under which, through the centuries, various recurring legal issues have been dealt with in that particular forum. This division have survived centuries of legal reform. We will now examine those individual courts in detail.

Criminal procedure flow chart

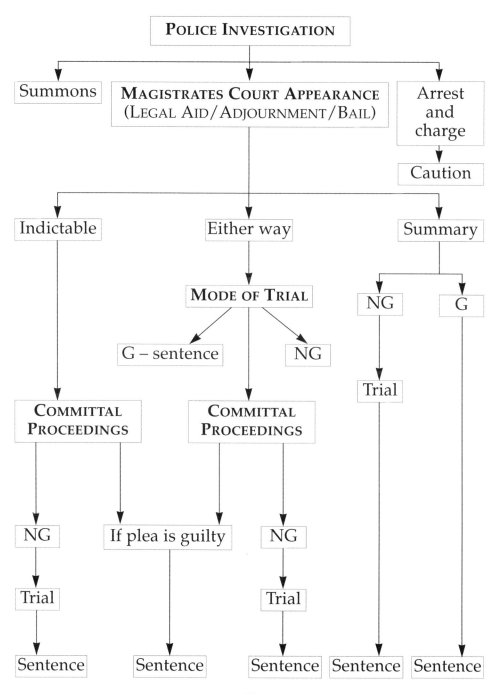

UK civil and criminal courts

These are divided, as set out below.

Criminal courts

These are primarily concerned with the prosecution of persons for criminal offences:

Magistrates' courts

These are the inferior criminal courts. They are supervised by legal qualified clerks and either lay or stipendiary magistrates. Formerly described as 'petty sessional' courts, they deal with the minor criminal offences, such as assaults, burglary and breach of the peace, as well as committal proceedings, sending the more serious offenders to Crown Court for trial.

A major part of the work of the magistrates' courts is to operate as youth courts dealing with juvenile justice. Appeals lie from the magistrates' courts to the Crown Court.

Crown Courts

Lord Beeching's Commission in 1966 set up the Assizes and Quarter Sessions courts, which, under the Courts Act 1971, became known as Crown Courts. In these courts, trial is by judge, who deals with legal questions, and a jury, 12 lay persons who consider the facts and determine whether the defendant is guilty or not guilty. These courts are supervised by either High Court, or normally circuit judges, or recorders/assistant recorders (part-time judges). Organised on circuits, six in the UK, Crown Courts deal with the serious criminal offences, such as murder, manslaughter, rape, serious assault, fraud, robbery and conspiracy, and so on. Appeals from the Crown Court on points of law lie to the High Court.

Civil courts

These are concerned with the resolution of disputes amongst complainant parties:

Magistrates' courts

Magistrates' courts, despite primarily having a criminal jurisdiction, have a civil remit. In particular, they have an extensive role in family and child law. Their powers include making financial orders or protecting the welfare of children. These are fully discussed in detail in Part II of this text. Magistrates also have civil duties in terms of enforcing the payment of rates, the collection of taxes and licensing and gaming registration. In civil matters, appeal lies from a magistrates' courts to the county or High Court.

County courts

County courts were set up under the County Courts Act 1846. Subsequently, the UK has been divided into districts, making up various local registries for dealing with civil disputes. Over 260 county courts currently exist within the UK.

Cases are heard by either a district or circuit judges, depending upon their nature and jurisdiction. The disputes heard range from contractual matters, to land disputes, to probate and family matters, and admiralty claims. Matters amounting to under less than the value of £50,000 are heard in county courts, with disputes of less than £3,000 being classified as small claims, denoting a special procedure where costs are not awarded against the loser. Appeals on civil matters over the value of £50,000 are heard in the High Court.

The High Court

Not peculiar to the UK system, but very distinct from other jurisdictions, the High Court has both a civil and criminal jurisdiction.

In civil matters, it hears cases to the value of £50,000 or above. In criminal matters it hears appeals against conviction or sentence. To assist this dual role, the High Court, part of the Supreme Court of England and Wales, is divided into three separate divisions:

- Queen's Bench Division (QBD)

  Considers claims in contract and tort and hears criminal appeals, as well as judicial review applications and proceedings. It has an Admiralty Court and Commercial Court to dispense with its business.

- Chancery Division (Ch)

  Considers matters about property, trusts, probate and business matters. The Vice Chancellor presides over this division.

- Family Division (Fam Div)

  Considers matrimonial and domestic causes, such as adoption, wardship and divorce. It is presided over by a President.

It should be noted that building and civil engineering matters are dealt with by the court in what is termed 'Official Referees' matters.

In the High Court, the first rank of senior judges, called High Court judges, who are appointed by the Monarch and knighted on appointment, hear cases and are referred to as Mr/Mrs Justice whomever. Appeals from the High Court to lie to the higher courts.

The Appeal Court

To simplify matters, appeals in the higher courts are divided between their respective divisions – civil or criminal.

In the Court of Appeal (Criminal Division), the Lord Chief Justice (LCJ), presently Lord Bingham, presides, accompanied by another two judges. Whilst in the Court of Appeal (Civil Division) is presided over by the Master of the Rolls (MR), currently Lord Woolf, who also sits with two other judges.

All appeals must be on grounds of law and are heard by three judges, all of whom are Lord Justices. Appeals lie, with leave, to the House of Lords or the European Court of Justice (ECJ). The Court of Appeal sits in the Royal Courts of Justice, The Strand, London.

House of Lords

The highest court in the UK is the House of Lords, which hears appeals from all the courts below, such as the Court of Appeal, the High Court and others, including the Northern Irish and Scottish courts.

All appeals are heard by at least three Law Lords, normally five, with each Law Lord expressing his opinion of the case. The House of Lords since 1833 also has an extra-jurisdiction, in so far as it is the Judicial Committee of the Privy Council, which hears appeals from former British colonies' courts.

Civil courts reform and Lord Woolf

Lord Woolf's Report, entitled 'Access to Justice', into persons access to civil justice (ie suing/other civil litigation) in its Final Report set out the following proposals:

- establish a fast track procedure for all cases up to £10,000;

- maximum legal costs for the fast track cases to be £2,500;

- alternative dispute resolution is to be enhanced, in order to encourage more co-operation between the parties to achieve settlements in civil litigation.

Tribunals

Since the 18th century, tribunals of some description have been in existence, either as an extra-judicial or quasi-judicial form of court. Following the Franks Report 1957, tribunals and enquiries have grown into many public spheres. Under the Tribunal and Inquiries Act 1958, as later amended in 1971 and 1992, a Council on Tribunals has been established to oversee the workings of these various tribunals, in terms of their composition, rules and purposes and remits. In contrast to courts, tribunals are free, and informal.

Within the UK, at present, there are over some 60 types of tribunals, ranging from issues about, *inter alia*, housing, criminal injuries, social security benefits, immigration, education and employment matters. In Chapter 25, we examine some of these tribunals in detail. At various points throughout this text, reference will be made to both the appropriate courts and tribunals applicable.

The law officers

Due to the historical events which have occurred in the English legal tradition, various law officers exists. The significance of these are set out below:

Lord Chancellor

The Lord Chancellor, the highest judge, a cabinet minister and Speaker in the House of Lords, holds responsibility for the administration of the courts, the supervision of legal aid and the making of judicial appointments within the UK legal system. Under the Courts and Legal Services Act 1990, in addition to his historical powers, the Lord Chancellor is responsible for legal education and conduct, the ombudsmen system and legal reform. In his roles, the Lord Chancellor is assisted by his Department, the Lord Chancellor's Department (LCD) which since the 1950s has grown in size into a large administrative department employing over 12,000 staff. Since 1992, the Lord Chancellor has also had a Parliamentary Secretary in the House of Commons, who is an MP of junior minister rank, to answer questions on his behalf. The current Lord Chancellor is Lord Irvine of Lairg QC, and his Parliamentary Secretary is Mr Geoff Hoon MP.

Attorney General

The Attorney General (AG) is the most senior law officer in the UK. The AG is both a cabinet minister, usually an MP, who represents the government, the Crown as it is officially termed in these proceedings, before the European Court of Human Rights in Strasbourg, and the International Court in the Hague, or more commonly in the High Court or above. The AG may either institute proceedings, or consent to the commencement of various cases in the public interest, as well as preventing trials from taking place at all. The AG is responsible for the Director of Public Prosecutions, the Crown prosecution Service (CPS), and the Serious Fraud Office (SFO). In his work, the AG is assisted by a deputy, the Solicitor General (SG), usually an MP or peer, and a legal secretariat. The current AG is John Morris QC MP and the SG is Lord Falconer QC.

Director of Public Prosecutions

The office of the Director of Public Prosecutions (DPP) has existed since 1879. The duties of the DPP are statutorily defined in the Prosecution of Offences Act 1985. The DPP must be a lawyer of 10 years' experience. The DPP is responsible for the day-to-day conduct of the CPS and the SFO, established in 1985 and 1987 respectively. The DPP may represent the Crown in appeals in the Court of Appeal or above. The current DPP is Mrs Barbara Mills QC.

Official Solicitor

Some social workers will already be familiar with this law officer, or at least are likely to encounter it sometime during their practice. The Official Solicitor (OS), like the DPP, must also be a lawyer of 10 years standing. Appointed under s 71 of the Courts and Legal Services Act 1990, they are responsible for: the application of habeas corpus and bail matters; representing wards of court in wardship proceedings; conducting litigation for children and mental patients; the administration of the intestate estates of deceased persons; and assisting the court as *amicus curiae*.

Home Secretary

Whilst the Home Secretary is usually seen as the cabinet minister responsible for law and order, in Law Officer's terms, the Secretary of State is also responsible for prisons and the reform of criminal law under the remit of the Criminal Law Revision Committee. It is also the Home Secretary who can recommend the exercise of the royal pardon by the Monarch, so as to quash a conviction or part of one.

The British judiciary

A remarkable characteristic of the British judiciary is that much of it, over 50,000 members of it, are lay people.

The laity

The laity plays a significant, but limited role in the British judiciary as: magistrates (ie lay magistrates); or as members of various tribunals.

As magistrates, they deal with 98% of criminal matters and other civil disputes, as discussed above. Established since 1361 under the Justices of the Peace Act, magistrates are unpaid and receive the letters patent 'JP' after their name. They can sit in magistrates' courts or with a judge in the Crown Court. They are appointed by the Crown under the supervision of the Lord Chancellor or the

Chancellor of the Duchy of Lancaster, for Lancashire, Greater Manchester and Merseyside, and local advisory committees. The only qualifications are that JPs reside within 15 miles of the court where appointed; of good standing; and are not a bankrupt.

As tribunals' members they are appointed regionally and sit in local tribunals. Again, they receive no payment, except travel expenses. Both magistrates and members of tribunals receive training and monitoring and are assisted by legally qualified clerks in the magistrates' courts and Chairpersons in the tribunals.

The professionals

Most of the British judiciary are appointed from the legal profession. They are therefore legally qualified and are often referred to as the 'professional' judiciary.

Of this professional judiciary, over 100 are stipendiary magistrates; chairmen/women of tribunals; circuit judges (10 years' standing, see Courts Act 1971); district judges (seven years standing); recorders/assistant recorders (part-time judges); or the higher ranking senior judiciary.

The higher or senior judiciary are recruited from the most experienced practitioners, usually QCs. As with all judges, they are appointed by the Lord Chancellor. Yet promotion from the High Court to a higher court is done so on the advice of the Prime Minister.

All judges hold office until their retirement at 70 years of age, unless they are removed for misconduct. The senior judges can be removed by petition of both Houses of Parliament on a motion of censure. They all undergo training and monitoring. Their training is governed by the Judicial Studies Board.

The UK legal profession

Unlike elsewhere in Europe and the United States of America, within the UK its legal profession, in other words its lawyers or legal services, are divided into two distinct branches: solicitors and barristers.

Solicitors

Established and regulated since 1605, solicitors make up the largest of the two branches within the UK legal profession. Governed by the Law Society, under the Solicitors Acts of 1843 and 1974. As general practitioners of law, solicitors can advise the public directly on a range of both criminal and civil matters. Though, in reality, most solicitors' firms now specialise. Today, though true to their historical roots, solicitors administer legal aid and can represent clients before the courts upto the Crown Court, subject to obtaining the requisite certification.

Barristers

Governed by the Bar Council and the Four Inns of Court (Gray's, Inner, Lincoln's and Middle), barristers have existed since medieval days. As the advocates of the UK legal profession, Barristers hold rights of audience before all the courts within the UK.

In terms of legal education, however, members of both branches of the UK legal profession must hold an academic qualification in law and have passed professional examinations, regulated by their respective professional bodies, and undertake continuing post-qualification professional education. With regard to quality of service, complaints about either solicitors or barristers can be made to their professional bodies or the legal services ombudsman.

Criticisms of the UK judiciary and legal profession

Social workers ought to be aware that many criticisms have been levied towards the UK legal profession and judiciary over the years, regarding their representativeness of society. These criticisms have concerned issues about the social background, gender and race inequality.

Various reports have shown that in both the profession and in particular, the judiciary, there are:

- too few women (only one female judge sits in the Court of Appeal and no higher);

- too few representatives from ethnic minorities are judges or senior members of the legal profession.

Clearly, both branches professional bodies, the Equal Opportunities Commission and the Commission for Racial Equality are concerned about this. Moreover, the Judicial Studies Board, which trains judges has sought in more recent years, under the directorship of Dyson J to undertake equal opportunities awareness and training. Whilst, many of the groups outlined feel under-represented, at least the issues are being raised and give rise to optimism in the future.

The 'ombudsman' system

An 'ombudsman' is in its simplest form a complaints body, or as its name translated form its Scandinavian origin notes 'a grievance man'. Following the Whyatt Report 1961, the first ombudsman was introduced within the UK. The Parliamentary Commissioner for Administration (PCA), under the PCA Act

1967, seeks to redress any 'maladministration' proven to have been suffered by members of the public. 'Maladministration' is defined as consisting of neglect, bias, delay, incompetence, arbitrariness, perversity and turpitude. Consequently, citizens who feel aggrieved by the actions of any government department can complain to their MP. Requesting that he or she passes their complaint onto the PCA for investigation. Having investigated the matter, the PCA will issue a Report and make recommendations, should any be necessary. Whilst the PCA cannot provide a direct remedy, he or she can recommend one.

Of importance to social work is the Health Services Commissioner (HSC), or 'ombudsman'. Formerly a role undertaken by the PCA, in 1993 this grievance body was separated from the work of the PCA and given its own office by an Act of Parliament (see the Health Services Commissioner Act 1993). Like the PCA, the HSC investigates into health service provision. Giving reports and making recommendations to the Department of Health. Furthermore, the local government ombudsman, who have existed since 1972 under the Local Government Act, seek to investigate complaints which concern local authorities' services, including social services. In contrast, to the PCA and HSC, members of the public can complain direct to the local government ombudsmen. Moreover, the local government ombudsmen system operates on a regional basis and eight in all exist in the UK. They deal with issues of housing and education, and important local issues.

However, in the 1990s, under a new regime of public management, several ombudsmen, relevant to various service provisions, have been introduced. For examples, *inter alia*, the legal services, building societies, prisons, pensions, banking and insurance ombudsmen. Clearly the advent of well-defined charters of service levels and quality of delivery, now requires various complaints and regulatory bodies. Hence, from its historical form, the ombudsman has become a system rather than a person, to whom the general public can turn when they have problems with the service they are using. Social workers ought to be aware of them and use them appropriately in the interests of their clients.

Community law

As already discussed in Chapter 1, the pervasive nature of EU law is ever grow-ing. As Lord Denning once described it: 'an ever-flowing tide.' This tide has been trickling away since 1957 under the then Treaty of Rome. Within this Treaty, now modified as the Treaty on European Union, laws are made which affect the UK, following its membership since 1973. To that end, Community law is supreme and prevails over UK law.

EU institutions

Under the Treaty of Rome 1957, which established the EU, four principal institutions were listed, they are:

The EU Commission

The Commission is the permanent officials of the EU, similar to the UK Civil Service, based in Brussels. It consists of 20 Commissioners, each a representative of a Member State (with the five major EU Member States having two rather than one). Sir Leon Brittan and Neil Kinnock are the UK Commissioners at present. Each Commissioner takes charge over an area of policy and the directorate general, department, responsible. Directorate generals range from external affairs, economic affairs, internal market, social affairs, agriculture, transport, fisheries to regional policy, energy, science, budgets and development. The role of the Commission is to draft legislation and enforce it, where they hold the powers to do so.

The EU Council

According to the Treaty, the Council shall consist of 'a representative of each Member State' responsible for the policy area being discussed. Hence, the composition of this institution varies according to which issue is being discussed, with the Ministers responsible from each Member State attending the discussion to put their country's view in the debate. For examples, when financial or economic matters are being discussed, the UK would send the Chancellor of the Exchequer, and for farming issues the UK Agriculture minister would attend. Member States also take it in turns to chair the Council meetings on a six monthly basis. This chairship is termed the 'Presidency' of the Council. This institution is assisted by a permanent secretariat of civil servants and advisers and a Committee of permanent representatives. The latter, known as COREPER, consists of each Member State's ambassador to the EU, who represent their countries in the EU on a daily basis.

The European Parliament

The European Parliament (EP) is the democratically elected organ of the EU. This institution is composed of elected Members of the European Parliament (MEPs). There are 624 in all, directly elected since 1979, from 15 Member States. MEPs sit in political groupings, like the UK Parliamentary but in an EU sense. The main EU political groupings in the EP are: the Socialist group (including UK Labour Party); the Christian Democrats (including the UK Conservative Party); the Liberal Democratic and Reformist group (including the UK Liberal Democrats); the Greens; the Rainbow Alliance group; the Fascists; the Radical

Left group, and other small groups. The EP has a legislative role with its various committees structure which can either approve or reject the EU Commission's and Council's proposals. It also debates important issues in its plenary sessions, one week per month, in either Strasbourg or Brussels.

The European Court of Justice

The European Court of Justice (ECJ), located in Luxembourg, heralds the legal institution of the EU. Composed of the Court of First Instance which hears competition cases and internal staff matters, and the court itself, its role is to interpret and uphold the Treaty. This judicial function includes ensuring that all Member States have properly implemented the law. In terms of enforcement, the ECJ is assisted by the Commission who initiates proceedings against violating Member States. There are 15 judges in all. The ECJ only gives one collegiate judgment upon which the ECJ has agreed. The ECJ is assisted by an independent rapporteur, an Advocate General who advises the ECJ and gives his opinion. The court either chooses to accept that opinion or not. Since 1957, the ECJ has developed a long case law, by which it is not bound in future cases. This unusual lack of precedence, in an English law context, makes the court both unpredictable as well as robust in its rulings.

Other institutions in the EU include the Court of Auditors, responsible for the EU's budget and accounting; the European Council, this is when the Heads of government, namely Prime Ministers or Presidents, of the Member States meet to discuss matters; the Economic and Social Committee is an advisory body to both the EU Commission and Council which represents business and the unions and issues opinions reports on various proposed legislation; and the Committee of the Regions, the newest of the institutions, represents regional and local bodies, such as councils, and again is an advisory body which issues reports on various issues and proposed legislation.

Clearly, the EU is a supranational body with a superstructure of multi-faceted institutions which have the task of policy-making and law-making within the EU. Obviously, this legislative competence includes social care and that is one area which is becoming critically evaluated and present and one where legislation at EU level is very much likely in the future, as already discussed above. Social workers, therefore, for two reasons, ought to have an understanding of the EU, namely: first, they ought to recognise the future importance of the EU and how they can lobby the institutions; and second and importantly, they should recognise that in legal terms, EU law overrides UK law.

The European Convention and Court of Human Rights

Outside the remit of Community, or EU law, lies an international human rights dimension under the UN's Universal Declaration of Human Rights, as well as at a European level, the 1950 European Convention on Human Rights (ECHR). Drafted in 1949, the ECHR covers the following, *inter alia*, fundamental human rights:

- the right to life;

- freedom from inhuman and degrading treatment;

- the right to liberty and security of person;

- the right to a fair and public hearing;

- the right to privacy;

- freedom of expression;

- the right to protest; and

- the right to marry and have a family.

Consequently, this Convention, of which the UK is a signatory, has had an immense impact on British law. In particular, as Chapter 22 will later discuss, the ECHR has had an enormous impact upon prisoners' rights, as well as police powers, within the UK.

At present the ECHR has not been incorporated into English law, despite many previous attempts by notable human rights campaigners, such as Lord Lester QC. However, the newly-elected UK government has recently confirmed that it intends to fully incorporate the ECHR into English law. Thus, ending the debate about its legal status and affirming the courts long held view that when English law is ambiguous, then the ECHR ought to be applied anyway (see *Derbyshire County Council* (1993) *The Times*, 19 February).

So important are these rights that social workers must be aware that clients might have recourse to the law in a human rights context, under the ECHR. Thus, social workers ought to be aware that the Commission of Human Rights, the filtering body which decides whether cases will be heard or not, and the European Court of Human Rights, in Strasbourg, seeks to enforce these human rights. The relevance of this will be developed at various, relevant points throughout the text.

Practice points

Social workers should:
- be able to recognise the system of law applicable to their practice (ie they should know which jurisidiction they are acting in, English/Welsh, Northern Irish or Scottish);

- familiarise themselves with the courts' structure in their respective jurisdiction;

- know the powers of the judges in each court within the system in which they operate;

- understand the relationships between the British and EU courts (including the European Court of Justice in Luxembourg and the European Court of Human Rights in Strasbourg);

- fully understand the procedures and types of cases heard by each court;

- be aware of the other complaints mechanisms outside the courts – which ombudsman or other regulatory body applies to the complaint concerned;

- be aware of the European Convention of Human Rights and understand how these rights might affect their practice and their clients and apply these rights where necessary, when in their own judgment a client's human rights have been violated.

Further reading

Clements, L, *European Human Rights – Taking a case under the Convention*, 1994, London: Sweet and Maxwell.

Craig, P and De Burca, G, *EC Law: Text, Cases and Materials*, 1995, Oxford: Oxford University Press.

Slapper, G and Kelly, D, *English Legal System*, 1997, London: Cavendish Publishing.

Smith, P and Bailey, S, *The Modern English Legal System*, 1996, London: Sweet and Maxwell.

Tillotson, J, *EC Law: Text, Cases and Materials*, 2nd edn, 1996, London: Cavendish Publishing.

PART II

SOCIAL WORK LAW:
CHILDREN AND FAMILIES IN PRACTICE

3   Children and the law

The care and protection of children is the most visible of a social worker's professional responsibilities. Even as we write this chapter, a cursory glance through the day's newspapers produces a range of dramatic headlines condemning yet again the professional competence of social workers in another case which has been subjected to the full glare of media exposure. Even the sober *Daily Telegraph* runs a headline proclaiming 'Social workers failed to stop killer' – the views of the tabloids are not worth recording. In the public's perception the latest incident is just another episode in a long catalogue of professional disasters to add to the names of Jasmine Beckford, Cleveland, Kimberley Carlile and many others, where the competence of social workers has been found to be wholly inadequate.

The media's concentration on the sensational means that the public only receive a snapshot of a social worker's responsibilities in child protection work. The thousands of successful outcomes and the years of hard work in child care are never considered because they don't make good newspaper copy or dramatic news items on television or radio.

Yet as all of us who work in the field of child care know only too well, that in your professional capacity you confront the full horrors of family life on a daily basis – the kind of horrors that most members of the public would never dare to contemplate even in their darkest moments. To use a well-known phrase, in these matters, a social worker has responsibility without power.

In combatting the evils of child abuse and consolidating the law and practice relating to the care of children generally, the Children Act 1989 represented a new start for social work practitioners, lawyers, parents, children and society as a whole. The Act is as comprehensive in the range of issues it seeks to address as it is voluminous. The Queen's Printers copy of the Act is 218 pages long, divided into 12 parts and has 15 schedules. This is without even considering the multitude of regulations, circulars and guidance that have been issued to simplify, clarify and explain the legislation.

Such is the significance of the Children Act 1989 in your professional life that we have devoted an entire section of the book to examine its most important provisions. As a result, we look at the provisions of the Act in the following way: this chapter is intended to explain the background of the legislation and introduce you to the important concepts. In Chapter 4 we look at the duties local authorities owe in relation to the provision of services under Part III of the Act and finally and perhaps most important of all, in Chapter 5 we deal with practice and procedure of children at risk.

Social workers and the Children Act 1989 – the legal framework

The Children Act 1989 received Royal Assent on 16 November 1989 and came into force on the 14 October 1991. It is the most comprehensive piece of legislation Parliament has enacted about children and forms the basis of the modern law relating to the care and welfare of children.

The Act provides a radical innovation to the legal regulation of the care and upbringing of children in that:

- it consolidates and simplifies existing legislation to produce a more practical and consistent body of law;

- it consolidated the substantive law and procedure relating to private individuals with the responsibilities of public authorities, most notably, social service agencies;

- it unifies public and private law child care remedies including the public law remedies of supervision orders; care orders and emergency protection orders and private child care law remedies of residence orders; contact orders; prohibited steps orders;

- the court system and procedure dealing with child care cases is streamlined and simplified;

- when making decisions under the Act the court is required to consider that the child's welfare is of paramount importance;

- the Act explicitly recognises that children are best looked after by both parents playing a full part in the family and introduces the concept of 'parental responsibility'.

In relation to the role of public authorities and children, the Act provides that:

- intervention by 'public agencies' including the courts, the social services agency and the NSPCC should occur only where it is in the best interests of the child and where possible without recourse to legal proceedings;

- local authorities' have a duty to give support to children and their families;

- local authorities' have a duty to return a child looked after them to the family unless this is against his or her interests;

- local authorities' have a duty to ensure contact with the child's parents whenever the child is being looked after by the local authority away from the parental home.

- co-operation between relevant public agencies is encouraged where necessary to promote and protect the welfare of children.

The background to the Children Act 1989

Parliament and the courts have long recognised the importance the law plays in providing protection for children against abuse and exploitation and more positively, as a means of promoting their welfare. Over a century ago the Guardianship of Infants Act 1886 required the court, when deciding custody cases, to have regard, in part, to the child's interests, as well as those of the parents. A wider range of concerns were reflected in the passing of the 1989 Act in that the legislation attempted to provide a new legal basis for state intervention in family life; the restoration of public confidence in child care practise and procedure; an increased recognition of children's rights and wishes in relation to their upbringing, the so-called 'Gillick' principle, following the landmark decision in *Gillick v West Norfolk and Wisbech Area Health Authority* [1986] AC 112, and finally a recognition of the importance of family life in providing for and promoting the child's welfare. Each of these finds a voice in the substantive provisions of the Children Act 1989.

Essential concepts under the Children Act 1989

To apply the law in its practical context, you need to be aware of the Act's three central concepts – the paramount importance of the child's welfare; the principle of non-intervention and the avoidance of delay in the Children Act 1989 proceedings. Each will be considered in detail below.

The child's welfare

Section 1 sets out the principles which guide the court when determining any question about the upbringing of a child or the administration of the child's income or property – the Act requires that 'the child's welfare shall be of paramount importance'.

The key words to the operation of s 1 are 'welfare' and 'paramount'. In relation to the meaning of 'welfare' the following points should be noted:

- 'welfare' is not defined in the Act but as a general matter of judicial interpretation, the word is given a wide meaning to include not only material factors but also moral, emotional and psychological considerations;

- the welfare principle means that the court is required to make its decision which promotes the child's welfare and is in the child's best interests;

- s 1(3) provides a checklist to guide the courts in deciding the welfare issue, to include:

  (a) the ascertainable wishes and feelings of the child (subject to the child's age, understanding, maturity etc);

  (b) the child's physical, emotional and educational needs;

  (c) the likely effect on him of any change in his circumstances;

  (d) the child's age, sex, background and any characteristics which the court considers relevant;

  (e) any harm which he or she has suffered or is at risk of suffering;

  (f) how capable each of the child's parents and any other relevant party is, in meeting the child's needs;

  (g) the range of powers available to the court under the Act and the proceedings in question.

The list is not exhaustive, nor are many of the factors new to the Children Act 1989 as the basis for their inclusion derives from court decisions made under previous legislation.

You should be aware that the 'welfare' requirement applies to most but not all issues dealt with under the Act. The welfare requirement will apply in the following situations:

- a child assessment order;

- a direction to a local authority to investigate a child's circumstances;

- an emergency protection order;

- a care order;

- a supervision order;

- an interim care or supervision order;

- an education supervision order.

The welfare requirement does not have to be of paramount importance when the court makes a decision in the following situations:

- orders for financial relief;

- orders for ancillary relief in matrimonial proceedings;

- an application for leave to apply for a s 8 order;

- an application to be joined as a party in proceedings;

- an application for a secure accommodation order;

- proceedings under the Adoption Act 1976;

- applications under the Child Abduction and Custody Act 1985;

- the granting of an injunction to restrict publicity.

Nor does the welfare principle take precedence over time limits imposed by the court or well-established principles of law.

Where there is a conflict between the interests of one child in the proceedings and the interests of another child, the court will balance the interests of one child against the other (see *Re T and E (Conflicting Interests)* [1995] 1 Fam LR 581).

Where there is more than one child involved in the proceedings, the welfare principle will be applied in relation to the child who is the subject of the proceedings (see *Birmingham City Council v H (A Minor)* [1994] 2 AC 212; *F v Leeds City Council* [1994] 2 Fam LR 60; *Re T and E (Conflicting Interests)* [1995] 1 Fam LR 581).

Two final points need to be considered. First, in determining the wishes of the child, where a guardian *ad litem* has been appointed, there is no obligation on the judge to interview the child, as the child's views will have been fully expressed by the guardian *ad litem* or the welfare officer (see *Re R (A Minor) (Residence: Religion)* [1993] 2 Fam LR 163). Second, the classic definition of what amounts to a 'paramount consideration' is to be found in the case of *J v C* [1969] 1 All ER 788 in which Lord McDermott made the following observation:

> They connote a process whereby when all the relevant facts, relationships, claims and wishes of the parents, risks choices and other circumstances are taken into account and weighed, the course to be followed will be that which is most in the interests of the child's welfare.

The principle of 'non-intervention'

The second central concept to the workings of the Children Act 1989 is the principle of 'non-intervention'. In practical terms this means that the court should not make an order under the Act unless it considers that it is in the child's best interests to do so. The provision is founded on the belief that children are best looked after within their family by both parents. The courts should intervene in private family life as a final resort. For an illustration of the principle in practice, see *Re H (Shared Residence: Parental Responsibility)* [1995] 2 Fam LR 883.

The court shall have regard to any delay in bringing the proceedings

Section 1(2) of the Act requires the court to take the view that any delay in determining a question which relates to the upbringing of the child is likely to prejudice his or her welfare. The rule applies to any proceedings where the welfare of a child is concerned. The requirement encourages the parties in a case and the courts to take decisions about children without delay.

The 'delay' principle is strictly applied. Even in such extreme situations as cases of murder, it is not necessarily preferable for the trial to take place before care proceedings unless there are exceptional circumstances for the court to take into account (see *Re S (Care Order: Criminal Proceedings)* [1995] 1 Fam LR 151 and *Re TB (Care Proceedings: Criminal Trial)* [1995] 2 Fam LR 801).

Not all delays will be penalised by the courts. A 'planned and purposeful delay' may be acceptable as would a delay caused by the parties seeking an agreed settlement of the matters in dispute. A delay may also be acceptable where the court needs to be fully informed before deciding whether to cut off contact between a parent and child (see *Re W (A Minor) (Welfare Reports)* [1995] 3 Fam LR 793).

Parental responsibility

In addition to the factors already discussed, the concept of 'parental responsibility' is another of the Act's key phrases. It is defined in s 3(1) as: 'all the rights, powers, authority and duty of parents in relation to a child and his property.'

The meaning of 'parental responsibility'

Parental responsibility is the collection of duties, rights and authority which a parent has in respect of the upbringing and property of his or her child.

The exercise of parental responsibility is left to the parent's discretion subject to the general duty that:

- a parent should care for the child; and

- protect and promote the child's moral, physical and emotional health.

Parental responsibility is also subject to:

- the minimum standards of care imposed by the criminal law, provided by the Children and Young Persons Act 1933 and 1969, the Child Care Act 1980 and the civil law remedies in respect of the child's welfare; and

- the 'Gillick' principle that establishes that parental responsibility diminishes as the child gains sufficient understanding to make his or her own decisions see *Gillick v West Norfolk and Wisbech Health Authority* [1986] AC 112.

Who can exercise parental responsibility?

Section 2(1) and s 2(2) provides that where a child's parents have been married or were married at the time of conception, they each have parental responsibility. In other circumstances the mother has parental responsibility.

The child's father can only acquire parental responsibility by:

- entering into a 'parental responsibility agreement' with the child's mother; or

- by applying to the court for an order which gives him parental responsibility under s 4(1).

Parental responsibility can also be assumed by others (including the child's father) in the following way:

- Guardianship: a guardian may be appointed to take over parental responsibility for a child when the parent with parental responsibility dies. The Act requires that the guardian must be an individual. A guardian cannot be a local authority or voluntary organisation.

The effect of parental responsibility

Where a person(s) has parental responsibility, it empowers the person to take decisions in the child's life. Parental responsibility does not have the same meaning in law as being the child's parent, in that where a person has parental responsibility it does not automatically make him or her the child's parent nor does the person acquire the rights of a parent, for example the right to inherit the child's property, or to assume the duties of a parent, for example the duty to maintain the child.

The Act importantly distinguishes between where a person has 'care' but not 'parental responsibility'. The person who has the care of the child is required to act for the benefit of his or her welfare but not in any way which conflicts with the duties and philosophy of the Act.

Parental responsibility also has the following characteristics in that where someone else acquires parental responsibility the parent's duties remain unaffected, in much the same way that parental responsibility is unaffected by divorce subject to any orders made by the court. Parental responsibility cannot be passed to someone else or otherwise given up but the person may arrange for parental responsibility to be exercised by a third party whilst that person is unable to act through illness or other incapacity. Where more than person has parental responsibility, each can act independently of the other to meet that responsibility (s 2(5) and (7)). This provision is subject to the important exception of where the child is in care. In this situation, the local authority decides to what extent parental responsibility can be shared with another person.

The duties of parental responsibility

The duties of parental responsibility are not defined. The concept is flexible and will change with the circumstances of each case – not least the age, maturity and understanding of the child. By way of guidance, the following are generally considered to be duties assumed by the person(s) with parental responsibility:

- determining the child's religion;

- deciding the child's name;

- determining the child's education;

- appointing the child's guardian;

- consenting or not to medical treatment;

- consenting or not to marriage;

- representing the child in legal proceedings;

- lawfully correcting the child;

- arranging the child's emigration;

- protecting and maintaining the child;

- administering the child's property;

- physical possession of the child;

- contact with the child;

- consenting to the child being interviewed;

- allowing the disclosure of confidential information about the child; and

- in the case of a deceased child, arranging for burial or cremation.

Courts and procedures under the Children Act 1989

One of the primary considerations behind the passing of the Children Act was to clarify and unify court procedures and remedies available in proceedings relating to children. The previous law reflected the primary division between civil and criminal jurisdictions, which according to the Law Commission Report No 172: Guardianship and Custody (1988) resulted in the law lacking direction and was unintelligible to both professional and lay participants. As a result, the Act introduced the following reforms.

The establishment of a unified court system

As well as streamlining and consolidating the substantive law relating to children, the Act unifies the court structure and procedure into the High Court, county courts and family proceedings court.

Commencing at the bottom of the hierarchy, the courts have the following jurisdictions:

HOUSE OF LORDS
Appeals from Court of Appeal

COURT OF APPEAL
(CIVIL DIVISION)
Appeals from High Court and County Court

HIGH COURT
(FAMILY DIVISION)
Public and private law cases involving complex points or issues of law

Private law applications made by children

Applications when there are pending proceedings, or vary, extend or discharge existing orders of the court

Appeals under CA 1989 from Family Proceedings Court

Inherent jurisdiction – Wardship

COUNTY COURT
(FAMILY DIVISION)

Care centre circuit judge
Transferred public law cases
Private law cases

Family hearing centre judge
Private law cases

District judge
Directions in public and private law cases

Limited and agreed orders in public and private law cases

District judge
Private law cases

FAMILY PROCEEDINGS COURT
Most public law cases are commenced here

Private law cases may be commenced here

Family proceedings courts

Most public law and many private law cases are commenced in the court, including:

- applications for care orders;

- supervision orders;

- other specified proceedings under the 1989 Act;

- adoption applications;

- it has power to transfer more complicated cases to the county court and to consolidate cases where necessary.

The county court

A county court will be designated as a care centre and a family hearing centre and a divorce centre.

Under its jurisdiction as a care centre, the court may:

- hear all applications under the Children Act;

- hear public law applications transferred from the family proceedings court or the high court;

- give directions in public and private law family cases;

- deal with transfer applications refused by family proceedings courts that have been referred for reconsideration;

- make limited or agreed orders in public and private law cases.

Under its jurisdiction as a family hearing centre it may:

- hear applications under Parts I, II and Schedule I of the Children Act 1989.

Under its jurisdiction as a divorce centre a county court may:

- hear applications under Parts I, II and Schedule I to the Children Act 1989, with the exception s 8 applications which must be transferred to a family hearing centre.

The High Court

The High Court will hear:

- public and private law cases involving difficult or complex points of law;

- private law applications brought by children;

- applications to vary existing court orders;

- appeals under the Children Act 1989 from the family proceedings court;

- exercise the inherent jurisdiction of the High Court.

The Court of Appeal (Civil Division)

The Court of Appeal will hear appeals from the High Court and county court.

The House of Lords

The House of Lords will hear appeals from the Court of Appeal.

The allocation of cases

The criteria which determines which court is the most appropriate venue to commence proceedings in is contained in the Children (Allocation of Proceedings) Order 1991 based on the following factors:

(a) the presumption in s 1(2) of the Act that delay in the conduct of the proceedings is prejudicial to the interests of the child and which venue will allow the proceedings to be conducted as expeditiously as possible. In addition to s 1(2) the following factors, provided for by Article 7(2) of the 1991 Allocation Order, are relevant;

(b) the length, importance and complexity of the case;

(c) the urgency of the case; and

(d) the need to consolidate the case with other proceedings which may be pending.

Court personnel

For proceedings under the Act, the High Court will be staffed by Family Division judges; the county court will be staffed by district judges and selected circuit judges and the family proceedings court are staffed by magistrates.

Correspondence to the court

Letters sent to the High Court should be addressed to the Chief Clerk, Principal Registry of the Family Division. Letters addressed to the county court should be addressed to the Chief Clerk and letters sent to the magistrates' court should be addressed to the Clerk to the Justices and in Inner London to the Senior Clerk.

Delays in court proceedings

In recent years both social workers and lawyers have expressed concern at the delay encountered by the courts when dealing with cases. In response to this criticism Dame Margaret Booth was commissioned by the President of the Family Division to report on the Delay in Public Law Cases. In her interim report Dame Booth identified seven reasons for the delay as:

- lack of adequate resources;

- poor administration;

- lax procedures transferring cases from the family proceedings court;

- lack of proper control over the preparation of cases;

- difficulties encountered with certain procedures such as the instruction of experts;

- the listing of cases to be heard by the courts;

- lengthy court hearings.

In response to the interim report, the courts have taken the initiative through a number of measures to alleviate the delay. These initiatives include the courts taking a more proactive role in proceedings under the Children Act 1989 the preparation and conduct of hearings. The courts will apply its discretion to limit the number of documents in case and the length of the parties' submissions. There will be less time allowed for the examination and cross-examination of witnesses and that a witness's evidence apart from expert witnesses, shall be confined to issues of fact not opinion and the source of any hearsay evidence must be disclosed. A party's legal advisers are required to give a full and frank disclosure to confine the issues in the case to essential matters in order to reduce the number of areas where expert evidence is required. The parties should also seek to reach agreement with each other before the hearing, about the main areas of agreement and disagreement.

Child support

To ensure that absent parents, either married or unmarried, contribute to the financial support of their children, the Child Support Act (CS Act) 1991 was enacted and came into force in April 1993. Readers should note that where an order for property or a lump sum for the benefit of a child, application must be made to the court under the Matrimonial Causes Act (MCA) 1973, the Children Act 1989 or the Domestic Proceedings and Magistrates' Court Act (DP&MCA) 1978, depending upon the relevant action and applicable court. The CS Act applies to a child under 16 or under 19 (if in full-time education) years of age. An exception to this rule is where the child is or has been married (see s 55 of the CS Act 1991). A 'qualifying child', therefore, as they are termed under the CS Act 1991 (see s 3(1)) includes adopted and artificially inseminated children (see the Human Fertilisation and Embryology Act 1990).

The CS Act 1991 applies where one or both of the 'qualifying' child's parents is absent as a parent (see s 3(2) of the CS Act 1991). Whilst the Child Support Agency has a role (to be discussed below), it is usually the 'person with care' (see s 3(3) of the CS Act 1991), described as the person with whom the child lives; and is provided day-to-day care for the child. A local authority, for the purposes of the CS Act 1991, is not considered to be a 'person with care', though local authorities can recover the cost of caring for a child under the Children Act 1989 (this will be discussed in the following chapters).

Child Support Agency

The Child Support Agency (CSA) has a statutory duty to trace absent parents and to investigate parents' financial means, as well as enforce the maintenance for the child. Under the CS Act 1991, both parents are required to complete a financial circumstances enquiry form. This returned and completed information is applied to a formula which determines the appropriate level of maintenance for the child concerned. All readers will be aware that it is this formula which has been subject to much public concern.

The formula is based on the income of the parents and the child's needs. It should be noted that where one parent is on social security benefits, they will be treated as having no income (see Schedule 1 to the CS Act 1991). In cases where the carer parent is receiving social security benefits, they are required to authorise the benefits agency, under the auspices of the CSA, to recover maintenance from absent parents. Should the carer parents refuse to consent to the CSA pursuing maintenance from the absent parent or their failure to provide the necessary information, then their benefits will be reduced accordingly, as the CS Officer thinks fit in the circumstances.

Social workers should be aware that CS Officers have a wide discretion under the CS Act 1991. Yet in their duties they should 'have regard to the welfare of the child' at all times (see s 2 of the CS Act 1991). Also, all CS Act assessments will be reviewed at two-yearly intervals.

CS Act assessments – reviews and appeals

Where an assessment is considered unsatisfactory, any parent can request a review or appeal the decision. For a detailed discussion of appeals and the Child Support Appeal Tribunal (CSAT), see Chapter 25, below.

Practice points

Social workers should:

- know the purpose and philosophy behind the passing of the Children Act 1989;

- understand the changes to child care law and practice the Act introduced;

- be aware of the meaning of the Act's key concepts: 'the child's welfare' principle; the 'non-intervention' principle; and the 'delay' principle;

- be able to recognise and apply these concepts to your social work practice;

- know the legal meaning and duties of 'parental responsibility';

- be aware of the practice, procedure and the powers of the courts dealing with Children Act cases;

- know the role of the CSA and be able to advise the client of its practice and procedures where appropriate.

Further reading

Cobley, C, *Child Abuse and the Law*, 1995, London: Cavendish Publishing.

Lockton, D, *Children and the Law*, 1994, London: Cavendish Publishing.

Social Services Inspectorate, 'Challenge of partnership in child protection: practice guide', January 1995, HMSO.

Social Services Inspectorate, 'Reporting to court under the Children Act: a handbook for social services', January 1996, CI(96)01, HMSO.

4 Local authority support for children in need and their families

Part III of the Children Act 1989 requires local authorities to provide a range of services and facilities for specified categories of children and their families. These categories are:

- children in need;

- children under five whether or not they are in need;

- other children, whether or not under five or in need.

In this chapter, we will consider a social worker's duties in relation to children in need and their families and then examine a social service agency's other responsibilities under Part III – the provision of day care, family centres and accommodation for children and young people living in local authority accommodation.

The provision of services for children and their families

A significant change introduced by the Children Act 1989 was a recognition that the interests and welfare of children are most effectively protected when they are living in a family with their parents. As a result, the primary responsibility for the welfare and upbringing of children remains with the parents, and where a local authority is required to exercise its powers under Part III, it will do so in partnership with the parents. The legislation therefore seeks to support the parent's involvement in the child's upbringing and not undermine the parent's role. To promote these ideals, Part III of the Act provides a number of general and specific powers and duties owed by local authorities which will enable them to work in partnership with the child and/or his or her family which will satisfy this requirement.

Children in need

The primary duties of a local authority under Part III are owed to 'children in need'. A 'child in need' is defined by s 17(10) where:

(a) the child is unlikely to achieve or maintain, or have the opportunity of achieving or maintaining a reasonable standard of health or development without the provision for him or her of services by a local authority under this Part;

(b) the child's health or development is likely to be significantly impaired, without the provision for him or her of services by a local authority under this Part; or

(c) the child is disabled.

Section 17(11) defines 'development' as 'physical, intellectual, emotional, social or behavioural development'; and 'health' means 'physical or mental health'.

A child is disabled under s 17(11) if 'if he or she is blind, deaf or dumb or suffers from mental disorder of any kind or is substantially or permanently handicapped by illness, injury or congenital deformity or such other disability as may be prescribed'.

Whilst there is no specific guidance as to who determines whether a child is in need, where the child meets the criteria laid down in s 17(10) and s 17(11), the threshold is satisfied and the child is classified as being 'in need'. The normal procedure is for the local authority to decide whether in its opinion the child is 'in need'. The child's parents will then be notified of the decision and where they do not accept the assessment they have the right to challenge the decision through representation or judicial review.

Where a child has been recognised as being 'in need', a local authority has a general duty to first, safeguard and promote the welfare of children within their area who are in need, and second, so far as is consistent with that duty, to promote the upbringing of such children by their families, by providing a range and level of services appropriate to those children's needs.

It is important to be aware that 'family' is widely defined to include not only 'blood' relatives but any person having parental responsibility and also any other person with whom the child has been living. The services may be given to the family rather than the child as an individual provided they are given to safeguard and promote the child's interests.

The services available for a child in need

Once a child is classified by a local authority as being a 'child in need', it gives the child a legal entitlement to a wide range of social, educational, health, housing and other public services found in Schedule 2 to the Act.

A local authority's duties under Schedule 2 include:

* Taking reasonable steps to identify the extent to which children are in need in their area, Schedule 2, para 1(2).

- Publishing information about the services available for the benefit of potential recipients from local authorities and voluntary organisations and take reasonable steps to ensure that those who may benefit from the services receive the information which is relevant to them, Schedule 2, para 1(2).

- Maintaining a register of disabled children in their area, Schedule 2, para 2.

- Providing an assessment of the needs of the child who is in need may be carried out at the same time as an assessment under other relevant legislation, such as the Disabled Persons (Services, Consultation and Representation) Act 1986, Schedule 2, para 3.

- Taking reasonable steps through the provision of services to prevent children in their area suffering neglect or ill-treatment, Schedule 2, para 1.

- Taking reasonable steps to reduce court proceedings in respect of a supervision or care order being made in respect of children in their area, or criminal proceedings being taken or proceedings in the High Court.

- Taking reasonable steps to encourage children in their area not to commit criminal offences and avoid them being placed in secure accommodation, Schedule 2, para 7.

- Conducting an investigation into the circumstances of children who might be at risk and where appropriate, seek compulsory powers to remove such children from their homes.

- Providing, as a local authority considers appropriate, a range of services available for children in need who live with their families: advice, guidance, counselling, home help (including laundry facilities) and assistance with travelling to use a service provided under the Act; assistance to enable the child and his or her family to have a holiday, Schedule 2, para (8).

- Providing family centres as they consider appropriate. A family centre is a centre at which the child, his or her parents or anyone with parental responsibility or who is caring for the child may attend for activities, advice, guidance and counselling, (during which time they may be provided with accommodation), Schedule 2, para 9.

- Where a child who is living away from his family, taking such steps that are reasonably practicable to enable a child to live with his or her family or to promote contact between the child and his or her family, if it is necessary to safeguard or promote his or her welfare, Schedule 2, para 10.

Whilst Schedule 2 provides a broad umbrella of powers which enables a local authority to discharge its duties under Part III it is unclear what level of services a local authority has to provide to satisfactorily fulfil its legal obligations. Freeman in his book, *Children, Their Families and the Law* (1992, Macmillan), suggests that a local authority cannot be expected to meet the need of every individual. The Act only requires them to take 'reasonable steps' which will be judged in the light of the financial and other resources available. The question will be also be judged in the context of the racial, ethnic, cultural, religious and linguistic needs of their area.

Inter-agency co-operation

The Children Act 1989 places great emphasis on inter-agency co-operation in the provision of services under Part III. Section 27 imposes a duty on local authorities to consider whether public authorities providing education, health and other related services can assist in the exercise of its functions in this area. When requested to do so other local authorities are required to provide the assistance as requested unless it would be incompatible with its own duties and functions or would unduly prejudice the discharge of its own functions. There is also now a requirement for a greater role for voluntary organisations and input from the private sector. For guidance as to how the courts approach the refusal from a local authority to co-operate with social services (*R v Northavon District Council ex p Smith* [1994] 2 Fam LR 671).

Financial assistance

In safeguarding and promoting children's welfare under the Act, s 17(6) provides that a local authority may give assistance in kind or cash in the exercise of their functions. An important change from the old law is that the assistance may be conditional on a full or partial repayment, s 17(7), except charges imposed for advice, guidance and counselling which are exempt from the repayment provisions. Before requiring repayment, the authority must have regard to the means of the child and his or her parents (s 17(8)). Under s 17(9), a person is not liable to repay any assistance where they are in receipt of income support or family credit, or where a person's means are insufficient to repay the full amount, he or she should not repay more than a reasonable amount. Under s 29(1) and (4) the charge can be recovered from the child where he or she is over 16 or from the child's parents.

A local authority may also make a contribution to the cost of looking after a child who is living with a person under a residence order – except where the child is being cared for by a parent or step-parent, Schedule 1, para 15.

It is unlikely that the court has any power to direct a local authority to provide financial assistance. The decision remains at the discretion of the local authority, for guidance (see *Re K and A (Local Authority: Child Maintenance)* [1995] 1 Fam LR 688).

The provision of day care or supervised activities

Section 18(1) imposes a duty on a local authority to provide appropriate day care in their area for children aged five or under and not yet attending school. The section further requires that a local authority should provide appropriate care and supervised activities outside school hours and during school holidays for any child. When arranging these activities, the local authority must take into account the different racial groups to which the children in their area belong.

'Day care' is defined in s 18, as 'any form of care or supervised activity provided for children during the day' and a 'supervised activities' are activities which are supervised by a responsible person.

To ensure that the children are supervised by well-trained and motivated staff, a local authority should also provide guidance, advice, training, counselling and other facilities for those who care for children in day care or who accompany children while they are in day care.

In discharging its functions under s 18, the social services agency is required to review, with the local education authority, the provision of day care and other services.

Family centres

Every local authority is required to provide family centres as it considers appropriate in their area. A family centre is where a child or any person looking after the child, including the child's parents or the person exercising parental responsibility, can attend for:

- occupational activities;

- social cultural and recreational activities;

- advice, guidance and counselling;

- accommodation whilst receiving advice, guidance and counselling.

There will three main types of family centre. These include therapeutic centres where social workers carry out intensive work with families experiencing problems; community centres being a neighbourhood facility for parents to use as a meeting place and where community activities are held; and a self-help centre which is normally run on a co-operative basis and will provide support and advice to families in an informal and structured way.

Accommodation for children

Under the Children Act 1989 the social services agency has a range of duties and obligations when providing accommodation for children and young people in their area. Where a child or young person is provided with accommodation under the Act, he or she is being 'looked after' by the local authority.

Accommodation will be provided in the following situations: where the child or young person is accommodated as 'a child in need'; or is accommodated under a care order; or where the child is being accommodated on the direction of the police or a court; or where the accommodation is provided to safeguard or promote the child or young person's welfare. The duties of the social services agency in relation to each category of accommodation will now be considered.

Where a child is accommodated as a 'child in need'

Under s 20(1), a local authority must provide accommodation for a child in need who requires accommodation where:

- no one is available to exercise parental responsibility for the child; or

- the child is lost or abandoned; or

- the person who has been caring for the child is prevented, either temporarily or permanently from providing the child with secure accommodation; or

- there is no one with parental responsibility for the child.

Whilst the local authority is under a duty to provide accommodation for a child in need, it does not acquire parental responsibility. Where it is in the interests of the child that parental responsibility should be assumed by the local authority, an application will have to be made for a care order or an emergency protection order.

Where the child is being accommodated under a care order

Where the child is in care, the local authority assumes parental responsibility. For the practice and procedure in relation to care orders see Chapter 7.

Where the child is being accommodated on the direction of the police or a court

A local authority must provide accommodation for a child where:

- the child has been taken into police protection and the local authority is requested to provide accommodation;

- the child has been arrested and the custody officer authorises his detention and makes arrangements for the child to be accommodated by the local authority;

- the child has been made the subject of a criminal supervision order, with a requirement that the child lives in local authority accommodation.

Where the child or young person is being accommodated to safeguard or promote the child or young person's welfare

A local authority may provide accommodation for:

- any child within its area, s 20(4); and

- any person who is over 16 but under 21;

- where the local authority considers it would safeguard or promote the child or young person's welfare.

A local authority will accommodate a young person aged 16–21 in a community home. Children who are accommodated under s 20 are 'looked after' by a local authority and the accommodation is provided on a voluntary basis. In these situations a local authority, and as far as is reasonably practicable and consistent with the child's welfare, will ascertain the wishes of the child regarding the accommodation to be provided and give the child's wishes appropriate weight having regard to his age and understanding (s 20(6)).

Guidance and regulations issued under the Act stress the importance of written arrangements being made with the child, the child's parents or anyone else who was looking after the child before he or she was taken into local authority accommodation.

The document will set out the following information:

- the purpose of the child's stay in local authority accommodation;

- the arrangements for any contact with the child;

- the delegation of any parental responsibility;

- that it is in the child's interests for plans to be made to return to his or her family.

Where the child who is accommodated under s 20 is normally resident in another social services area, the other authority can take over responsibility for looking after the child within three months of being notified in writing that the child is being accommodated (s 20(2)).

Objecting to the child being accommodated by the local authority

Whether the local authority has the legal right to provide accommodation is subject to the views of any person exercising parental responsibility over the child.

Where the person who exercises parental responsibility objects to the local authority providing accommodation and is able and willing to provide adequate accommodation, under s 20(7), the local authority may not provide accommodation for the child.

There appears to be no procedure or criteria to decide whether the person who exercises parental responsibility is capable of providing suitable accommodation for the child. Where the local authority believes that the person will not provide suitable accommodation, an application will have to be made to the court for a care or emergency protection order because without these orders, the local authority is powerless to prevent the child being removed from its accommodation.

There are two situations where the rights and duties of the local authority in this respect take precedence over other people. First, the right of a person with parental responsibility to object to the child being accommodated by a local authority will be deferred where:

- there is a residence order in force in respect of the child and the person in whose favour the residence order was made does not object to the child being accommodated by the local authority; or

- where there is an existing order in force determining who has care and control of the child and the person in whose favour the order is made does not object to the child being accommodated by the local authority; or

- where a person has the care and control of the child vested in him or her by the High Court and that person does not object to the child being accommodated by the local authority;

- where the child is at least 16 and agrees to live in accommodation provided for him or her by the local authority.

The second exception is where the person who objects to accommodation being provided by the local authority, does not have parental responsibility, for example the child's unmarried father and other family members. In these circumstances, the rights and obligations of the local authority have priority.

Removing the child from local authority accommodation

Apart from in the situations described above, the person who has parental responsibility may remove the child from local authority accommodation at any time and without giving notice. Where the local authority objects to the child being removed from their accommodation, the only remedy is to apply to the court for a care order or an emergency protection order, where of course, the grounds exist for making the application (see *Nottinghamshire County Council v J* (unreported, 26 November 1993) where the court decided that the local authority would be powerless to prevent the removal of the child from their accommodation without obtaining a court order).

The provision of accommodation – a local authority's duties

The Children Act 1989 imposes a number of duties and responsibilities on a local authority before it provides accommodation. Most of these duties apply to all children or young people being accommodated by a local authority, whether under a care order or in the other situations described above. Some of the most significant duties are as follows:

The proposed accommodation should be consistent with the child's welfare

Any proposal that the local authority has in relation to the accommodation of a child is subject to the general duty that the proposed accommodation is consistent with the child's welfare.

The proposed accommodation should be consistent with the child's planning arrangements

The local authority is required to make immediate and long-term planning arrangements which are consistent with the child's welfare. The matters to be included are:

- the arrangements for contact with the child's family and others;

- whether a change in the child's status is required;

- the type of accommodation to be provided;

- the details of services to be provided;

- delegation of parental responsibility;

- the expected duration of the arrangements.

The local authority is also required to review the child's plan on an ongoing basis.

The duty to consult

Before taking a decision in respect of a child whom they are looking after or proposing to look after, the local authority must as far as is reasonably practicable:

- ascertain the wishes of the child; and/or

- ascertain the wishes of the child's parents; and/or

- ascertain the wishes of any other person having parental responsibility; and/or

- ascertain the wishes of any other person whom the local authority considers to be relevant (s 22(4)).

The duties described above are not absolute duties, as it will not always be practicable to ascertain the wishes of those people mentioned. The Act does not provide guidance as to how these people will communicate their views to the local authority.

It is important to note that the wishes of the child have become increasingly influential since the House of Lords' decision in *Gillick v West Norfolk and Wisbech Health Authority* [1986] AC 112. Under the 'Gillick' principle, the significance of the child's input to the decision-making process will depend upon the child's age, maturity and understanding, but in many cases, they must nevertheless be given serious consideration.

The proposed accommodation should allow the child to maintain contact with home, family and culture

This comprises a number of important considerations including the requirement that, where it is reasonably practicable and in the interests of the child's welfare, the accommodation should be near the child's home. The accommodation should also be located to encourage and facilitate contact with the child's brothers and/or sisters. The Act imposes a statutory requirement on the local authority, under s 22(5), to give due consideration to the child's racial, ethnic, cultural and linguistic background.

The proposed accommodation should not restrict the child's liberty

The proposed accommodation should only be chosen as secure accommodation as the local authority's last resort. The Children Act Guidance and Regulations Volume 1 provides:

> Restricting the liberty of children is a serious step which must be taken only when there is no genuine alternative which would be appropriate. It must be a last resort, in the sense that all else must first have been comprehensively considered

and rejected – never because no other placement was available at the relevant time, because of the inadequacies in staffing, because the child is simply being a nuisance or runs away from his accommodation and is not likely to suffer harm in doing so, and never as a form of punishment.

The type of accommodation provided by the local authority

Where the child is being looked after by the local authority, the accommodation provided will be in one of the following: a foster home, a registered children's home, a community home or in secure accommodation.

Under s 25 Children Act 1989, a secure accommodation order can be made in proceedings by the following courts: the youth court, the magistrates' court, the Crown Court, the family proceedings court, the High Court, or the county court.

Secure accommodation – the application procedure

An application to place a child in secure accommodation can be made by:

- a local authority; or

- a health authority; or

- national health service trust; or

- local education authority; or

- a person carrying on in the business of a residential care home, nursing home or mental nursing home.

Most applications will be made to the family proceedings court. The following people will be respondents and should be notified of the application:

- every person with parental responsibility;

- every person with parental responsibility prior to the care order;

- the child.

Where appropriate, it will also be necessary to serve copies of the application on the local authority where it is providing accommodation and/or the person with whom the child was living. The notice must be served at least one day before the hearing. It is unlikely that the court will hold a directions hearing. It is more likely that an interim care order will be obtained and adjourn the application with directions that the respondent(s) may file an answer. The full hearing follows the same procedure as an application for care or supervision order.

The grounds for granting a secure accommodation order

The law recognises that restricting the liberty of a child is a serious step. Therefore, as a general rule, a child may not be placed or kept in secure accommodation unless he or she:

•   has a history of absconding; or

•   is likely to abscond if secure accommodation is not provided and will suffer significant harm, or will injure himself or herself or others, if he or she does abscond.

Where either of these conditions are satisfied, a child may be kept in secure accommodation for a maximum of 72 hours without court authority. After this period has ended, an application must be made to the court.

Contributions to maintenance

Where a local authority is looking after a child, it is required to consider whether or not to recover contributions towards the cost of the child's maintenance from the child's parent, or, where the child is aged 16 or over, from the child himself or herself.

The local authority is not required to consider whether to recover contributions in respect of a child's maintenance where the child is looked after:

• under an interim care order; or

• under an emergency protection order; or

• under certain other criminal provisions, Schedule 2, para 21.

Contributions may only be recovered where the authority considers it reasonable to do so. Contributions should not be recovered where the parent is in receipt of:

• income support;

• family credit; or

• while the child lives with his or her parent, Schedule 2, para 21(2)–(4).

The procedure to recover contributions

Where a local authority seeks to recover contributions, it must comply with the following procedure:

- serve a contribution notice on the contributor;

- the notice must specify the weekly sum to be repaid;

- the weekly sum should not be any greater than the sum would pay to foster parents for looking after a similar child and which is reasonable to expect the contributor to pay;

- the notice must state the proposed arrangements for the repayment;

- where the parent withdraws from a voluntary agreement, the authority may apply for a contribution order.

After-care when a child ceases to be looked after

Before a child/young person ceases to be looked after by the local authority, steps should be taken to prepare the child for when he or she is not looked after by a local authority.

Under the Act, local authorities are required to advise, assist and befriend each child/young person when he or she ceases to be looked after by the local authority, with a view to promoting his welfare (s 24(1)). A child/young person will be entitled to advise, assist and befriend a child where:

- the child/young person lives in the area of the local authority who will give the advice and assistance; and

- is under 21; and

- at any time after reaching 16 but while a child is still:

    (a)   looked after by a local authority; or

    (b)   accommodated by or on behalf of voluntary organisation; or

    (c)   accommodated in a registered children's home; or

    (d)   accommodated –

        (i) by a health authority; or

        (ii) in any residential care home, nursing home or mental nursing home, for a consecutive period of at least three months; or

    (e)   was privately fostered;

    (f)   but is no longer looked after, accommodated or fostered.

Representation procedures

Each local authority is required to establish procedures for considering representations and complaints in respect of the discharge of their functions under Part III. Section 26(8) requires that the representation procedures receive adequate publicity.

Representations can be made by:

- a child who is being looked after by a local authority;

- any child in need;

- any other person who is considered by the authority to have an interest in the child's welfare;

- the child's parents;

- any other person who has parental responsibility;

- a local authority foster parent.

Section 24(6), requires that the representation procedures must have an independent element in that a person who is not associated with the local authority must take part in the discussions in relation to any action that may be taken as a result of the representations made to them. Local authorities will be required to monitor the representation procedures to ensure that they comply with the regulations issued under Part III.

Once the representation procedures have been completed, the local authority must have due regard to the findings of the committee set up to hear such representations, and reasonable steps must be taken to notify the person who has made representations about the action that has been taken. People who should be notified of the committee's decision include:

- the person who made the representations;

- the child where he or she has sufficient understanding of the matters under discussion;

- anyone else who is likely to be affected by the local authority's decision (s 26(7)).

An alternative approach for your client if he or she is dissatisfied by the way in which a local authority acted in relation to its powers under Part III and Schedule 2, is to seek judicial review in the Queens Bench Division of the High Court.

Practice points

Social workers should:

- know the purpose behind the passing of Part III of the Act;

- be aware of the categories of children and their families entitled to receive support and assistance;

- understand the meaning of 'children in need' and be able to apply to your social work practice;

- be aware of the services and support available to 'children in need' and their families;

- understand the role of inter-agency cooperation;

- understand the role of the person exercising parental responsibility in relation to Part III and apply to your social work practice;

- be aware of the representation procedures required by Part III.

Further reading

Burton, F, *Guide to the Family Law Act 1996*, 1996, London: Cavendish Publishing.

Lockton, D, *Domestic Violence*, 1997, London: Cavendish Publishing.

Social Services Inspectorate, 'Domestic violence and social care', April 1996, CI(96)06, HMSO.

5   The protection of children at risk under the Children Act 1989

Parts III, IV and V of the Children Act 1989 provide local authorities and other agencies such as the NSPCC with wide-ranging legal powers to protect children who are considered to be at risk. It is convenient to describe these powers as 'preventative' in that the matters dealt with in Part III, such as the maintenance of child protection registers and case conferences seek to identify children at risk and prevent physical and/or sexual abuse occurring.

The powers contained in Part V can be described as 'proactive' in that they allow social workers and other professionals to take quick, decisive action to remove the child from danger or other situations not conducive to their welfare by using one or more of three emergency orders: an emergency protection order; a child assessment order and a recovery order.

Part IV contains reactive powers, in that the local authority, NSPCC and other relevant parties, may apply for a care order, which allows the applicant to take the child into care and assume parental responsibility for the child and also seek a supervision order which enables a local authority, NSPCC or other relevant parties to appoint a supervisor to befriend the child.

In this chapter therefore we make a detailed examination of the preventative, proactive and reactive powers available under the Children Act 1989 to protect children at risk.

Preventing neglect and abuse under Part III

Under Part III of the Children Act 1989, a local authority has a specific duty to prevent children in their area suffering abuse or neglect. This involves the social services agency in engaging in a number of activities:

Informing other local authorities

Where a social services agency believes that a child within its area is likely to suffer harm, and the child is going to live or is considering living in another area, it must inform the social services agency for that area about the child. The agency must also be informed of the kind of harm the child may suffer and the child's address or proposed address.

Checking criminal convictions

In accordance with the circular 'Protection of Children: Disclosure of Criminal Background of Those with Access to Children', a local authority or voluntary organisation is required to check with local police forces about the possible criminal backgrounds of those people who apply to work with children including prospective members of staff, volunteers, child minders, those providing day care and foster parents.

Where the person has been appointed to a position which will give them substantial opportunity for access to children, the police will check details of any convictions, spent convictions under the Rehabilitation of Offenders Act 1974, bind-overs and cautions against the person's name.

The local authority and any voluntary organisation will also check with the Department of Health Consultancy Service which contains information not contained in police records. In many cases it will also be appropriate to do a 'List 99' check. 'List 99' is a register maintained by the Department of Education and Science which provides the names of people who are regarded as being unsuitable to work with children.

In recognition of the overall philosophy of modern child care of inter-agency co-operation, information should be regularly maintained with other relevant bodies such as the General Medical Council and the United Kingdom Central Council for Nursing Midwifery and Health Visiting.

The child protection register

Each local authority is required to maintain a register in their area which lists all the children in its area which it considers to be suffering from or likely to suffer significant harm and for whom there is a child protection plan.

The maintenance of the register has two purposes. First, it provides evidence of all the children who are the subject of an inter-agency protection plan and second, it ensures that each plan is reviewed on a six-monthly basis.

The information to be provided on the register is to be found in the handbook 'Working Together' published in 1991, which requires the register shall contain the following information:

- the child's name;

- date of birth;

- address;

- legal status;

- the name of other people living in the household;

- the nature of abuse;

- the date of the first referral;

- the name of the key worker;

- the name of the child's GP;

- the name of the child's health visitor;

- the name of the child's school;

- details of the review procedure;

- details of regular visitors to the child's home;

- information about relevant offences committed by people in the child's home. A relevant offence is a reason which leads to the child being placed on the register.

The register should be managed by an experienced social worker who is known as the register custodian. When a child moves to the area of another social services agency, the register custodian is required to contact his or her counterpart for the area to which the child is moving to confirm the child's details.

The child's name should then be entered on the register in the new area and a child protection conference should be held to discuss the case. As an exception to the normal procedure, described below, the child's name can be placed on the protection register before the child protection conference in the child's new social services area, which is required at a later date to confirm the decision.

Criteria for placing a child on a child protection register

A child's name can only be placed on the child protection register where the decision has been taken at a child protection conference. In deciding whether a child should be placed on the register the conference has to be satisfied that there is or is a likelihood of significant harm occurring to the child.

In para 6.39 of 'Working Together', the requirements for the 'significant harm' test to be satisfied are described in this way:

(i) There must have been one or more identifiable incidents which can be described as having adversely affected the child. They may be acts of commission or omission. They can either be physical, sexual, emotional or neglectful. It is important to identify a specific occasion or occasions when the incident has occurred professional judgment is that further incidents are likely, or

(ii) Significant harm is expected on the basis of professional judgment of findings of the investigation in this individual case or on research evidence.

Paragraph 6.40 provides five categories of treatment which will lead to a child's name being put on the register:

- **neglect** – being persistent or severe neglect or failure to protect or carry out important aspects of care which results in significant impairment of the child's health or development;

- **physical injury** – actual or likely physical injury, or failure to prevent physical injury or suffering, including deliberate poisoning, suffocation and Munchausen's syndrome by proxy;

- **sexual abuse** – actual or likely physical exploitation of a child or adolescent, where the child is dependent or developmentally immature;

- **emotional abuse** – caused by persistent or severe emotional ill-treatment or rejection.

It is important to emphasise that the list is neither exhaustive nor prescriptive and that in most cases the reason for the child being placed on the protection register will be obvious. Also, the social services authority is not under a duty to formally record the reasons for its decision. The specific reasons for the decision will be found in the written minutes of the case conference.

The child protection register – the proper exercise of discretion

Parliament has provided social service agencies with wide legal powers to protect children at risk in their areas. In discharging this responsibility, it appears that the courts will give a broad discretion as to how the legal responsibilities are discharged. According to *R v Harrow London Borough ex p M* [1989] QB 619, whilst the decision to place a child on the protection register can be judicially reviewed by the courts, judicial intervention will be rare. Provided the correct procedure is followed in that the decision to place the child on the register is taken by a case conference, the courts will not normally interfere with the reasons for the decision.

As an illustration of this approach in *R v East Sussex County Council* [1990] JPN 597 the social service agency placed a child's name on the register where the child had suffered non-serious injuries as a result of a reprimand, the court confirmed the decision to be reasonable as the local authority was exercising its statutory duty to care for children within its area. A similarly wide discretion was confirmed on local authority by *R v Devon County Council ex p L* [1991] 2 Fam LR 541.

Register of child abusers

In addition to maintaining the 'at risk' register it is becoming increasing common for the social service agency and/or the probation service to compile a register of convicted or suspected child abusers and paedophiles.

As extension of this development and following the example of the so-called 'Megan's Law' from the United States, many parents and child protection pressure groups are demanding that social service agencies and the police should have a positive duty to inform people when a convicted or suspected child abuser comes to live in their community.

From September 1997, under strict guidelines issued by the Home Office, the police are allowed to inform schools, community groups and members of the public about convicted paedophiles living in their area. Disclosure under the rules will be limited to 'exceptional circumstances' only, where, for example, the offender is believed to pose a continuing risk to children in the community. Also, under the Sex Offenders Act 1997, a central register is to be established which will provide details of over 9,000 sex offenders in prison or on probation. Anyone jailed for more than 30 months in respect of a sex offence will be entered on the register for life. Those sentenced to between six and 30 months custody will be 'registered' for 10 years and offenders who go to prison for less than six months will be registered for seven years. A non-custodial sentence will result in the offender being registered for five years.

Child protection case conferences

In discharging its responsibilities under the Children Act 1989, the social services agency is required to engage in discussion and decision with other relevant parties in respect of children considered to be at risk. Add this requirement to the importance of inter-agency co-operation and action and it is clear why, since the 1970s, case conferences have been widely used as the multi-disciplinary forum in which discussion and decisions take place on a case by case basis.

As para 6.1 of 'Working Together' confirms, child protection case conferences are '... the prime forum for sharing information and concerns, analysing risk and recommending responsibility for action'. Any agency or professional may initiate a child protection conference but only the social services agency or NSPCC have the legal power to set the conference up. It should also be remembered that there are two types of conference: the initial child protection conference and the child protection review.

The initial child protection conference

The only decision that will be taken at the initial child protection conference is whether or not to put the child's name on the 'at risk' register. It discusses and records a proposed plan of action and it is the responsibility of each agency representative to decide whether he or she accepts or rejects the proposals.

The child protection review

The main responsibilities of the child protection review are:

- to review the arrangements agreed for the protection of the child;

- to examine the current level of risk to the child;

- to ensure that the child continues to be adequately protected;

- assess the effectiveness of inter-agency co-ordination;

- to review the protection plan;

- to consider whether the child's name should be removed from the at risk register.

In many cases, the review conference will be the occasion when the full child protection plan is produced and discussed.

Case conference practice and procedure

Social work practice is divided between social work agencies as to the purpose of holding a case conference. All agencies are required to hold an initial child protection conference to decide, where the criteria is met, whether the child should be put on the at risk register. Some agencies also use case conferences to decide who should be the key worker, to decide whether to seek a care order or to attempt reconciliation between parent(s) and child. By way of illustration the following paragraph concentrates on the practice and procedure at an initial child protection conference.

As para 6.4 of 'Working Together' identifies an initial child protection conference should only be called after an investigation under s 47 of the Children Act has been made in respect of an incident or where abuse is suspected. There appears however to be a wide variation as to the criteria applied when deciding whether to convene a case conference. The guidance suggests the following criteria for an initial child protection conference to be held:

- when there is sufficient evidence, which is not rejected during the investigation, that a child is likely to suffer significant harm, so that a child protection plan may be considered;

- when information is made available to the social services agency or any other child protection organisation concerning the pregnancy of a parent whose previous child had been very seriously harmed or died as a result of unexplained injuries or proved child abuse;

- when the agreed child protection plan cannot be implemented or is ineffective;

- where there is strong dissent following investigation about the need for a child protection conference.

The time span between referral and the conference will vary according to the precise circumstances of the case. As a general rule, the initial conference will normally take place within eight working days of referral, with the maximum period being 15 working days where it has not been possible to convene the conference earlier.

The conference should be chaired by an experienced member of the social work agency staff. Invariably, the success of the conference and the effectiveness of the protection provided for the child is dependent on the skill of the chair in setting clear and agreed objectives for meeting, harnessing the wide range of skills and experience assembled; and to focus the skills and experience in a way that is most beneficial to the child's interests. It is also desirable that the same person is chair for all conferences about the child and has detailed personal knowledge about the circumstances of the case.

'Working Together' suggests that all those agencies which have specific responsibilities for child protection should be represented at the conference and any other relevant body that can make a positive contribution to protecting the child should be invited to attend. The vast majority of child protection conferences will have representatives from the following organisations:

- social services;

- NSPCC (where active in the area);

- police;

- education authority (where the child is of school age);

- health authority;

- probation service;

- the child's general practitioner;

- health visiting service;

- probation service.

Joint research undertaken by the Department of Health, the BMA and the Conference of Medical Royal Colleges in 1994 indicated that in the survey sample, GPs could only attend 19% of conferences they were invited to and other doctor's attendance was about 20%. Where it is not possible for the conference to have the direct benefit of medical advice, a written report might be submitted in the absence of a personal attendance.

An effective conference will proceed in the following structured way:

Stage 1 will be concerned with the sharing of information to ensure that all the representatives are participating on the basis of a common factual context.

Stage 2 will require the conference to assess the immediate, medium- and long-term risks to the child.

Stage 3 is the decision-making stage. The essential issue to be decided is whether the conference recommends that the child should be the subject of an inter-agency child protection plan and placed on the child protection register. In some conferences the decision will be taken by a formal vote. On other occasions the mood of the meeting will be the determining factor.

It is important to be aware that the decision of the conference is a recommendation only. In practice it should be seen as a recommendation to the individual agencies for action. In *R v Norfolk County Council, ex p M* [1989] 2 All ER 359, the court confirmed the view that the main function of a case conference was to advise rather than direct. The final decision as to what action to take lies with the local authority social services agency.

The involvement of parents and child

It used to be the case that parents (or anyone exercising parental responsibility) were barred from attending and participating in case conferences. Two important influences on child care law and practice have challenged the traditional view. First, the Cleveland Report at p 246 (para 4(e)) states: 'Parents should be informed of case conferences and be invited to attend for all or part of the conference unless, in the view of the chairman of the conference, their presence would preclude a full and proper discussion of the child's interests.' Second, 'Working Together' at para 6.14 provides: 'It is important that the Area Child Protection Committee should formally agree the principle of including parents and children in all conferences.'

As a matter of practice before a decision can be taken to invite the parents to attend, the agreement of all the agencies attending the conference must be obtained.

Where the child is of sufficient age and understanding he or she should also be invited to attend the whole or part of the conference where it is consistent with safeguarding and promoting the child's interests. 'Working Together' also provides guidance as to the considerations to apply when deciding whether to exclude parent(s):

> While there are exceptional occasions when it will not be right to invite one or other parent to attend a case conference in whole or in part, exclusion should be kept to a minimum and needs to be especially justified. The procedure should lay down criteria for this, including the evidence required. A strong risk of violence with supporting evidence, by the parents towards the professionals or the child might be one example or evidence that the conference would be likely to be disrupted. The possibility that one of the parents may be prosecuted for an offence against the child does not in itself justify exclusion.

The decision to exclude the parents rests with the conference chair after hearing the views of the other professionals attending. Where it is decided to exclude the parents, the decision should be noted on the child's file and recorded in the conference minutes.

The role of the legal adviser at the conference

In April 1994, the Law Society, the solicitor's governing body in England and Wales, issued a guidance document outlining the role of the local authority solicitor at the case conference. It should be noted that the solicitor attends as a legal adviser to the conference rather than as a full member. The solicitor is required to be aware that he or she should not later be able to benefit from their presence at the conference by raising matters in court which may have been referred to in confidence or in support of their case during the conference. The guidance also considered that it was good practice for the parent's or the child's legal adviser to be present at the conference.

The role of the key worker

Where the initial child protection conference has recommended the child's name should be entered onto the at risk register, it will be necessary to appoint a 'key worker'. The 'key worker' who will either be a social services field worker or NSPCC officer has three main functions. First, he or she is required to draw up the child protection plan which will embody the multi-agency, multidisciplinary approach for the child's protection required by the Children Act. Second, the key worker will play the lead role in co-ordinating the inter-agency activities. Third, the key worker is required to ensure that the parents and/or the child are fully involved in the implementation of the child protection plan.

Implementation and review

Where the child has been registered on the child protection register and the protection plan has been agreed, the plan should be implemented. Formal review of the protection plan is required to be undertaken at least every six months at the child protection review.

Taking the child off the register

The decision to remove a child from the child protection register will usually be made at the child protection review. Paragraph 6.45 of 'Working Together' identifies the reasons for removing the child from the register to include:

- a child who has been removed from home where the risk of abuse has been reduced;

- the child has been placed away from home and the abuser no longer has access to the child or is no longer considered to be a risk to the child;

- where the abuser is no longer in the same household or there no longer is contact between the child and the abuser;

- a comprehensive assessment of the child has taken place and it shows that there is no longer a need for the child to be registered.

Other reasons for de-registration include:

- the child has permanently moved to another area and that area's social services agency has assumed responsibility for the child;

- the person by legal definition is no longer a child;

- the child has died.

Area child protection committees

As part of the inter-agency approach to child care, area child protection committees provide a multi-disciplinary approach to establishing agreed procedures, policy and practice in the designated area. Membership of the committee will include representatives from:

- social services agency;

- health authority;

- police;

- education authority;

- police;

- probation service;

- health authority.

It is a requirement that the committee shall be chaired by an officer of the social services agency and in the discharge of its duties it is required to review policy and procedure and to report annually. The committee should pay particular attention to the following matters:

- monitor the implementation of legal procedures;

- establish guidelines to deal with cases;

- review the effectiveness of child protection procedures;

- review the effectiveness of inter-agency cooperation;

- to conduct reviews as required by Part 8 of 'Working Together'.

The non-criminal detention of children by the police

A police officer has the power under s 46 of the Children Act 1989 to take a child into 'police protection'. This power was formerly contained in s 28 of the Children and Young Persons Act 1969 where the police had power to take the child to a place of safety. The police can exercise their power under s 47 where the following conditions apply:

- the officer must have reasonable cause to believe that if the child was not taken into police protection they would otherwise be likely to suffer 'significant harm';

- 'police protection' can mean either:

    (a) removing the child to suitable accommodation and to keep him or her there; or

    (b) take such steps as are reasonable to ensure that the child's removal from any hospital or other place in which he is then being accommodated is prevented;

- a 'child' for the purpose of s 47 is a person under 18 years;

- 'harm' includes impairment of development and development is widely interpreted to mean physical, intellectual, emotional, social or behavioural development (s 39(1));

- where an officer has exercised powers under s 47, the child is in 'police protection' not police custody or detention;

- no child can be kept in police protection for longer than 72 hours;

- as soon as is practicable after the child is put in police protection, the officer must ensure that the case is inquired into by the officer designated for such duties by the chief constable;

- where the inquiry is completed the child must be released from police protection unless there is still reasonable cause to believe that the child would still be likely to suffer significant harm.

The officer is also required, as soon as possible to:

(a) inform the local authority for the area in which the child was found of the steps taken or to be taken;

(b) tell the local authority for the area in which the child is ordinarily resident, where the child is being kept in police protection;

(c) where appropriate, inform the child of the steps which have been taken and will be taken in respect of their welfare;

(d) where appropriate, take reasonably practicable steps to discover the child's wishes;

(e) ensure that the child is taken to secure accommodation provided by the local authority;

(f) the officer must also take reasonably practicable steps to inform:

(i) the child's parents;

(ii) the person who has parental responsibility; and

(iii) any other person with whom the child was living immediately before being taken into police protection;

of the steps taken in respect of the child and the reasons for taking them (s 46(3) and (4)).

- where the child is in police protection, the officer may apply on behalf of the local authority for an emergency protection order under s 44 of the Children Act;

- where an emergency protection order is applied for, the maximum period that the order can run is eight days;

- the period of eight days runs from the time the child was taken into police protection under s 46;

- the police do not assume parental responsibility under the Children Act 1989 for the time the child spends in police protection;

- the police are under a general duty to safeguard the child's welfare;

- the child's parents or anyone else with parental responsibility or anyone with whom the child was living before being taken into police protection or anyone in whose favour a contact order has been made, should be allowed to have such contact with the child as the designated officer considers is reasonable and in the child's best interests.

Powers of investigation by local authorities

Many referrals of children considered to be at risk arise out of a local authority's powers of investigation under s 47. A local authority is under a duty to investigate in one or more of the following five circumstances:

(a) where they have reasonable cause to suspect that a child who lives or is found in their area is suffering or is likely to suffer significant harm (s 47(1)(b));

(b) where they have obtained an emergency protection order in respect of a child (s 47(2));

(c) where they are informed that a child who lives or is found in their area is subject to an emergency protection order or is police protection (s 47(1)(a));

(d) where a court in family proceedings directs them to investigate a child's circumstances (s 37(1));

(e) where a local education authority notify them that a child is persistently failing to comply with directions given under an education supervision order (Schedule 3, para 19).

Local authority responsibilities

In relation to their responsibilities under s 47, detailed at (a), (b) and (c) above, a local authority is required to make such inquiries as it considers necessary or instruct another agency such as the NSPCC to conduct the inquiries on its behalf. The purpose of the inquiry is to enable the local authority to decide whether they should take any action to promote or safeguard the child's interests. After having made the necessary inquiries, the local authority have to decide what action (if any) should be taken.

Where action is required the social worker has a range of options available including making an application for a care or supervision order or to offer services to the child and his or her family under Part III of the Children Act 1989.

The powers available where the social worker is denied access to the premises

If, when making inquiries under s 47, you are denied access to the premises where the child is living to assess whether the child is at risk, s 47(4) provides that you are required to take steps which ensure that you gain access to the property or that you ensure that another person, for example a doctor, obtains access. Where access is denied, you can apply for a court order protecting the child unless the child's welfare can be satisfactorily protected by other means.

In this situation you can apply to the court for the following orders:

- emergency protection order; or

- child assessment order; or

- care order; or

- supervision order.

The action to be taken where the child is living with someone who may mistreat the child

Where it is discovered that the child is living with the abuser in the same household:

- the child may be removed from the premises; or

- the person who poses the threat to the child can be provided with assistance, financial or otherwise to find alternative accommodation (Schedule 2, para 5); or

- you may assist the husband/wife/cohabitee of the person posing the threat to apply for a court order excluding the person from the home (s 47(8)).

Further investigative duties

Where an emergency protection order has been made in respect of the child, and the child is not in local authority accommodation, the local authority are required to consider whether the child should be in such accommodation (s 47(3)(b)). Where the child has been taken into police protection, the local authority is required to consider whether they should ask the police to apply on the local authority's behalf for an emergency protection order (s 47(3)(c));

Where the local authority consider that the child's education needs to be investigated, s 47(5) requires they should consult the local education authority.

What happens when no emergency action is taken?

Where it is decided not to take emergency action, s 47(7) requires that the local authority should consider whether to review the child's case at a later date. Where the decision is taken to review the child's case a date must be fixed for the review to begin.

Court orders under the Children Act 1989

The Act confers on the courts a wide range of powers to make the following orders to protect children.

Emergency protection order – s 44 of the Children Act 1989

As the name suggests, the order is the appropriate course of action where it is necessary to act quickly in order to safeguard the physical, moral or emotional well being of a child.

The applicant, usually the social services agency or the NSPCC, will apply to the court for an order under s 44 which will only be granted if the court is satisfied that:

(a) there is reasonable cause to believe that the child is likely to suffer significant harm if –

  (i) he or she is not removed to accommodation provided by or on behalf of the applicant; or

  (ii) he or she does not remain in the place in which he is then being accommodated; and

(b) in the case of an application by a local authority –

  (i) inquiries are being made in respect to the child under s 47(1)(b); and

  (ii) those inquiries are being frustrated by access to the child being unreasonably refused to a person authorised to seek access and that the applicant has reasonable cause to believe that access to the child is required as a matter of urgency; or

(c) in the case of an application made by an authorised person –

(i)   the applicant has reasonable cause to suspect that a child is suffering, or is likely to suffer, significant harm;

(ii) the applicant is making inquiries with respect to the child's welfare; and

(iii) those inquiries are being frustrated by access to the child being unreasonably refused to a person authorised to seek access and the applicant has reasonable cause to believe that access to the child is required as a matter of urgency.

Where a court makes an emergency protection order, the applicant assumes parental responsibility for the duration of the order. The person is required to exercise parental responsibility in such a way which will safeguard and promote the welfare of the child and/or to remove the child to alternative accommodation and/or to prevent the child's removal from her/his present accommodation.

An emergency protection order is a short-term order which enables a child to be made safe when he or she might otherwise suffer harm.

In exercising its powers under s 44, the court will take into account the following factors:

- the court is required to be satisfied that there is reasonable cause to believe that the child will suffer significant harm;

- the test is based on the likely future treatment of the child;

- evidence of harm which occurred in the past is not by itself sufficient unless it is indicative that harm in the future is more likely to occur;

- 'significant harm' includes ill-treatment as well as impairment of health or development;

- the order will often specify where the child should be detained, for example in hospital, and who would likely to suffer 'significant harm' if he or she was allowed to return home.

The effect of an emergency protection order

Where an emergency protection order is granted by the court, it has the following effects:

- it requires any person with power to do so, to produce the child to the applicant; and

- it authorises the removal of the child to accommodation provided by or on behalf of the applicant; and/or

80

- prohibits the removal of the child from a hospital or another place where the child was living or staying at the time the order was made.

A person commits a criminal offence where he or she obstructs the exercise of these powers.

The duration of an emergency protection order

- The emergency protection order is limited to a maximum of eight days;

- the duration can be less than eight days where the court considers it appropriate;

- before the expiration of eight days, the applicant should apply for any other relevant order;

- any other relevant order will include: an interim care order; or an extension to the emergency protection order for a further seven days.

Who may apply for an emergency protection order?

The following may apply for an emergency protection order:

- any person;

- local authority;

- an authorised person such as the NSPCC;

- a police officer who is a designated officer where a child is in police protection.

The application procedure

- the party seeking the order is known as the applicant;

- the other side is known as the respondent;

- applications can be made *ex parte* which means that it is not necessary to give notice to the respondent(s);

- where the application is made *ex parte* the applicant is required to serve notice on the respondent(s) a copy of the application within 48 hours of the order being made;

- where the order is made *ex parte* the respondent(s) may apply to the court for the order to be discharged 72 hours after it began. The application can also be made *inter partes*, ie with notice being given to the respondent(s);

- one day's notice is required for the service of the application on the respondents – the court has discretion to shorten the notice procedure;

- where there has been an *inter partes* hearing at the making of the emergency protection order and the respondent was present, the respondent cannot apply for the order to be discharged.

There is no appeal against the making or refusal of an emergency protection order.

Who can be respondents?

The following can be respondents in an application for an emergency protection order:

- the child; and

- any person who has parental responsibility; or

- any person who had parental responsibility immediately prior to the making of the emergency protection order.

Who is required to be notified by the applicant

In addition to which parties can be the respondent, the following also have to be notified of the application:

- every person whom the applicant believes to be a parent of the child; and

- any local authority providing accommodation for the child; and

- any person with whom the child was living at the time of the proceedings were commenced; and

- where the child is living in a refuge for children at risk, the person providing the refuge.

Which court to use

An application for an emergency protection order will normally be made in the family proceedings court but may also be made in the county court or the High Court where there are proceedings pending in respect of the child.

After the order is made

Where the order is made a copy of the order is served upon the child by either serving the order on the child's solicitor or where there is no solicitor, the guardian *ad litem* or with leave of the court, the child.

The appointment of the guardian *ad litem*

It is important that the court appoints a guardian *ad litem* at the earliest opportunity. The guardian should then instruct a solicitor and be available to accept service of any application and notices. The guardian's appointment terminates on the making of the order.

A child assessment order – s 44 of the Children Act 1989

According to the Department of Health guidance, a child assessment order:

> ... deals with the single issue of enabling an assessment of the child to be made where significant harm is suspected, but the child is not thought to be at risk (requiring his removal or keeping him in hospital), the local authority or authorised person considers that an assessment is required and the parents or other persons responsible for him have refused to cooperate. Its purpose is to allow the local authority or authorised person to ascertain enough about the state of the child's health or development or the way in which he has been treated to decide what further action, if any, is required.

A child assessment order will therefore be appropriate in situations of non-cooperation by parents or the child's carers, and there is no evidence to indicate the need to apply for an alternative order. The order will enable an assessment to be made of the child in respect of her/his medical, psychiatric or social development, where it has not been possible to make the assessment with the consent and co-operation of the child's parents or carers.

Grounds for making a child assessment order

The grounds for making the order are found in s 43(1). The application can be made by a local authority or authorised person in respect of a child, and the court will only make the order if, it is satisfied that:

(a) the applicant has reasonable cause to suspect that the child is suffering, or is likely to suffer significant harm; and

(b) an assessment of the state of the child's health or development, or the way in which he or she has been treated, is required to enable the applicant to determine whether or not the child is suffering or is likely to suffer significant harm; and

(c) it is unlikely that such an assessment will be made, or be satisfactory, in the absence of an order under this section.

In addition to the factors provided by s 43, the court will also take into account when deciding to make an order, the paramountcy of the child's welfare under s 1 and the no order principle under s 1(5).

In virtually all cases, an application for a child assessment order will have been preceded by an investigation under s 47 and that steps that have been taken to persuade the child's parents or carer to co-operate with any investigation.

The effect of a child assessment order

A child assessment order can last up to a maximum of seven days from the date specified in the order:

- the order will require any person who is able to do so to produce the child to enable an assessment to be made of her/his medical, psychiatric or social development;

- the order will state the nature of the assessment required and the manner in which it will be undertaken;

- where appropriate it will be necessary for the child to be kept away from home for the duration of the assessment (s 49(3)).

Who may apply for a child assessment order

The local authority and or a specified person may apply for a child assessment order.

The respondents in an application for a child protection order

The respondents are:

- every person with parental responsibility;

- the child;

- where the child is subject to a care order, every person who had parental responsibility prior to the making of the care order.

The procedure for making a child assessment order

The application will normally be made in the family proceedings court unless:

- the application arises out of an investigation of the child's circumstances under s 37(1) in which case it should be made to the court that directed the investigation; or

- there are other proceedings pending in which case it should be made to the court where the proceedings are pending.

The application will be made after giving notice to the respondents. When the application has been made the court will appoint the guardian *ad litem*.

The notice of the application must be sent to the following:

- the parents;

- every person caring for the child;

- every person who has a contact order in force with respect to the child;

- every person allowed to have contact with the child under s 34;

- any local authority providing accommodation for the child;

- any person with whom the child is living at the time the proceedings are commenced;

- if the child is living in a refuge for children at risk, the person providing the refuge;

There is no right of appeal when the order has been made or the refusal of the court to make an order.

Variation of a child assessment order

An application to vary a child assessment order must be sent to the court which made the original order. The application can be made by any of the following parties:

- the local authority and or a specified person;

- every person with parental responsibility;

- the child;

- where the child is subject to a care order, every person who had parental responsibility prior to the making of the care order;

- the parents;

- every person caring for the child;

- every person who has a contact order in force with respect to the child;

- every person allowed to have contact with the child under s 34;

- any local authority providing accommodation for the child;

- any person with whom the child is living at the time the proceedings are commenced;

- if the child is living in a refuge for children at risk, the person providing the refuge.

Recovery order – s 50 of the Children Act 1989

A recovery order will be appropriate where the child is:

- in the care of the local authority; or

- subject to an emergency protection order; or

- in police protection; *and*

- there is reason to believe that the child has been unlawfully taken:

    (a)   from the care of a responsible person; or

    (b)   has run away; or

    (c)   is staying away; or

    (d)   is missing.

The powers available under s 50 are often used in two situations. First, where the child has run away from local authority care because, for example he or she wishes to be independent or is unhappy in the foster home or residential accommodation an application can be made under s 50 to secure the child's return, where the child's whereabouts are known. As well as seeking the child's return, the guardian *ad litem* should investigate the reasons for the child running away and where necessary, act upon its findings so that the child does not have a reason to run away again. The second situation where the powers available under s 50 can be used is to combat the increasing problem of child abduction. About 200 children each year are abducted within the UK and about the same number of children are taken abroad.

Procedure for applying for a recovery order

A recovery order can be made either by giving notice to the other side or without giving notice depending on the circumstances of the case. The application will usually be made on short notice to the family proceedings court unless there are other proceedings pending. In these circumstances it will be unlikely whether there will be sufficient time for the guardian to become involved in an investigation.

Care order and supervision orders – s 31 of the Children Act 1989

Care and supervision orders are the main public law orders available under the Children Act. A care order takes the child away from home and places him or her in the care of a local authority home or foster parents. Under a care order the local authority acquires parental responsibility for the child, but does not generally displace the parental responsibility of the child's parents.

A supervision order puts the child under the supervision of a local authority or probation officer.

Many care or supervision orders are made following a 's 37 inquiry'. This means that any court which is hearing family proceedings in which the question arises about the welfare of a child may direct a local authority to investigate the child's circumstances where it appears that a care or supervision order might be the appropriate course of action to follow.

Where the court direct that an investigation should be held, the social services agency is under a duty to consider the appropriate action to take in respect of the child and to report its decision to the court. Provided the investigation is carried out, the final decision whether to apply for an order under s 31 rests with the local authority. In *Nottinghamshire County Council v P* [1993] 3 WLR 637 it was decided that following an investigation, where the local authority decides not to apply for a care or supervision order, the court cannot require them to do so, no matter how strongly the court believes an application for the order should be made. A care or supervision order can only be made in respect of a child aged below 17, or 16 where the child is married.

The orders are mutually exclusive in that a child can be the subject of either a care order or a supervision order but not both of them at the same time. Finally, do not confuse a supervision order under the Children Act 1989 and a sanction of the criminal court in respect of a young person under the Children and Young Persons Act 1969.

Who can apply for a care or supervision order?

An application for a care or supervision order can only be made by:

- a local authority; or

- an authorised person.

An 'authorised person' includes a NSPCC officer and the officer of any other organisation authorised by the Secretary of State. Under the previous law, both the police and the local education authority could make an application. This provision no longer applies.

The conditions for making a care or supervision order

A care or supervision order should not be made unless the following conditions are satisfied:

- that the child is suffering, or is likely to suffer, significant harm; and

- that the harm, or likelihood of harm, is attributable to –

  (i) the care given to the child, or likely to be given to him if the order were not made, not being what it would be reasonable to expect a parent to give to him; or

  (ii) the child being beyond parental control.

Even where the relevant conditions apply, the court is not bound to make an order. In making its decision, the court is required to take into account the factors provided by s 1 of the Act, including:

- the child's welfare;

- the presumption that no order should be made;

- the 'no delay' principle.

'Harm' includes both ill-treatment, including sexual and physical and also non-physical abuse such as emotional and psychological mistreatment; and

- the impairment of health and development including the child's physical and/or mental health and/or development her/his physical, intellectual, emotional, social or behavioural development.

In applying its powers under s 31 to the facts of each case, the court should take a flexible approach and not be restricted by a strict legalistic analysis. This is especially significant when deciding whether the threshold criteria for making the order has been met. An order can be made either where the harm or the impairment of health and development of the child is existing at the time of the application or the court considers that it may occur in the future. The House of Lords decided in *Re M (A Minor) (Care Order: threshold conditions)* [1994] 3 All ER 298, that the court could look back at the circumstances which necessitated the social services agency to rescue the child from danger in deciding whether the child 'is suffering' significant harm. Similarly, when looking for harm likely to occur to the child in the future, the House of Lords decided in *Re H (Minors) (Sexual Abuse: Standard of Proof)* [1996] 2 WLR 8 that it is sufficient to show that there is a real possibility of harm and a possibility of harm that cannot be ignored based on the present facts and the inferences that arise out of those facts (see also *Manchester City Council v B* [1996] 1 Fam LR 324).

To justify making an order it must be shown that the harm was 'significant'. What amounts to 'significant' will depend on the circumstances of each case. For example, a child may have specific physical or emotional needs which, where these needs are not being satisfied, may result in a care or supervision order being made.

In other cases, in deciding whether the impairment of health or development is significant, the court will compare the health or development of the child in question with the health and development of a hypothetical child with the same attributes and needs. In *Re O (A Minor) (Care Order: Education: Procedure)* [1992] 1 WLR 912, where a 15 year old girl was failing to attend school, the court decided that she should be compared with a child of equivalent intellectual and social development who had attended school.

The second condition is that the harm suffered or likely to be suffered is attributable to the absence of reasonable standard of parental care. Only where there is such a standard of parental care will the court be able to justify state intervention to take over parental responsibility for the child. The child's parents are judged by what a reasonable parent would do for the child in question.

It is worth noting that the private law remedy of a s 8 order can be made as an alternative to a care or supervision order.

The application procedure for a care or supervision order

The applicants, the local authority or NSPCC are required to serve:

- a copy of the application; and

- a notice giving the date, time, place of the hearing on the respondents at least three days before the court hearing.

The respondents will be:

- any person exercising parental responsibility;

- the child; and any other relevant party including the person with whom the child was living at the time the proceedings were commenced.

The court will fix a date for the hearing, giving at least seven days' notice to the parties and the guardian *ad litem*.

Interim orders

An interim care or supervision order will be made where the court is not in a position to decide whether to make a supervision or care order. Under the Children Act 1989 the following interim orders can be made:

- a s 8 order made for a specific period;

- an interim care order; or

- an interim supervision order (s 38(1)).

An example of an interim s 8 order would be a residence order which will not last beyond the date of the full care or supervision order. An interim order has the same effect as a full order in that the local authority has the same responsibilities towards the child as where a full order is made and the conditions that apply for the court to make an interim order remain the same as full orders, in that the court cannot make an interim order unless the court:

- has reasonable grounds for believing that:

- the child is suffering or is likely to suffer, significant harm; and

- that the harm, or likelihood of harm is attributable to –

  (i) the care given to the child, or likely to be given to him if the order were not made, not being what it would be reasonable to expect a parent to give to him; or

  (ii) the child being beyond parental control.

There important difference between an interim and final order is that the court may make certain directions and the duration of the orders is more restrictive.

When making an interim order or when an interim order has been made, the court may make directions as to any appropriate assessment of the child. The purpose of these directions is to promote the interests of the child as well as the other parties to the proceedings.

Practice points

Social workers should:

- be aware of the legal powers in contained in Part III, Part IV and Part V of the Children Act 1989 and be able to apply to their social work practice;

- know that a local authority has a duty to prevent children suffering neglect and abuse;

- be aware of the following and be able to apply to your social work practice where appropriate: child protection registers; child protection committees; powers of the police to detain a child at risk; local authority's powers of investigation; the action to be taken following an investigation; case conference practice, procedure and purpose;

- know when and how to apply for: an emergency protection order; a child assessment order and a recovery order; care and supervision orders.

Further reading

Barton C and Douglas G, *Law and Parenthood*, 1995, London: Butterworths.

Bloy D, *Child Law*, 1996, London: Cavendish Publishing.

Cobley C, *Child Abuse and the Law*, 1995, London: Cavendish Publishing.

Lockton D, *Children and the Law*, 1994, London: Cavendish Publishing.

Mitchels B, *Child Care and Protection Law and Practice*, 1996, London: Cavendish Publishing.

6 Guardian *ad litems*

The independent representation of children and young people in legal proceedings is a well-established practice. For example, where a minor sues in civil litigation in the High Court or county court, he or she is represented on the court record by an adult to protect his or her interests.

The Children Act 1989 extended the role of the guardian and increased its prominence. The anticipated extent of the guardian's involvement in specified proceedings was raised by Lord Mackay, the Lord Chancellor during a debate in the Act's passage in the Lords when he stated: 'We accept that the courts are unlikely to find many cases in which it would be inappropriate to appoint a guardian *ad litem*.'

As a result, a local authority has a duty to maintain a panel of guardians for their area drawn from a panel of: self employed social workers; local authority employees; voluntary organisation's employees; and probation officers.

There are 54 panels covering England and eight covering Wales. The powers and duties of the guardian are set out in the Children Act 1989; the Family Proceedings Rules 1991 (Part IV); and the Family Proceedings Court (Children Act 1989) Rules 1991. To act in public law cases the guardian must be a member of a panel of guardians; or the Official Solicitor.

The guardian is appointed in 'specified' proceedings to represent and safeguard the interests of the child and to advise the courts on the allocation of business, timetabling, case management and how to keep delays to the minimum in the interests of the child's welfare. 'Specified' proceedings are defined by s 46, and include applications in relation to a care or supervision orders, a child assessment order or a recovery order, secure accommodation order, changing the surname of a child in care, and removing a child in care from the UK.

The guardian is required to remain an independent adviser to the child and to the court. A guardian shall be appointed in all specified proceedings unless the court is satisfied that it is not necessary to do so in order to safeguard the interests of the child. Where the guardian is appointed, the appointment should be made as soon as practicable after the proceedings have been commenced and will continue for the duration of the proceedings.

The powers and duties of the guardian *ad litem*

Section 41(2) requires that:

The guardian *ad litem* shall –

(a) be appointed in accordance with the rules of the court; and

(b) be under a duty to safeguard the interests of the child in the manner prescribed by such rules.

The guardian's powers and duties are set out in rule 11 of the Family Proceedings Court (Children Act 1989) Rules 1991 and rule 4.11 of the Family Proceedings Rules 1991.

The rules require that:

- the guardian should be an independent adviser;

- the guardian should be consulted throughout the proceedings;

- the court must take account of the guardian's advice and recommendations;

- the court should follow the guardian's recommendations and according to *Re W (A minor) (Secure Accommodation Order)* [1993] 1 Fam LR 692 where it fails to do so, it must give its reasons;

- where the guardian's recommendation is not followed the court must give its reasons for not doing so, see *S v Oxfordshire CC* [1993] 1 Fam LR 452 and *Devon County Council v Glancy* [1985] 1 Fam LR 20.

When carrying out his or her duties the court rules require that the guardian shall have regard to the matters set out in s 1(3)(a)–(f) of the Act. These are known as the 'welfare checklist' which are as follows:

(a) the ascertainable wishes and feelings of the child concerned considered in the light of his age and understanding;

(b) the child's physical, emotional and educational needs;

(c) the likely effect on the child of any change in her/his circumstances;

(d) the child's age, sex, background and any characteristics which the court considers relevant;

(e) any harm which the child has suffered or is at risk of suffering;

(f) the capability of the child's parent(s), and any other person whom the court considers to be relevant in meeting the child's needs.

The guardian is also required to consider the provision of s 1(3)(g):

(g) the range of powers available to the court under the Children Act in relation to the proceedings in question.

Appointment as a guardian – the first steps

Once appointed as a guardian you will receive written confirmation of the appointment and copies of the papers submitted to the court. You should check the papers carefully to ensure that you have the following information:

- the name of the child;

- the nature and grounds of the application;

- the name and address of the child's solicitor (where appointed);

- details of the child's family, including those people with parental responsibility;

- the outline child protection plan.

Where an appointment has not already been made, you should appoint a solicitor to act on behalf of the child. Where you have been appointed as guardian *ad litem* there is no requirement for the court to appoint a welfare officer to report to the court as well (see *Re S (A Minor) (Guardian ad litem/Welfare Officer)* [1993] 1 Fam LR 110).

Appointment of a solicitor

The guardian will normally appoint a solicitor for the child, although where the guardian is not available immediately at the commencement of proceedings, the child's solicitor can be appointed by the court or where appropriate, the child can appoint his or her own solicitor. The guardian may apply to the court to dispense with the solicitor's advice but he or she must explain to the court the reasons for this decision. The solicitor and, where appropriate, the child is permitted to address the court on the decision.

Instructing the solicitor

The guardian will normally instruct the solicitor, unless the child is judged capable of instructing the solicitor. The solicitor should only accept instructions from the child where the solicitor is convinced that the child has sufficient understanding of the nature of the proceedings and is capable of giving instructions independently.

Where there is conflict between the guardian's instructions and the instructions given by the child, the court will ultimately be required to decide the issue. It will be for the court to ultimately rule on the child's capacity in this respect. Where the conflict continues the guardian should consider applying to the court for separate legal representation, for which the local authority will liable to meet the costs.

Directions, appointments and hearings

You will be expected to attend all directions appointments which prepare the parties for the full hearing. At the directions hearing you will advise the court. Where you do not attend the hearing in person and give oral advice, it may be possible for the advice to be given in writing. You should have a good reason for not attending in person. What amounts to a 'good reason' includes where you are involved in another case at the same time. Where there is a conflict, you should contact the court to explain the reason for your absence. The court may either direct that your advice can be given in writing or the date and time of the directions hearing will be changed.

Where your report is to be given in writing it will be necessary for copies of your advice to be sent to all the other parties in the case and you must ensure that the child's solicitor is fully briefed to be in a position to advise the court.

You will be expected play an influential role at the directions hearing as the parties prepare to focus on the full hearing. The matters that you will be required to advise the court on include:

- the child's wishes and feelings (depending on the child's maturity and understanding);

- the child's attendance at the court hearing;

- whether the child has sufficient understanding, maturity to give informed consent to medical or psychiatric treatment or any other kind of assessment;

- the requirement for expert evidence and the nature of the expert evidence required;

- whether the proceedings are in the appropriate court (following consultation with the child's solicitor);

- whether there should be a delay (known as a constructive delay) before the full hearing, for example where the case is particularly complex;

- whether it is appropriate for the court to make an interim order;

- where the child should reside before the hearing;

- any other appropriate matter upon which you can assist the court.

Advising possible parties

Where it is considered necessary to safeguard the interests of the child, you may notify a party of their prospective right to be joined in the proceedings. A prospective party may include:

- a parent who does not have parental responsibility;

- grandparents;

- step-parent.

Before considering the two most important functions of the guardian's role, namely your powers of investigation and the report, be aware of the following:

The duties of the local authority

You should be consulted by the local authority before it makes any decision about the child during the period of your appointment. It is important to note that the local authority cannot withdraw its application for a care or supervision order without the consent of the court. In deciding whether to give its consent, the court is required to hear your views on the matter.

Acceptance of documents

As the guardian, you can accept service of documents on the child's behalf where no solicitor represents the child.

Other parties – the right of cross-examination

When embarking on your investigation and the subsequent report, you should always remember that at the court hearing, the other parties have the right to cross-examine you about any evidence, written or oral advice that you place before the court. So, for your own peace of mind and professional credibility, ensure that you could justify and defend any view that you put forward.

The guardian's investigation

The Children Act 1989 and its attendant regulations gives you wide powers of investigation in relation to the interviewing of witnesses and the inspection and possession of documents and records. In particular the regulations provide that the guardian may:

- contact or seek to interview any person whom you consider to be appropriate to be interviewed;

- interview any person whom the court directs you should interview;

- inspect any records referred to in s 42; including –

  (a) obtaining such professional assistance which you think is appropriate;

  (b) obtaining such professional assistance as the justice's clerk directs you to obtain.

The purpose of your investigation is to collect and assimilate as much information as possible in order to prepare your report for the court. As indicated above, you are given wide powers to interview all 'relevant' individuals including the child's family and those with a professional involvement in the case. In order to get the issues absolutely clear, you can interview the same witness more than once. Where it is relevant to do so, observe the interaction between the child and his or her immediate family. At each interview, take careful note of what you are told and as soon as possible after the interview revise what you have been told. Always remember that you are collecting evidence which, at the hearing, will play a vital role in assisting the court to come to a decision. Also take advantage of your wide legal powers to inspect local authority files, records and other important documents.

At the end of your investigation you should be in a position to:

- advise the court of the facts of the case;

- have interviewed all relevant people involved in the case;

- inspected all relevant documentary evidence relating to the case;

- communicate the child's wishes to the court;

- present a full assessment of the child's needs;

- evaluate the local authority's plans for the child;

- consider the options available to the court;

- make a recommendation as to the decision the court should make.

The guardian's report

Your report will be read by people from a wide range of backgrounds including the child, the parties, magistrates, the court clerk, lawyers, expert witnesses, social workers and the judge. In terms of style, the essential quality that your report must have is that it should be capable of being read and understood by any one who is required to see it. It should, therefore, be written in clear, concise style and differentiate between professional opinion, undisputed fact and disputed fact. The layout of your report should be carefully structured to assist those reading it to fully understand its contents.

The report should also reflect the primary purpose of the guardian's role in that you should give a fair and balanced view of the relevant issues which will assist the court in making its decision. You should be careful not to allow your report to stray into areas which go beyond your expertise as a social worker. This is especially important as your credibility will be undermined if you were cross-examined by the other parties on matters of which you have no professional knowledge. Most important of all it is not your responsibility to decide the main issue in the case, for example, whether a child has been abused or not. That decision falls firmly within the exclusive competence of the court.

You are required to file (deliver) to the court your report no later than seven days before the date of the final hearing. There may be some occasions where the court will direct that your report should be filed at a different time but normally it will be expected that the parties should receive your report at least seven days before the hearing.

The guardian *ad litem's* responsibilities – a conclusion

The Children Act 1989 provides an extension to the scope of and the influence of the role of the guardian *ad litem*. The guardian has two roles to fulfil – to safeguard, promote and represent the child's interest and to provide experienced, independent advice to the court by taking an overview of the proceedings.

Practice points

Social workers should:

- know the role of the guardian;

- be aware of what are 'specified proceedings';

- know when it is appropriate to appoint a solicitor;

- be aware of the purpose of directions appointments and hearings and how to prepare for them;

- be aware of the guardian's wide powers of investigations and be able to apply them to you social work practice;

- develop the skills to be able to write an effective guardian's report.

Further reading

A Guide for Guardians *ad Litem* in Public Law proceedings Under the Children Act 1989, 1995, HMSO.

Family Court Proceedings, 1995, London: Jordan.

Monro P and Forrester L, *The Guardian Ad Litem*, 1995, London: Family Law.

7 The Children Act and 'private' family law orders

One of the underlying purposes of the Children Act 1989 was to provide courts with a greater range of flexible powers enabling it to deal more effectively with the specific needs of individual cases. Part II of the Children Act 1989 confers powers on the court to make 's 8 orders'. The term 's 8 orders', which primarily arise in the jurisdiction of private law, is the general term which describes three types of orders: a contact order; a prohibited steps order; a residence order; a specific issue order which are defined by s 8(1) in the following way (see Appendix 1 for s 8 order).

- **Contact order** – This requires the person with whom the child lives, or is to live, to allow the child to stay with or visit the person named in the order, or for that person and the child to otherwise have contact with each other. The aim of the residence order is to settle the arrangements to be made as to with whom the child is to live.

- **Prohibited steps order** – No step can be taken by a parent in meeting his or her parental responsibility for a child, and which is of a kind specified in the court order, shall be taken by any person without the consent of the court. A prohibited steps order therefore prohibits any person, without the consent of the court, from taking any step specified in the court order which could be taken by a parent in meeting his parental responsibility to a child. The order cannot be made to prevent a person from having contact with a child because this is not an issue of parental responsibility (see *R v Croydon London Borough Council v A* [1992] Fam LR 169).

- **Residence order** – This settles the arrangements to be made as to whom the person is to live.

- **Specific issue order** – Gives directions for the purpose of determining a specific question which has arisen, or which may arise, in connection with any aspect of parental responsibility for a child.

It was intended that s 8 orders would be a flexible combination of court orders to deal with any issue which might arise about the welfare of the child. They are regarded as providing a practical solution to the child's problems and to encourage the child's parents to maintain their involvement in the child's life and so they have the following characteristics.

- s 8 orders can be for a specified period;

- conditions can be attached to s 8 orders;

- directions can be imposed as to how the s 8 order should be carried out (s 11(7));

- s 8 orders can be interim orders where the court is not in a position to finally dispose of the matter;

- an order can be made at any time up until a child's 18th birthday but only exceptionally after they have reached 16 (s 9(7)).

A contact order can be used to determine issues of access. Contact in this context means more than face-to-face experience of access and where appropriate will be extended to other forms of contact including telephone calls, letter writing etc. A residence order, formerly known as a custody order, is usually applied for after the separation or divorce of the child's parents and it is not clear where the child is to live. In deciding whether to grant the order, the court applies the welfare principle and the statutory checklist. The effect of a residence order is that it confers parental responsibility upon the applicant, where the applicant does not already have parental responsibility although where a parent does not obtain an order, he or she continue to exercise parental responsibility.

Where it is in the best interests of the child, a residence order can be made in favour of more than one person even where the people specified in the order do not live together (s 11(4)).

As an illustration of a residence order, consider the following cases. In *Re H (Shared Residence: Parental Responsibility)* [1995] 2 Fam LR 883, the mother of two boys appealed against a shared residence order made in favour of herself and her husband. He was the father of the younger child but not the older, who was 14. The husband had always treated the 14 year old as 'his own' and had good relations with both children. The judge had made the shared order to enable the father, who was considered to be a good and committed parent, to continue having a positive influence in the child's life. The Court of Appeal upheld the shared residence order in this case, but made the wider observation that in some situations a shared order might confuse the child and even where an applicant had parental responsibility would not always justify the making of a shared order.

In *Re R (Residence Order: Finance)* [1995] 2 Fam LR 4, the parents of a three year old boy separated. During the week, the boy lived with his father and lived with his mother at weekends and during school holidays. After deciding to give up working, the mother applied for a residence order. The Welfare Officer found that the existing arrangements had been working satisfactorily. The trial

judge made a shared residence order with the existing arrangements to continue, which the Court of Appeal upheld.

In *Re D (Residence: Imposition of Conditions)* [1996] 2 Fam LR 281, the Court of
Appeal decided that a court cannot prevent a parent from having the partner of
his or her choice living with them, by attaching conditions to a residence order
under s 11(7). The true question to be determined by the court is whether, having regard to the presence of the partner, is it right for the children to live with
that parent.

Contact order

As we have already seen, the effect of a contact order is that it requires the person
with whom the child lives or stays, to allow the child to have contact with
another person or persons named in the contact order. This order reinforces one
of the fundamental principles of the Children Act 1989 that children are best
looked after by their parents and where this is not possible, to have as much
contact as possible with either or both parents. There is a presumption that it is
in the child's best interests to retain as much contact with their parents as possible. This principle is illustrated by *RH* [1994] 2 Fam LR 776, where the court
would only make an order terminating contact where if it was wholly satisfied
that it is in the interests of the child for contact to cease. In *Re W (A Minor)
(Contact)* [1994] 2 Fam LR 441, the court stated that 'contact with a parent was a
fundamental right of a child, save in wholly exceptional circumstances'. A case
which illustrates what amounts to wholly 'exceptional circumstances' is *R v F
(Minors) (Denial of Contact)* [1993] 2 Fam LR 677, in which two boys aged 12 and
nine did not wish to have contact with their father who was a transsexual. The
court agreed that no order should be made. Another example of what amounts
to 'wholly exceptional' circumstances is *Re G and M (Child Orders: Restricting
Applications)* [1995] 2 Fam LR 416. The father of three young children was convicted of serious sexual offences against young boys. After the children were
taken into care, the mother, with the support of the local authority, sought to
obtain a residence order which the court granted. The order was conditional
that, if on release, the children's father sought to make contact with her children, she would immediately notify the local authority. The court also made an
order of no contact with the father and under s 91(4) prohibited any further contact between him and the children.

An increasingly common situation that you will come across is where one
parent is opposed to the other parent having contact. This is known as a situation
of 'implacable hostility'. In theory the court's powers to make an order in the
face of 'implacable hostility' remains unaffected. However, as a practical solution
in promoting the welfare of the child is this approach to be encouraged? As a
guidance to these difficult situations the Court of Appeal in *Re M (Contact:*

Welfare Test) [1995] 1 Fam LR 274, have suggested the following test: are the fundamental emotional needs of the child to have an enduring relationship with both parents outweighed by the depth of harm which the child would be at risk of suffering by virtue of contact. Where, after applying this test, the judge considers that contact would cause harm to the child, it will not be necessary to make a contact order. The situation has become further complicated by a decision of the European Court of Human Rights in *Hokkanen v Finland* [1996] 1 Fam LR 289. In this case, the failure of the Finnish court to take a proactive and interventionist role in finding a solution to a situation of 'implacable hostility' is equivalent to colluding with the hostile parents and a breach of Article 8 of the European Convention of Human Rights 1950. For guidance as to the influence of the Convention in English law see Chapter 1.

Another area of potential conflict is the position in relation to grandparents. Grandparents do not have automatic right to apply for a s 8 order. They are required to seek leave and the issue is determined on the 'welfare principle'.

In *RF and R* [1995] 1 Fam LR 524, a grandmother sought contact with her four grandchildren following a family row. Her application was dismissed by the magistrates as they felt that contact would harmfully disrupt the children's lives. On appeal, the High Court decided that in determining the application, the magistrates should not have taken into account the family row unless there was clear evidence that contact with the grandmother would have a harmful effect on the child's welfare.

The following two cases illustrate that cases are decided very much on their individual circumstances and that it is difficult to lay down any clear guidelines. In *Re A* [1995] 2 Fam LR 153, a grandmother was denied contact with her grandchildren on the basis of great hostility between the grandmother and the children's mother. Yet in *Re S* [1996] 1 Fam LR 158, grandparents were granted a contact order despite the parent's opposition.

Specific issue order

This order is used to determine a specific issue that has arisen about any aspect of parental responsibility towards the child or will arise in the future. The situations where specific issue orders are granted are well-illustrated by the following cases:

Re R [1993] Fam LR 577. The local authority became aware that the child of two Jehovah's Witnesses needed a blood transfusion. They successfully sought a specific issue order allowing the transfusion to go ahead.

Prohibited steps order

This order restrains the actions of another person in relation to the child. The only steps that can be prohibited are those that could taken by a parent in meeting her/his parental responsibility.

The following cases provide an illustration of the application of a prohibited steps order. In *Re R* [1932] Fam LR 312, an unmarried mother wanted to take her three year old child to Tenerife for three months to see whether she wanted to live with her Spanish fiancee. The child's father objected and sought a prohibited steps order. The order was made and upheld on appeal. The High Court stated that 'an application for the removal of a child from the jurisdiction requires the profoundest thought and the most careful planning before being launched'. The High Court considered that a two week stay in Tenerife was enough time to allow the mother to decide if she wanted to live there.

In *Re B (Change of Surname)* [1996] 1 Fam LR 791, the Court of Appeal stated that as a general rule, the courts will be reluctant to allow a change of surname where it remains a vital link with the child's natural parent. In this case, the court refused to allow the change even where the teenaged children wanted the change to be made.

In *Re D (PSO)* [1996] 2 Fam LR 273, the parents of three children were involved in an acrimonious divorce. The father was working in Paris; the children and mother had returned to the UK. The mother applied for a prohibited steps order to prevent the father from staying overnight in the matrimonial home when visiting the children at weekends. The Court of Appeal overturned the order on the basis that the court had no jurisdiction to make it.

Section 8 orders – the application procedure

The Act distinguishes between those parties who can automatically apply for a s 8 order and those who can apply for an order only with the leave or permission of the court (s 10(1)(a) and (2)). The child's parents and any person in whose favour a residence order is in force (s 10(4)) can automatically make an application to the court for any s 8 order.

The following can automatically apply for a residence order or contact order without the leave of the court (s 10(5)):

- a child's step-parent;

- a person with whom the child has lived for at least three years out of the last five years where the period has not necessarily been continuous but should not have ended more than three months previously;

- any other person who:

  (i) where the child is subject to a residence order and the person has the consent of each of those in whose favour the residence order is made;

  (ii) where the child is in care and the person has the consent of the local authority in whose care the child is; or

- in any other case, the consent of those who have parental responsibility for the child.

The categories of people who can apply with leave

Anyone who is not detailed above can apply for a s 8 order. This is known as the open door policy which recognises that any person who is genuinely concerned with the child should be able to ask the court to make an order in relation to the child's welfare. Included in this category, is the child him or herself where the following conditions where the child has sufficient understanding to make the application (s 10(9)).

In the case of other applicants the court must have regard to the following factors in deciding whether to grant leave:

- the nature of the proposed application for a s 8 order;

- the applicant's connection with the child;

- whether the child might be harmed by the proposed disruption in his or her life the order might make;

- where the child is being looked after by a local authority, the authority's plans for the child's future and the wishes and feelings of the child's parents.

The requirement for obtaining leave is to ensure that the child and his or her family are protected against unwarranted interference with their comfort and security, while ensuring the child's interests are properly respected. In practical terms, the leave procedure acts as a filter mechanism ensuring that it is granted only where it is in the best interests of the child.

The Law Commission foresaw the leave procedure working in this way: 'leave will scarcely be a hurdle at all to close relatives ... who wish to care or visit the child.' In other circumstances however:

> ... there will hardly ever be a good reason for interfering in the parent's exercise of their responsibilities unless the child's welfare is seriously at risk from their decision to take, or more probably not to take, a particular step, and the only people involved in taking that step for them would have the required degree of interest.

The obvious example in such a situation would be in terms of medical treatment.

Variation or discharge of s 8 orders

The same rules apply in relation to the leave procedure where an applicant who seeks to vary or discharge a s 8 order.

Where the child is in care

In spite of promoting an open door policy in respect of s 8 orders, s 9 of the Children Act 1989 imposes important restrictions on children who are being looked after by local authorities:

- where the child is in care, the only s 8 order that can be made is a residence order (s 9(1));

- an application for a residence or contact order may not be made by a local authority (s 9(2));

- a person who has been a local authority foster parent of a child within the last six months may not apply for leave unless he or she has the local authority's consent or he is a relative of the child or the child has lived with him for three out of the last five years.

Practice points

Social workers should:

- be aware of the purpose and philosophy behind the passing of Part II of the Children Act 1989;

- be aware of the practice and procedure relating to contact orders; prohibited steps order; residence orders; and specific issues orders;

- be able to apply and advise about s 8 orders in your social practice.

Further reading

Bloy D, *Child Law*, 1996, London: Cavendish Publishing.

8 Family breakdown

The UK has the highest divorce rate in Europe. During an average year 41% of marriages end in divorce and many clients will seek your advice and guidance about the law relating to family breakdown. In this chapter therefore we provide a brief survey of divorce and the law, practice and procedure relating to domestic violence.

Divorce

A marriage can be brought to an end in one of three ways: an application for a decree of nullity; judicial separation and divorce. In practical terms, nullity and judicial separation are so rare that divorce is the only method of terminating marriage that you need to be aware of. We will therefore begin by introducing you to some divorce terminology. The spouse seeking the divorce is known as the petitioner. The other spouse is known as the respondent. In adultery cases, the party with whom the respondent committed adultery is the co-respondent. A vital point to be aware of is that proceedings for divorce cannot be commenced within the first year of marriage.

A divorce is commenced by the petitioner completing a court document known as the petition and will include details of the ground(s) upon which the divorce is sought and any other orders which the petitioner is seeking as part of the divorce settlement. The petition will normally be prepared by a solicitor. The petition and other supporting documents will then be presented to any divorce county court or the divorce registry of the High Court in London, which for practical purposes is treated as a divorce county court. The fee for presenting a divorce petition to the court is £80.

The ground for divorce

There is only one ground for divorce: the marriage between the parties has irretrievably broken down (s 1(1) Matrimonial Causes Act (MCA) 1973).

The 'five' facts

In determining whether the marriage has irretrievably broken down, the petitioner has to prove one or more of the 'five' facts set out in s 1(2) of the MCA 1973. These are:

- that the respondent has committed adultery and the petitioner finds it intolerable to live with the respondent (s 1(2)(a));

- that the respondent has behaved in such a way that the petitioner cannot reasonably be expected to live with the respondent (s 1(2)(b));

- that the respondent has deserted the petitioner for a continuous period of at least two years immediately preceding the presentation of the petition (s 1(2)(c));

- that the parties to the marriage have lived apart for a continuous period of at least two years immediately preceding the presentation of the petition and the respondent consents to the decree being presented (s 1(2)(d));

- that the parties to the marriage have lived apart for a continuous period of at least five years immediately preceding the presentation of the petition (s 1(2)(e)).

Proving the 'five' facts

Adultery: s 1(2)(a)

Where the petitioner relies on adultery to prove irretrievable breakdown he or she must prove two points:

- the respondent has committed adultery; and

- the petitioner finds it intolerable to live with the respondent.

Adultery is voluntary sexual intercourse between a man and a woman who are not married to each other but one of whom at least is married. Adultery can also be proven by findings in other proceedings, including where:

- the husband has been found to be the father of a child in proceedings brought under s 1 of the Children Act 1989 for a lump sum order, or a transfer of property order; or

- the Child Support Agency has brought an action for maintenance for a child; or

- a finding of adultery has been made in family proceedings; or

- where the husband has been convicted of rape.

The person with whom the alleged adultery occurred, the co-respondent, will usually be joined as a party to the proceedings. The test of whether the petitioner finds it intolerable to live with respondent is subjective not objective, ie does the petitioner as a person find it intolerable to live with the respondent? Where the petitioner continues to live with the respondent for a period or periods together of not more than six months after she or he has discovered the fact of the adultery will not prevent the petitioner from relying on the adultery.

Behaviour: s 1(2)(b)

Where the petitioner relies on 'behaviour' to prove the fact of irretrievable breakdown she or he must prove that the respondent has behaved in such a way that the petitioner cannot reasonably be expected to live with the respondent.

The test has both objective and subjective elements. In effect, would a right-thinking person come to the conclusion that this husband/wife has behaved in such a way that the petitioner cannot be reasonably expected to live with him or her. In determining this question, the court will take into account the whole factual circumstances of the case including the personalities of both petitioner and respondent.

'Behaviour' is commonly used in situations of domestic violence and other anti-social behaviour. The court will also be entitled to take into account isolated incidents which might be trivial in themselves but incremental add-up to significant acts of anti-social behaviour.

Where the petitioner has become bored with her/his partner or disillusioned with the marriage will not be a sufficient ground to prove irretrievable breakdown.

Where the petitioner continues to live with the respondent for a period or periods together of not more than six months after the last incident of behaviour relied on, can be disregarded in determining whether the petitioner cannot reasonably be expected to live with petitioner.

Desertion: s 1(2)(c)

Where the petitioner relies on the fact of 'desertion' to prove irretrievable breakdown, two factors must be proven:

- the respondent has deserted the petitioner; and

- the desertion has gone on for a continuous period of at least two years immediately preceding the presentation of the petition.

In practice desertion is rarely used – not least because the petitioner has to prove the four following elements:

- that cohabitation with the respondent has ceased; and

- the respondent intended to bring the cohabitation to an end; and

111

- the petitioner does not consent to the cohabitation ceasing; and

- the respondent must not have any reasonable cause to bring the cohabitation to an end.

Where the petitioner continues to live with the respondent for a period or periods together of not more than six months will not prevent the petitioner from relying on the fact of desertion but the period of cohabitation will not count towards the period of desertion.

Two years' separation with consent: s 1(2)(d)

Where the petitioner relies on the fact of two years separation with consent, the petitioner is required to prove:

- that the petitioner and respondent have lived apart for a continuous period of at least two years immediately preceding the presentation of the petition; and

- the respondent consents to the decree being granted.

The following should be noted:

- the respondent will signify his or her consent on acknowledgment of the service form;

- the respondent can seek to hold up the decree absolute until her/his financial position after the divorce has been considered by the court (s 10(2) of the MCA 1973).

Where the petitioner continues to live with the respondent for a period or periods together of not more than six months will not prevent the petitioner from relying on the fact of the separation but the period of cohabitation will not count towards the period of separation.

Five years' separation: s 1(2)(e)

Where the petitioner relies on the fact of five years separation, the only matter which must be proven is that immediately preceding the presentation of the petition, the petitioner and the respondent have been living apart for a continuous period of at least five years.

It does not matter whether the respondent consents to the decree or not. The respondent can seek to hold up the decree absolute until his or her financial position after the divorce has been considered by the court (s 10(2) of the MCA 1973).

Where the petitioner continues to live with the respondent for a period or periods together of not more than six months will not prevent the petitioner from relying on the fact of the separation but the period of cohabitation will not count towards the period of separation.

The procedure after presenting the petition

The procedure will vary depending on whether the respondent decides to defend the proceedings. The vast majority of divorces are now undefended and will be dealt with under the 'special procedure' provisions, to enable a marriage to be ended as speedily as circumstances allow.

An undefended divorce under the special procedure provisions will take the following course after the petition has been served. The respondent will complete and return the acknowledgment of service within eight days of receipt indicating:

- that he or she has received the petition;

- in adultery cases the respondent may admit the adultery; or

- in cases involving two years' separation the respondent may give his or her consent to the petition being granted and that the petition will not be defended.

The petitioner's solicitor will request directions for trial. The district judge will then give directions for trial which involves:

- the case being entered on the special cause or special procedure list and the case is allocated a date for the court hearing;

- at the court hearing, a district judge pronounces decree nisi – it is not necessary for either party to be present;

- before the matter can proceed further a district judge must be satisfied about the proposed arrangements for the petitioner's and respondent's children;

- *decree absolute* is pounced in open court on the petitioner's application at least six weeks after the decree nisi.

Fewer than 100 divorces are defended each year. The most common reason for defending is financial hardship.

Reform of the divorce laws: Family Law Act 1996

The existing law and procedure on divorce is considered to be highly unsatisfactory. As a result, Parliament has passed the Family Law Act 1996, which, among other things, introduces a number of radical changes. The requirement for mediation is given high priority by the legislation but once a couple have decided that their marriage has come to an end, the new law and procedure seeks to ensure that divorce does not necessarily have to be a painful or costly experience. The reform of divorce laws by the 1996 Act are not expected to be introduced until the middle of 1998 at the earliest.

Domestic violence

Part IV of the Family Law Act 1996 (not yet in force at the time of writing), which deals with domestic violence, provides a simpler and more unified system for the legal protection of victims of domestic violence. Much of the old law, contained in the Domestic Violence and Matrimonial Proceedings Act 1976, ss 16–18 of the Domestic Proceedings and Magistrates' Courts Act 1978, the Matrimonial Homes Act 1983 and s 8(4)(c) and (f) of the Children Act 1989, will have been repealed.

Where your client has been the victim of domestic violence you should take immediate action to protect them from any further harm by taking the following action:

- inform the police;

- place your client and his or her children in temporary accommodation; or

- seek the exclusion of the violent or abusive person;

- seek legal advice about obtaining an occupation order or a non-molestation order against the violent or abusive person.

Legal protection against domestic violence

Under the Family Law Act 1996, the legal protection against domestic violence is provided by two orders: an 'occupation order' and a 'non-molestation order' (see Appendix 1). The orders are available from either the High Court, a county court or magistrates' court.

An occupation order

An occupation order which gives the applicant a legal right to occupy the home and will usually exclude the other party from the party's home. The order can be applied for in other family proceedings or as an independent remedy against domestic violence without other proceedings being commenced. The person seeking an occupation order is known as the applicant and the person against whom the order is sought is the respondent.

The categories of people entitled to make an application

For the first time in domestic violence legislation, the Act clarifies the legal rights and obligations of each party in situations of domestic violence in relation to specific categories of people including:

- where the applicant is entitled to occupy the home through the general law or by virtue of the matrimonial home rights; or

- where the applicant is a former spouse; or

- where the applicant is a cohabitant or former cohabitant of the home.

The order may be applied for against any person with whom the applicant is associated and where the property was at any time intended to be their home.

The factors to be considered

In deciding whether to grant an occupation order, the court is required to consider all relevant factors including:

(1) the housing needs and resources of each party and any relevant child

- a relevant child means a child who is living with a party; or

- who might reasonably be expected to live with either party; or

- an adopted child; or

- any other child whose interests the court considers to be relevant (s 62(2)).

(2) the financial resources of each party;

(3) the likely effect of the court exercising or deciding not to exercise its powers to make an order on the health, safety or well-being of the parties or of any relevant child;

(4) the conduct of the parties in relation to each other and otherwise (s 33(6)).

The court is also required to consider these factors alongside the 'harm' test provided for by s 33(7) which requires the court should make an order where:

(1) it appears that the applicant and/or a relevant child is likely to suffer significant harm if the order is not made; and

(2) the significant harm is attributable to the conduct of the respondent.

How long will the order last?

There is no maximum duration for the order. The order can be made:

- for a specified period; or

- until the happening of a specified event; or

- until the making of a further order.

The declaratory order

The court may also make a declaratory order which establishes the right of one party of their entitlement to occupy the home. The court may further declare that where a party enjoys matrimonial home rights, those rights will not be brought to an end by the death of the other spouse or the termination of the marriage.

Ancillary orders

When making an occupation order the court may under s 40 make an ancillary order imposing certain obligations on either party. These obligations may include:

- the payment of rent or mortgage instalments;

- the maintenance of the home;

- to allow the other party possession of furniture and so on.

The factors to be considered

In deciding whether to exercise its powers under s 40 the court will take into account the following factors:

- the financial needs and resources of the parties; and

- the financial obligations which they have or are likely to have in the foreseeable future, including the financial obligations to each other and any relevant child.

A non-molestation order

Section 42 provides the court with power to make a non-molestation order. The order can relate to acts of molestation in general or to individual acts of molestation or both. The order can be made where the applicant makes a separate application or is ordered as part of other family proceedings. The order can be made for the benefit of the applicant and/or a relevant child.

The meaning of molestation

Molestation is not defined in the Act and reference will need to be made to decided cases under the old law. Molestation appears to include acts of physical and psychological violence towards another person.

The content of the order

Under s 42(1), a non-molestation order may contain one or both of the following:

- a provision prohibiting the respondent from molesting another person who is associated with the respondent;

- a provision prohibiting the respondent from molesting a relevant child.

The factors to be considered

In deciding whether to make a non-molestation order the court is required to have regard to all the circumstances of the case including the need to secure the health, safety and well-being of the applicant and/or any relevant child.

Factors common to both orders

It is important to be aware of the following provisions which apply to both an occupation order and a non-molestation order.

Children

The Act allows an application for an occupation order and/or a non-molestation order to be made by a child under the age of 16 where the leave of the court has been granted. The application will only be granted where the court is satisfied that the child has sufficient understanding to make the application.

Ex parte orders

The court has the power to make either order *ex parte*, ie without the knowledge of the respondent where it is just and equitable to do so. This power is especially useful in emergency situations where the applicant wants to catch the respondent by surprise.

Enforcement

The court is required to attach a power of arrest in respect of both orders (including *ex parte* applications) where it appears that the respondent has used or threatened violence against the applicant or a relevant person unless the applicant or the child will be adequately protected without a power of arrest.

Where the respondent breaches either order, the police can arrest the respondent without a warrant who must be brought before the court which made the orders within 24 hours of the arrest.

Adoption

In 1994, 6,329 adoption orders were made in the UK, of which 3,071 were made to step-parents. Adoption is the legal transfer of a child from one set of parents to another and all parental responsibility is passed to the adopting parents.

Adoption procedures are closely controlled by the law, and the child's new status is recognised by the law to the extent that a new birth certificate is issued to give legal effect to the child's new identity.

Your professional involvement with adoption will arise where your social services agency acts as an adoption agency, vetting prospective adopting parents who are usually childless couples or step-parents or a natural parent such as the child's unmarried father.

When deciding to allow the prospective parents to adopt the child, the adoption agency will have to give first consideration to the interests of the child and pay attention to the prospective parent's attitude to religious upbringing.

Whilst the court's role is to give formal recognition to the child's new status, it may be required to arbitrate in disputes between the adoption agency and the other parties. A common dilemma encountered by social workers is where the child's natural parents, usually an unmarried mother, is understandably reluctant to give her child up. In these circumstances the adoption agency can make a submission to the court that the child's natural parent is unreasonably withholding consent to the adoption and ask the court to override the parent's wishes. In deciding this desperately difficult issue, the court applies an objective test by considering whether a reasonable parent would see the adoption as being beneficial to the long-term interest of the child.

The law relating to adoption is undergoing change. The new adoption legislation includes:

- the need to obtain the agreement of a child over 12 to the adoption;

- the court can order an adoption where it is considered to be 'in the child's best interests';

- the present guidelines on the age, ethnicity and education of the prospective adopting parents would be relaxed and applied more flexibly.

The private fostering of children

Part IX of the Children Act 1989 deals with the private fostering of children. Under the Act the local authority must be notified of a private fostering arrangement where:

- the child is under the age of 16; and

- is living with someone other than the person with parental responsibility or another relative;

- for a period longer than 28 days.

To be brought within the provisions of the Act it is not necessary that fostering arrangements should involve the payment. However, excluded from the Act will be where the child is at boarding school or is being looked after by his or her grandparents. The most common fostering arrangement is where the child is taken into care and the social services agency itself places the child with foster parents.

Section 67 requires that a local authority should satisfy itself that the welfare of foster children within its area is being satisfactorily safeguarded and protected. In discharging this role, a local authority has the power to inspect foster homes and ensure that people who are disqualified from fostering children are not allowed to do so.

Wardship

Wardship is the inherent power of the High Court to assume responsibility over a child who becomes a 'ward of court'. As a result no major decision can be taken about the child's life without the consent of the court. A wardship application is appropriate where it is necessary to protect a child's interest in an emergency. It has been used in a wide variety of situations including whether a child should be allowed to live outside of the UK; or whether the child's life support system should be switched off or whether a mentally-retarded schoolgirl should be sterilised.

The Children Act 1989 has substantially reduced the importance of wardship in a social worker's professional life. Where you consider that wardship is the appropriate course of action you will have to:

- obtain the leave (permission) of the High Court; and

- show that the court orders available under the Children Act 1989 will not achieve the necessary results; and

- the child will suffer significant harm if she or he is not made a ward of court; and

- that you have a proper interest in the child's welfare.

Wardship takes place immediately even before the application is heard. The hearing must take place within three weeks of the application being made.

Practice points

Social workers should:

- be aware of the 'one year' rule;

- know the ground for divorce – 'irretrievable breakdown' and proof by one or more of the 'five' facts;

- be aware in outline of the practice and procedure for divorce and be able to apply to your social work practice;

- be aware of the proposed reform of the divorce laws under the Family law Act 1996;

- be aware of the practice, procedure and remedies available in relation to domestic violence and be able to apply them in your social work practice;

- know the practice and procedure in relation to fostering and adoption.

Further reading

Burton, F, *Family Law and Practice*, 1996, London: Cavendish Publishing.

Burton F, *Guide to the Family law Act 1996*, 1996, London: Cavendish Publishing.

Davies, R and Mornington, M, *Matrimonial Proceedings*, 2nd edn, 1991, London: Cavendish Publishing.

9   Local authorities and community care

Ever since the 18th century poor law legislation, the local authority's role in social services has been paramount. Over decades many separate statutes have established local authorities, in the guise of social services, as the main provider of social care and welfare. To that end, most, if not all, of these statutes have recognised that social services departments across the UK are for most children and families a substitute for care and support. Following the Seebohm Committee of 1965, after 1971 the administrative organisation of social services was transformed from children's, health and welfare departments under a single social services committee and department under the directorship of one head of social services in each local authority to cover:

- home help;
- mental health support;
- day care;
- child care services;
- care for the elderly;
- care for the homeless;
- care for disabled persons.

From this structure has grown the modern social services department with its following services:

- child protection and registration;
- residential care;
- home care services;
- community care;
- information services;
- day care services.

Some of these services being directly provided by the local authorities and others by contractors, or in partnerships with other local authorities or organisations.

This form of structure, modelled on Beveridge's 1942 'five giants' programme of social security, education, health, employment and housing, combining forces to combat mutual issues of concern.

Consequently, the role of the social worker has been reformed by sweeping legal reforms which diversifies their role further, and subsequently their practice. In light of these changes the role of the local authority as the employer of social worker has changed. Contracting-out has distanced this relationship further, with many social workers now being employed outside the Town Hall environment in private contractors, charitable or voluntary organisations. These changes were identified recently by the Court of Appeal in *Barret v Enfield LBC* (see (1997) *The Times*, 22 April), where it held that if a social worker was careless in implementing decisions relating to a child in care the local authority could be found to be vicariously liable for the resulting damage. Hence a local authority has a duty after a child has been placed in care. Yet had this involved a contractor, the individual social worker might have been liable, as well as her/his employer. The difference here being whether a statutory duty held by a statutory agency, a local authority, is being executed by such, or another agency. Thus, an interplay between the law of negligence (tort law) and employment law, the latter being determined by the employment relationships of the social worker and employer concerned, exists. In terms of powers, local authorities have immense duties, not only pursuant to s 17 of the Children Act 1989 to '... safeguard and promote the welfare of children within their area who are in need ...', but all in their geographical area in need.

Community care

According to Clements: 'Community care law results from a hotchpotch of statutes ...' (see Clements, *Community Care and the Law*, 1997, London: Legal Action Group). This is indeed true and such is reinforced by the fact that some form of community care has always existed in the UK. From Medieval days with the monasteries and churches providing shelter, through to the poor laws of Victorian England, to Beveridge establishing the 'modern welfare state' and to modern times, the issue of caring for the community has both existed and remained controversial. However, whatever decade is under discussion, the term 'community care' is concerned with adults (ie, persons over 18 years of age, since those below this age will be cared for under the provisions of the Children Act 1989) who comprise of the following groups within society: the elderly, disabled persons and persons who are mentally ill.

Often these groups within society are referred to as those most 'vulnerable', so as to implicitly reveal the major purpose of the provision now under investigation, that is the aspect of care or after-care.

For a number of decades now, social services, often in partnership with other agencies, such as housing agencies, health trusts, as well as charitable trusts and voluntary organisations, have been given a lead role in providing services for those persons listed above. In order to execute such a task, questions about needs, levels of service provision and resourcing prevails. Moreover, until 1993, these salient questions were answered by a collection of voluminous and various statutes.

In fact the legal structure for so-called 'community care' prior to 1990 consisted of seven statutes, identified as follows:

- National Assistance Act 1948;

- Health Services and Public Health Act 1968;

- Chronically Sick and Disabled Persons Act 1970;

- Local Authority Social Services Act 1970;

- National Health Services Act 1977;

- Mental Health Act 1983;

- Disabled Persons (Services, Consultation and Representation) Act 1986.

Consequently, it was found by those who used and provided these services that reform was needed, in order to provide some simplicity, if not clarity, amongst service providers. Eventually, the Audit Commission (see 'Making a reality of Community care', 1986, HMSO) investigated the need for reform as early as 1986 and produced a report recommending a mixed economy in community care, comprising a new statute setting out some general duties on key questions, such as assessment and care. In response to this report an enquiry was held by the government and a subsequent report was produced in 1988. The 1988 Griffiths Report, entitled *Community Care: An Agenda for Action*, noted that care provision needed greater transparency.

Moreover, Sir Roy Griffiths recommended:

- clarification in the role of central and local government in community care provision;

- the promotion of independent living;

- the need for local government to develop local priorities and undertake the assessment of local needs;

- the enhancement of the role of the health authority in community health service; and

- to transfer the responsibility of funding residential accommodation and nursing homes to local authorities.

Subsequently, a 'new' statutory framework was established in 1990. This change came under the auspices of the National Health Service and Community Care Act (NHS&CCA) 1990 which eventually came into force in April 1993. The key provisions contained in this Act are as follows:

- A statutory definition of 'community care' was provided. It includes service for:

  (a)   residential accommodation;

  (b)   welfare services;

  (c)   welfare of the elderly;

  (d)   domiciliary and day services;

  (e)   after-care; and

  (f)   services for the mentally ill and disabled (see s 46(3) of the NHS&CCA 1990).

- Charges for accommodation and welfare services were introduced (see ss 42–45 of the NHS&CCA 1990).

- The duty to prepare and publish community care plans (see s 46(1) of the NHS&CCA 1990).

- Establishes a duty to define, determine and assess a person's 'needs' (see s 47 of the NHS&CCA 1990).

- Establishes a duty to adhere to defined procedures determine a person's 'needs' (see s 47 of the NHS&CCA 1990).

- Inspection of premises used for community care services must be undertaken (see s 48 of the NHS&CCA 1990).

- Sets up the relevant framework for complaints procedures by users and the public in general.

More specifically, in terms of social work law, the key provisions in the statute listed above set out legal duties under Part III of the Act. In addition, in respect of children, duties to children in need are found in s 17 of the Children Act 1989.

The law and the costs of care

Recently, the controversial issue about the costs of care have been scrutinised by the courts in an attempt to resolve the long, on-going dispute between local authorities and government about the costs of social care. Most notably, the recent *Sefton* case (see *R v Sefton MBC, ex p Help the Aged* (1997) *The Times*, 26 March), in which the High Court ruled that a local authority was entitled to take its resources into account when assessing whether a person seeking accommodation was in need under the National Assistance Act 1948. This clearly established the relevance of costs when a local authority seeks to identify its priorities in organising social care within its area.

The *Sefton* case, now ensures the applicant's need to be assessed according to the provider's resources and costs. Fortunately for the local authority concerned this decision came after the House of Lords definitive judgement on costs in the *Barry* case (see *R v Gloucestershire CC, ex p Barry* [1997] 2 All ER 1, HL). In this three to two decision, with Lloyd and Steyn LJ dissenting, their Lordships held that in deciding how much weight was to be attached to the cost of providing care, the authority had to make an evaluation about the impact that cost would bear on its own resources.

So important is the cost of care that even the courts are now forced to accept that the overall costs of service provision ought to be borne in mind when determining, whether or not, to deliver the care provision required.

Working with the elderly

Over 10 million people in the UK are over 65 years of age. According to Age Concern this figure is likely to increase inevitably making an impact upon social care in Britain in the next millennium. Such an increase in older persons has over the last 10 years also promoted an increase in the number of agencies, some charities and others specialist providers, which provide residential care and social care support to these people. With the advent of the NHS&CCA 1990 the introduction of care management and intervention has also highlighted the greater needs of the growing elder populous. To this end, for over half of the workers employed in local authorities, social work now comprises of caring for the elderly. These adult specialists, experienced care workers or residential social workers, must be able to both clearly communicate with those under their care, as well as constantly assessing their needs. They should also, according to CCETSW '... have extensive knowledge of legislation affecting older people' (see CCETSW, 'Work with Older People', Paper 13, August 1993). Consequently, they should understand all of the legislation contained in this chapter, particularly the NHS&CCA 1990 and the National Assistance Act 1948, as outlined above. Moreover, those social workers working with disabled people should also familiarise themselves with the relevant legislation, as described above, as well as the Direct Payments Act 1996 and the Disability Discrimination Act 1995 examined in Chapter 23.

Carers and the law

In order for the NHS&CCA 1990 to succeed, the legislators recognised the need for crucial support to be provided by a vital network of carers. Whilst the legislation recognises the need for carers, the 1990 Act did very little to encourage professional care, since it promoted free care. Eventually, this omission was rescinded in 1995, when the then UK government enacted the Carers Act 1995. Under s 1 of the Carers (Recognition and Services) Act 1995, coupled with s 8 of the Disabled Persons (Services, Consultation and Representation) Act 1986, carers, though not statutorily defined, are to be involved in the assessment and are likely to be assessed by the assessor/social services as to their abilities to be a carer.

It should be noted that voluntary organisation employees and volunteers are excluded from the definition, for the purposes of either Acts, of 'carer'.

Circular LAC (96)7 covers local authorities interpretations of 'regular' and 'substantial' care. Moreover, Practice Guidance issued by the Social Services Inspectorate encourages the view that carers should participate in the assessment process. Whether the carers be parents, young carers, or even advocates, they can be supported by various services and organisations (see s 1 of the 1995 Act).

Residential accommodation and care

Social workers will be reminded of the importance of residential care by the Central Council for the Education and Training of Social Workers' (CCETSW) statement on 'Residential care', Paper 12, October 1993, which states that:

> Some children and adults with special needs require more support than their families can offer, or than they can provide themselves, even with the help of domiciliary and day care services; they need to live in residential homes, hostels, sheltered housing or some other form of group care.

Thus, many social workers will need to familiarise themselves with the powers and duties which a social services department holds in its provision of residential accommodation. These powers are primarily the result of ss 21 and 29 of the National Assistance Act 1948 (see Part III). Additionally, other residential care and accommodation are provided under either the Registered Homes Act 1984; the Mental Health Act 1983, to be discussed below in detail; or, under the NHS&CCA 1990 by NHS Trusts.

The two salient prerequisites for residential care are that the person must be 18 or over and must be in need of care and attention which is otherwise unavailable to them.

Again the formula, 'care and attention' are not defined by any of the statutes concerned. Likewise, the terms 'otherwise unavailable to them' conform to the usual legal catch or exclude all clause of phraseology which often confuses, due to the differing levels of discretion read into these terms, than clarifies. As a result, numerous cases have sought to interpret the terms (see *Steane v Chief Adjudication Officer* (1996) *The Times*, 8 August, HL). The overall conclusion of this case law being that the applicant must show that he or she is seeking accommodation from social services as a 'last resort'.

Subsequently, to meet the test as outlined above and to be considered by the courts in numerous cases, criteria is considered when a person applies for residential accommodation, as follows:

- age;

- illness;

- disability;

- whether the applicant is an expectant mother; and

- any other relevant circumstances.

Whilst the latter category remains vague and broad, it has become customary practice that it refers to, more often than not, any mental disorder or alcohol and/or drug dependency which the applicant might be suffering from.

Social workers should note that following the Housing Act 1996, the homeless are considered separately and the provisions of the 1996 Housing Act apply in the instant cases.

It remains in this section to deal with two outstanding related issues in this area of residential accommodation: first, what do we mean by residential accommodation and second, what duties do social services have in order to register and inspect homes that are at their disposal for residential care and accommodation?

In respect of what is residential accommodation, s 21 of the National Assistance Act 1948 places a duty on social services to make arrangements for providing residential accommodation. Residential accommodation can therefore be provided by either the social services department itself, or alternatively it can be provided by another social services department from another local authority; or by a voluntary organisation or private provider. Subject to s 26 of the National Assistance Act 1948 and the NHS&CCA 1990 a voluntary organisation or a private provider can provide residential accommodation. In any event, residential accommodation is categorised as accommodation which includes care and accommodation with nursing care.

The Registered Homes Act 1984 defines residential accommodation as: 'an establishment which provides or is intended to provide ... residential accommodation.' Consequently, all (with the exception of local authority homes) residential care homes must be registered (see s 1(5) of the Registered Homes Act 1984). In accordance with the Registered Homes (Amendment) Act 1991, even residential care homes with fewer than four residents must now also register.

Registration of homes for residential care involves the registration of the person who is to be or is in charge of the home (see s 3 of the Registered Homes Act 1984 and Circular LAC (95) 12).

More importantly, registration is only given were the applicant can establish:

- that the persons working the home are fit to do so;

- that the premises are fit to be used (ie considering the state of repair, staffing levels and equipment and facilities available);

- that the home will provide the services and facilities required.

In contrast, a 'nursing home' is defined under s 21 of the Registered Homes Act 1984 as: 'premises used for the reception of ... persons suffering from any sickness, injury or infirmity ...' (note s 22 defines a nursing home for the mentally disordered). As with residential homes, all nursing homes, including mental nursing homes, must be registered, but with the local NHS authority rather than social services. Like residential homes, the conditions listed above must be met and the services provided according to the medical and health needs of the residents (see Nursing Homes and Mental Nursing Homes Regulations 1984, in particular, Regulation 12).

Last, with regard to registration and inspection, all local authorities, namely social services have a duty to inspect all residential care homes (see s 17 of the Registered Homes Act 1984 and Regulation 18 of the Residential Care Homes Regulations 1984).

Any homes found operating without registration will be liable to prosecution and a fine. Inspections are merely intended to establish whether the service is managed and whether the home meets the standard required?

Guidance on inspection has been produced by the SSI, which ensures that social services' inspection and registration units are independent and undertake inspections objectively. In fact since the NHS&CCA 1990, these inspection powers have been extended to cover any premises from which community care services are provided.

As for nursing and mental nursing homes, inspection of this accommodation lies with the Secretary of State for Health.

The enforcement of the community care statutory duties

For aggrieved users of the community care services there lies two routes for enforcement: public and private remedies. Each depends on the circumstances of the complaint and the remedy sought. For instance, for negligence claims the private route would be taken. In contrast, to challenge a decision by a local authority not to provide a service, the alternative public route would be utilised.

It therefore very much depends upon the type of complaint. Also, not only should the nature of the complaint be considered, but also the available complaints bodies or mechanism. Since the 1990 Act requires local authorities to have a complaints procedure. In addition, various other statutes still provide remedies and appellate tribunals themselves, for example, the Registered Homes Tribunal. Furthermore, where necessary, some complainants might have rights under the European Convention on Human Rights 1950, based on a violation of their fundamental rights.

Mental health

As discussed in the last section of this chapter mental health belongs to the so-called 'vulnerable' group of persons within our society. Moreover, it is part of the law relating to community care. However, the law governing social workers' duties in respect of those who are mentally ill is the Mental Health Act 1983, which repeals the Mental Health Act 1959. Until 1990, social workers' interest in the provision of services for the mentally ill concerned institutionalised care rather than care in the community.

Defining 'mental illness'

The central term upon which the 1983 Act revolves is 'mental illness'. The 1983 Act defines mental illness as: '... arrested or incomplete development of the mind, psychopathic disorder and any other disorder or disability of mind.' Four key factors exist within this generic definition: mental impairment, severe mental impairment, mental disorder and psychopathic disorder.

It remains an anomaly that the central term 'mental illness' is not defined in the 1983 Act. However, for the purposes of the Act, 'mental impairment' is defined as:

> ... arrested or incomplete development of mind which includes significant impairment of intelligence and social functioning and is associated with abnormally aggressive or seriously irresponsible conduct on the part of the person concerned.

The concept of 'severe mental impairment' is also used which is defined as:

... arrested or incomplete development of mind which includes severe impairment of intelligence and social functioning and is associated with abnormally aggressive or seriously irresponsible conduct on the part of the person concerned.

In addition, 'psychopathic disorder' is defined as:

... a persistent disorder of mind (whether or not including significant impairment of intelligence) which results in abnormally aggressive or seriously irresponsible conduct on the part of the person concerned.

As already discussed in Part III of this text, certain rules within the criminal justice system apply to the mentally ill. For instance, see the powers of arrest and detention. More importantly, Chapter 14 showed that the mentally ill are not held liable for their acts within the UK criminal justice system. Here, for example, the criminal law provides some specific defences and also creates the new verdict of 'not guilty on evidence of mental disorder' under the Criminal Procedure (Insanity and Unfitness to Plead) Act 1991.

The role of approved social workers under the Mental Health Act 1983

Under s 145 of the Mental Health Act 1983 an approved social worker (ASW) scheme was created. This means that the ASW has extensive powers in relation to dealing with mentally ill persons. These powers include admitting a mentally ill person to hospital or guardianship. Each local authority is responsible for approving ASWs. There is also a statutory duty for each local authority to have sufficient ASWs to deal with the mentally ill in each regional area.

The legislation notes state that next to the ASW the so-called 'nearest relative' has rights over a mentally ill person. In particular, according to s 26 of the Mental Health Act 1983, where no 'nearest relative' exists: then a cohabitee (over six months); son or daughter; parent; brother or sister; grandparents; or an aunt and uncle can assume responsibilities for the mentally ill person.

It should be noted that compulsory admissions are carried out on the application of either the ASW or the nearest relative. Under s 2 of the Mental Health Act 1983, for the admission for assessment of a mentally ill person the authorisation of either the ASW or the 'nearest relative' is required, as well as the support of two doctors. One of the doctors should be a specialist in mental disorder.

'Sectioning' as it is termed, is undertaken when:

- the patient is suffering from mental disorder of a nature or degree which warrants the detention of the patient in a hospital for assessment;

- the patient ought to be so detained in the interests of his or her own health and safety or with a view to the protection of other persons.

On some occasions an emergency admission might be required. Again, before making an emergency admission the consent of one doctor is required under s 4 of the Mental Health Act 1983, though the same grounds as required by s 2 listed above are used. However, additionally, the doctor or 'nearest relative' must state that it is 'of urgent necessity for the patient to be admitted and detained under s 2' and that a s 2 application would involve 'undesirable delay'. Normally, these emergency detentions last for a maximum duration of 72 hours, but they might be automatically converted into a s 2 detention, comprising a 28-day duration, where the second doctor is obtained during the 72-hour period of the emergency order. It should also be noted that this emergency power under s 4 does not give authorisation to administer treatment without consent. Yet where the order is converted to a s 2 order such treatment will be permitted. Section 3 allows for treatment without consent.

Where the nearest relative objects to the 'sectioning' and gives notice of his or her objection under s 11(4), then an application to the county court must be made. The maximum duration of the order under s 3 is six months. Though, the court may be renewed on the advice of a consultant for a further six months and thereafter for a year at a time. Section 13(1) of the 1983 Act imposes a positive duty on the ASW to make an application for compulsory admission in certain circumstances, for instance:

- where the patient is physically present within the area covered by the social workers local authority;

- where the social worker is 'satisfied' that the application ought to be made;

- where the ASW is satisfied that the application should be made then he or she is under a duty to make such an application if he is of the opinion that 'it is necessary or proper for the application to be made by him' having regard to any wishes expressed by relatives of the patient or any other relevant circumstances.

Hospital detention and ASW procedures

Section 13(2) requires the ASW to 'interview the patient in a suitable manner and satisfy himself that the detention in a hospital is in all the circumstances of the case the most appropriate way of providing the care and medical treatment of which the patient stands in need'.

When applying for compulsory admission an ASW must have seen the patient within the 14 days prior to the application (see s 11(5)) or in the case of an emergency application within the 24 hours prior to the application.

Should a dispute arise between the opinion of the ASW to section and the 'nearest relative', as discussed above, the ASW must apply to the county court for authorisation. The powers of the county court in this area are found in s 29 of the 1983 Act. There are four grounds for obtaining the courts' authorisation against the wishes of the 'nearest relative'.

Guardianship in mental health

Guardianship in the context of 'mental health' is half way between full liberty in society and detention in hospital. Whilst the concept of 'guardianship' allows some element of control over the patient, it also allows for movement by the patient as she or he desires.

There are no age restrictions on the powers of compulsory admission under the 1983 Act. Yet no one under the age of 16 may be entered into guardianship under the 1983 Act (see ss 7(1) and 37(2)(a)(ii) of the Act).

In order to apply for guardianship, the social worker must believe that the person for whom he or she is applying for guardianship is suffering from mental illness, psychopathic disorder, severe mental impairment or mental impairment of a nature or degree which warrants his or her reception into guardianship. Again, two doctors must support the social worker's view, as well as be satisfied that reception into guardianship is necessary 'in the interests of the welfare of the patient or for the protection of other persons'.

Like 'sectioning', guardianship can also be ordered by a court. This guardianship order can be made on the basis of the patient suffering from mental impairment, psychopathic disorder or a severe mental impairment and that the court is satisfied that such an order is the most suitable method of dealing with the case in all the circumstances. As with a s 3 admission the nearest relative can oppose the ASW's application.

The powers of a guardian over a mental disordered person

The 1983 gives the guardian certain powers over the patient. These are:

- to require the patient to live at a specified place;

- to require the patient to attend at specified times and at specified places for the purposes of medical treatment, occupation, education or training;

- to require that access to the patient be given to any doctor, any ASW or any other specified person.

It should be noted that there is no legal sanction which can be brought to bear if a patient decides not to comply with such an order. Guardianship orders have a six months duration and can be further renewed for six months and thereafter at yearly intervals.

Mental Health Review Tribunals

As already suggested in Part I of this text, social workers should familiarise themselves with the various tribunals as well as courts within which they potentially operate. One tribunal of importance to social workers is the Mental Health Review Tribunal (MHRT).

Both a patient and in some cases the 'nearest relative' has the right to apply to an MHRT for discharge from hospital or guardianship. MHRT's have the power to order discharge from a hospital or from a guardianship order on the basis that the original criteria for detention are no longer justified.

A patient has the right to apply to the MHRT within 14 days of a s 2 admission and within six months of a s 3 admission.

The 'nearest relative' has the right to apply to the MHRT where he or she is prevented from discharging a patient by the application of a Registered Medical Officer. Such an application must be made within 28 days of being informed of the doctor's action.

Where a nearest relative is replaced on an order of the county court she or he may apply to an MHRT within 12 months of that decision. Where a patient is detained under a hospital order the nearest relative can apply after six months to the MHRT and once a year after that.

It is important to note that under s 132 of the 1983 Act hospital staff are under a statutory obligation to ensure that the patient is aware of her or his rights. This includes their appellate rights before a MHRT with regard to their correspondence, treatment and the grounds for their detention.

The Mental Health Act Code of Practice

Pursuant to s 118 of the 1983 Act, in the August of 1983 the Secretary of State for Health issued a Code of Practice. This code covers:

- assessment prior to admission;

- admission to hospital;

- admission to a guardian under the Act;

- treatment and care in hospital;

- leaving hospital;

- treatment of children and young people (ie under 18 years of age);

- treatment of those persons with learning disabilities.

The code came into force on 1 November 1993. Whilst there is no legal duty to comply with the code, failure to do so will be noted by any court of law or tribunal. In effect, the Code covers the gaps left open by the Act itself. To that end, most social workers adhere to this code. In fact, practitioners are advised to acquaint, if not reacquaint, themselves with the code.

Lastly, the Mental Health Commission continues to monitor the code's operation and revisions are made to the code, as and when necessary. Also, readers from Scotland should note that they should consult the Mental Health (Scotland) Act 1984 for the relevant law relating to mental health in Scotland.

Special needs education

Baroness Warnock chaired an inquiry into the education of handicapped children in 1978. Its underlying aim was to investigate the then common practice across Britain of refusing to educate special needs education children in mainstream schools, often excluding these children and making them attend what were termed 'special schools'. The Warnock Report's sweeping recommendations put an end to this discriminatory practice and, subject to certain conditions set out in s 160 of the 1993 Act, allowed for the special needs education child to be educated in an ordinary school, should the parent so desire. Consequently, the Warnock Report very much influenced the later Education Act 1981, which sought to resolve some of the concerns of parents and guardians of children with special educational needs. Now, Part III of the Education Act 1993 makes provision for the education of children with special needs in line with the proposals set out in the White Paper 'Choice and Diversity: A Framework for Schools' (see Cmnd 20221, 1992).

Section 156 of the 1993 Act defines a child as having special educational needs if they have 'a learning difficulty which calls for special educational provision to be made'. Moreover, s 156(2) states that a 'learning difficulty' is adjudged by the level of greater difficulty the child has which is significantly more than other children of her/his age; or, she or he has a disability which hinders that child from making use of educational facilities. Furthermore, s 156(2) refers to any child under five years of age who is or will be deemed as having a learning difficulty at school age.

In addition, under s 166 a local authority or health authority has a duty to help a local education authority to identify and assess children with special educational needs. Subsequently the Education (Special Educational Needs) Regulations 1994 SI 1994/1047 and a Code of Practice on the identification and assessment of needs 1994 (see Department of Education and Employment (DfEE), 1994, HMSO) were enacted which set out the procedures to be followed when undertaking an assessment. Quite clearly, at all stages the parent ought to be consulted and involved. In fact, the whole procedure commences with a formal notice being served on the parents. Should a local authority, having assessed the child, decide to provide special education, then a statement of need will be produced (see s 168(5) of the 1993 Act). Following an assessment, should a local authority decide not to provide any special education, then the parents have a right to appeal against the decision to the Special Educational Needs Tribunals. Parents also have a right to appeal against the contents of a statement, pursuant to s 170(3) of the 1993 Act.

Clearly, the law in this area is incredibly complex. Due to the perplexity of the legislation, the case law is often confusing. For instance, in *R v East Sussex CC, ex p T*, the High Court (*per* Keene J) recently held (see (1997) *The Times* 29 April) that in deciding what educational provision was suitable under s 298 of the Education Act 1993, regard should be had to the individual character of the child in question rather than to the local authority's financial resources. Although, resources were relevant in deciding between different forms of suitable provision. More recently, the High Court held that in deciding whether a particular school was suitable for a child with special educational needs, a local education authority did not need to carry out a balancing exercise between the degree of unsuitability of the school and the parents' wishes. In fact, Popplewell J ruled that the suitability of a school was a question of fact not fairness (see *Crane v Lancashire CC* (1997) *The Times*, 16 May).

However, the House of Lords gave a definitive ruling in *X (a Minor) and Others v Bedfordshire CC et al* (see [1995] 3 All ER 353, HL) suggests that in special educational needs cases, the success of an action for breach of statutory duty depends upon whether the statute intended such an action to be taken. Moreover, that a mere assertion of the careless exercise of a statutory power or duty is not sufficient in itself to give rise to a private law cause of action. The established current law on special educational needs cases, therefore, is that an action for vicarious liability against the local authority for the negligent advice of their professional employees, the staff being qualified or/and trained in special needs education, is likely to be more successful than a claim for a breach of statutory duty for failure to provide special needs education.

Clearly, the law deals with each case on its facts and merits. To that end, in special education needs cases, social workers can play a vital supportive role to the children and families concerned.

Education and the law

One would not do the law justice, if we pretended here to state all the current law governing education. That would certainly not be possible within the confines of this text. However, what we intend to do below to is alert social workers to the major statutes in this area and the major issues, such as attendance, exclusion and discrimination.

The duty to provide education grew out of the Education Act 1944. Yet it was this statute which recognised that parents and guardians of children also had obligations with regard to the education of children in their care. It was under this Act that the concept of *loco parentis* emerged, meaning that those who care for children of school age, either parents or guardians must ensure that they are educated and, moreover, that they are responsible for children when in their care. Thus, schools become liable for children during the school day. It was also made law that children must compulsorily attend school until the age of 16. However, under the Education Act 1980, parents and guardians now have a right to decide which school they wish their child to attend.

Where it is found that a child's school attendance is poor and where the school has informally attempted to seek an explanation or resolve the problems discovered to no avail, then subject to s 192 of the Education Act 1993 a notice will be served upon the parent requiring them, normally within 15 days, to ensure that the child concerned is receiving suitable education. Thereafter, should a local education authority remain concerned about an absent child, a school attendance order will be sought. Once such an order has been granted, then the parents should they default on the order are liable to prosecution before the local magistrates' court. The usual penalty being a fine. It remains a fact under s 36 of the Children Act 1989 that even where the parents are not prosecuted, a local education authority in consultation with its social services department and the requisite local authority committee may apply to the court for an education supervision order, which places the child's educational supervision under the responsibility of the local authority, thus abrogating the parent's duties. The supervising education officer, whilst placing the 'welfare of the child' first and foremost, will assist both the child and parents in ensuring that the child receives 'suitable education'. The courts require evidence of the need for an order in accordance with Department of Health Guidance and Regulation (The Children Act 1989) 1991. When granted these orders last for 12 months only and must then be renewed, if it is appropriate to do so.

Apart from poor attendance, another controversial issue in education at present is exclusion from school. Since the enactment of the Education Act 1993, amending the Education Act 1986, exclusions from schools can no longer be indefinite and, therefore, must be for fixed periods (see s 261 of the 1993 Act). Pursuant to the Department of Education's Circular 10/94, parents have a right to appeal against such exclusions to both the governing body and local education committee. Again here, it is the education social worker (ESW) who can play a vital role, since school exclusions can have damaging consequences on the child concerned, as well as the school. Moreover, it is worthy of note that children with behavioural problems will often be sent to the educational psychological services for assessment and any assistance. Here a vital interplay amongst the various services at the disposal of social services is critical and should not be overlooked. It should also be noted that none of these rules apply to a child with special educational needs, as discussed above.

The final contemporary educational issue at the moment in the UK is about discrimination in schools. Not only now does the national curriculum provide for an exchange and understanding of cultural views, but also for a discussion about non-discriminatory behaviour. To this end, schools, like other public services must operate in accordance with the Race and Sex Discrimination Acts 1976 and 1975, to be discussed later in Chapter 23. Also, special regulations govern schools in respect of disability. In more general terms, any racist or sexist behaviour in schools ought to be eradicated and the pupils disciplined accordingly.

A vital interface between education and social work is that of the education welfare officer (EWO). This office holder developed alongside compulsory education in the UK, in order to enforce school attendance. However, out of these narrow beginnings came the role of the ESW. The organisation of ESWs varies from one local authority to another. There roles are to:

- support schools and parents;

- ensure regular school attendance;

- investigate where a child is at risk or suffering from social deprivation or disadvantage.

The latter role proves often to be the most controversial. This is more than often due to the ambiguity of the law. For instance, what is meant by 'social deprivation and disadvantage' is left open to interpretation by the individual ESW concerned. Though, guidance provided defines such as behavioural problems, illness, abuse or risk of abuse and educational needs and support. More recently, this controversy has centred around child abuse and neglect by parents and others, exclusions of pupils from school, and child labour (this will be discussed later in Chapter 23). Due to the vast nature of the ESWs job, they are often working in partnership with the police, health visitors, teachers, community groups and the DSS. The ESWs role also covers the educational and behavioural difficulties of children, as well as the psychological services available for pupils.

Future reform?

The Queen's Speech following the 1997 General Election has noted that further reform of the NHS is to be introduced. The Bill has not yet been published and the proposed changes are not yet fully known. However, despite the ramifications which the ending of the internal market in the NHS will have on the existing social work framework, how these reforms will affect community care provision is currently speculative only. Though, it is likely that social care will be more integrated with health, as was the case prior to 1977. We await the Bill.

Practice points

Social workers should:

- be able to recognise the relevant statutes which provide a framework for community care provision within the UK;

- Recognise and apply their duties under ss 42–47 of the NHS& CCA 1990 to their social work practice;

- be fully aware of carers of their rights and responsibilities under the Carers Act 1995;

- be sensitive to the rights to your elderly and vulnerable clients;

- know all the major provisions contained in the Mental Health Act 1983 .

In particular, approved social workers, should:

- know the rights and responsibilities surrounding their role in mental health;

- appreciate the rights of the 'nearest relative';

- fully comprehend the rights and the role of medical professionals (Doctors) in mental health assessments.

With regard to education, social workers should be aware:

- of the rights of the parents and the education authorities concerned;

- of the welfare, in particular educational welfare, of the child, whether it be an issue of exclusion, non-attendance, bullying, poor conduct, anti-social behaviour or special needs provision;

- of the relevant Education Acts.

Further reading

CCETSW, *Educational welfare*, Paper 4, May 1996.

CCETSW, *Residential care*, Paper 12, October 1993.

CCETSW, *Work with disabled people*, Paper 14, May 1993.

CCETSW, *Work with older people*, Paper 13, August 1993.

Clements, L, *Community Care and the Law*, 1997, Legal Action Group

Clements, L, *Duties of social services departments*, September 1992, Legal Action Group.

Code of Practice, Mental Health Act 1983, HMSO.

Dimond, B, *Legal Aspects of Care in the Community*, 1997, London: Kingsley.

Fennell, P, 'The Beverly Lewis Case – was the law to blame?', 17 November 1989, *New Law Journal*.

Hoggett, B, *Mental Health Law*, 2nd edn, 1991, Chapters 1, 2, 3 and 4, London: Butterworths.

Mandelstam, M, *Community Care Practice and the Law*, 1996, London: Kingsley.

Social Services Inspectorate, *Development of Approved Social Worker Services*, 1991, CI(91)09, HMSO.

PART III

CRIMINAL PROCEDURE AND JUSTICE IN SOCIAL WORK

10   Criminal justice

A social worker's professional responsibilities in the criminal justice system require your involvement with the police and the courts in a unique way. At various times, you will work with the police as part of an inter-agency child protection team; negotiating and liaising with the police when a decision is made about what further action (if any) should be taken against your juvenile or 'vulnerable' client; receiving a child into your care where the child is the subject of a secure accommodation order; acting as an 'appropriate' adult at police interviews; appearing in court as a witness or providing support for a 'vulnerable' witness; and assisting the court in its sentencing decision by preparing a pre-sentence report. It is stating the obvious to say that the expectations of your professional competence are extremely high – not least because no other professional or lay person is required to play such a versatile and multi-faceted role.

In recognition of the significant part that criminal justice plays in your professional life, Part III of this book explains the background and context in which the criminal justice system operates and guides you through the essential law, practice and procedure. We have endeavoured, where possible, to keep the subject matter of each chapter in the chronological order in which the case would proceed in practice. Therefore, this chapter introduces the terminology of criminal justice; Chapter 11 deals with the theme of 'the social worker and the police' and includes a detailed examination of police powers; Chapter 12 considers the social worker's role at the police station; Chapter 13 deals with the criminal process of cautioning and court procedure; Chapter 14 outlines sentencing powers and Chapter 15 considers the controversial issue of juvenile justice.

The criminal justice system – the essential background

In recent years the criminal justice system has undergone fundamental change. It has become the focus of heated public debate and controversy, with political parties battling to seize the initiative in the war against the rising tide of lawlessness and anti-social behaviour that appears to be sweeping the UK.

In the wake of this political battle, Parliament has passed legislation which has extended coercive police powers and diluted or abolished a number of fundamental civil rights. Sentencing policy has been influenced by a greater emphasis on retribution against offenders as opposed to rehabilitation. Judicial independence has been threatened by the Crime Sentences Act 1997.

Before we consider how these changes have affected your professional involvement with the criminal justice system, we will take this opportunity of reminding you about the legal and social context in which the criminal justice system operates.

The classification of criminal offences

As a preliminary step it is important to remember that criminal offences can be classified in the following ways.

Common law and statutory offences

A basic distinction is made between common law and statutory offences – whether the criminal offence is created by the courts or Parliament. The vast majority of offences are now created by Parliament in the form of Acts to include:

- **Rape** – s 1(1) of the Sexual Offences Act 1956 which provides that 'it is an offence for a man to rape a woman or another man'.

- **Intercourse with a girl under 13** – s 5 of the Sexual Offences Act 1956.

- **Incest by a man** – s 10 of the Sexual Offences Act 1956.

- **Assault occasioning actual bodily harm** – s 47 of the Offences Against the Persons Act 1861.

Some important common law offences remain, including murder, manslaughter and common assault.

Arrestable or non-arrestable offences

Another significant way of classifying criminal offences is to describe them as either arrestable or non-arrestable.

An arrestable offence allows the immediate arrest, under s 24 of the Police and Criminal Evidence Act (PACE) 1984, of a person suspected of, or caught in the process of committing the offence, without the need to obtain a warrant from a magistrate. The most serious and many middle-ranking criminal offences are arrestable offences including: murder, rape, manslaughter, robbery, causing the prostitution of women and taking a motor vehicle without consent.

As a general rule, non-arrestable offences are those offences where an arrest cannot be made without obtaining a warrant from a magistrate, subject to the provisions of s 25 of the PACE 1984. Non-arrestable offences include most driving and minor regulatory offences.

Summary, 'either way' and indictable offences

Criminal offences can also be classified on the basis of where they are to be tried, ie where the issue of the accused's guilt or innocence is to be decided. Summary offences can only be tried in the magistrates' court. Included in this category are: taking a conveyance, s 12 of the Theft Act 1968; causing fear or provocation of violence, s 4 of the Public Order Act 1986; causing harassment, alarm or distress, s 5 of the Public Order Act 1986.

Offences triable either way

'Either way' offences can be tried either in the magistrates' court or in the Crown Court. The procedure to determine where the case will be tried is called the 'mode of trial' hearing and is provided for by ss 18–21 of the Magistrates' Court Act 1980. Examples of either way offences are: theft, s 1 of the Theft Act 1968; burglary, s 9 of the Theft Act 1968 and; assault occasioning actual bodily harm, s 47 of the Offences Against the Person Act 1861. For further details on the procedure to be followed regarding the mode of trial enquiry see Chapter 13.

Indictable offences

The most serious criminal offences are classified as indictable offences, to include rape, s 1 of the Sexual Offences Act 1956; murder and manslaughter as defined at common law and robbery, s 8 of the Theft Act 1968. Indictable offences are tried before a judge and jury at the Crown Court, provided the case has been sent there for trial by the magistrates' court. This procedure is known as committal proceedings and will be dealt with in detail in Chapter 14.

Serious arrestable and non-serious arrestable offences

Where a person has been arrested by the police in connection with a serious arrestable offence, the police have increased powers to detain the suspect and to temporarily deny the person some basic rights such as refusing him or her to inform a relative or friend of their arrest or access to professional legal advice. All serious offences are serious arrestable offences and many middle-ranking offences can become serious arrestable offences where the provisions of s 116 of the PACE 1984 applies.

The prosecution of criminal offences

The vast majority of criminal offences are prosecuted by the independent Crown Prosecution Service (CPS). The CPS was set up under the Prosecution of Offences Act 1985 and will assume control of the case from the police after the suspect has been formally charged or will advise the police whether there is sufficient evidence to charge the suspect.

When the CPS receives the papers from the police the evidence will be reviewed and a decision made as to whether there is a realistic prospect of conviction and, if so, whether 'it is in the public interest' to continue with the prosecution. In most cases the CPS will either continue with the prosecution or proceed with different charges, usually by reducing the seriousness of the charge, for example, from murder to manslaughter or decide to discontinue the prosecution. Figures for 1994 show that 160,000 or 11% of prosecutions were discontinued by the CPS.

The CPS is headed by the Director of Public Prosecutions, who is accountable to Parliament through the Attorney General. At the present time the organisation is divided into 13 regional areas, each of which is headed by a Chief Crown Prosecutor. In May 1997 plans were announced to reorganise the service into 42 areas – an area for each police force in England and Wales. The plans intended to promote an improved spirit of co-operation between the police and the CPS. Virtually all prosecutions are controlled from the area offices located in most major cities and towns. Some sensitive and complex cases are dealt with by the Director of Public Prosecutions, and these cases will have the case reference or citation as *DPP v Smith* for example.

Other public bodies such as local authorities and the Health and Safety Executive also prosecute criminal offences relating to housing, consumer protection and environmental health whilst the Serious Fraud Office prosecutes the most serious and complex cases of fraud in England, Wales and Northern Ireland.

The criminal courts

As indicated above, the trial of criminal offences will take place in either the magistrates' court (in the case of juveniles in the youth court) or the Crown Court depending on how the offence is classified. The vast majority of criminal cases, approximately 96%, will be tried in the magistrates' court. The most serious offences are tried before a judge and jury in the Crown Court.

The magistrates' court

Magistrates' courts are open to the public and media and are presided over by three lay magistrates, also known as justices of the peace. The magistrates are assisted by a legally qualified or trained clerk. There are about 30,000 lay magistrates and full-time, legally qualified, stipendiary magistrates who sit alone. Stipendiary magistrates usually sit in busy inner city courts. Most cases involving people under 18 are heard in a division of the magistrates' court known as the youth court, these are specialist courts which either sit apart from other courts or are held at a different time.

The Crown Court

The Crown Court was created by the Courts Act 1971. It deals with the more serious criminal offences including the most serious known as 'indictable' offences and middle range offences where it has been decided the case should be heard in the Crown Court.

There are 93 venues. Which case is heard by which court depends upon the classification of the case. The most serious cases, known as class 1 offences, are heard at 'first tier' courts; class 2, 3 and 4 offences are heard at second and third tier courts. They are presided over by High Court judges who hear the most serious cases and circuit judges, recorders and assistant recorders who hear the less serious cases.

The Crown Court also deals with appeals from the magistrates' court against conviction and/or sentence and sentences those offenders committed from the magistrates' court for sentencing. The Crown Court also has jurisdiction over certain civil matters including children, young persons and licensing matters.

Adults, juveniles and children

The words 'adults', 'juveniles', 'children', and 'young people' have their own meaning within the criminal justice system.

- An 'adult' is a person of 18 and over. Typically, these offenders will all be dealt with in the same way – there are certain kinds of sentences which may be imposed on an adult aged 18 to 20 but not available on offenders over 21.

- A 'juvenile' is the collective name for those people who are aged 17 and under.

- A 'young person' is aged between 14 and 17 inclusive.

- A 'child' is aged 13 and under.

These distinctions are important for the following reasons:

(a) the age of the alleged offender determines whether they can be held criminally responsible for their actions;

(b) the way in which they can give evidence in court, whether as the alleged offender, a witness or as a victim;

(c) the options available to the police or the courts of dealing with the offender.

The age of criminal responsibility

In addition to classifying 'juveniles' for the purpose of criminal procedure, the law also makes a distinction between the children and their presumed capacity to commit criminal offences.

Children under the age 10

The police have no powers to arrest children under the age of 10. The law conclusively presumes that children under the age of 10 cannot be guilty of a criminal offence (s 50 of the Children and Young Persons Act 1933). This has the following consequences:

- a child under the age of 10 years cannot be prosecuted in a court in respect of a criminal offence; but

- the police have powers to take them into police protection for up to 72 hours where 'there is reasonable cause to believe they may otherwise be likely to suffer significant harm';

- where the child has been involved in wrongdoing the police and/or social services may informally warn the child's parent or guardian;

- commence care proceedings under s 31 of the Children Act 1989;

- make an application for an emergency protection order under ss 44 and 45 of the Children Act 1989;

Children between 10–13 years old

There is a rebuttable presumption that children aged between 10–13 years old cannot commit a criminal offence. This is known as doli incapax which means incapable of crime. The rule presumes that such a child is incapable of having sufficient understanding to distinguish between right and wrong and is incapable of forming the necessary mental state to commit the crime (ie the *mens rea*).

This does not mean that a client aged between 10 and 13 years old will not be prosecuted for and/or found guilty of an offence. The presumption can be rebutted by the prosecution proving to the court beyond reasonable doubt that at the time the alleged offence was committed, the child appreciated not merely that what he or she was doing was not just mischievous or naughty but seriously wrong. This requires the prosecution to call positive evidence of: the child's background including, his or her home life and stability of family relationships; the child's character including his or her maturity, understanding, emotional development and any previous findings of guilt. The more serious the alleged offence, the easier it will be for the prosecution to overturn the presumption. The younger the child, the more difficult it will be for the prosecution to overturn the presumption.

As an illustration of this important point of law consider the following cases: In *IPH v Chief Constable of South Wales* [1987] Crim LR 42, an 11 year old boy was found guilty of damaging a van. He admitted to the police that he knew that damage would be caused to the vehicle by him pushing it. The prosecution submitted that any child of the defendant's age would recognise that pushing the van was wrong. On appeal, the conviction was quashed because whilst it was clear that the child knew the consequences of his actions, there was no evidence to indicate that he knew what he was doing was wrong.

The most recent case on *doli incapax* is the House of Lords' decision in *C v DPP* [1995] All ER 43. The facts of the case are as follows. C, who was aged 12 and another boy were seen by a police officer using a crowbar to tamper with a motor cycle on a private driveway. C ran away but was caught and arrested. The juvenile was charged with interfering with a motor vehicle with intention to commit theft. In the hearing before the magistrates, the defence alleged that *doli incapax* applied, and that the prosecution had failed to prove that C knew that what he was doing was wrong. The magistrates found C guilty on the basis that by running away when challenged by the officer, indicated that he knew what he was doing was wrong. The case eventually reached the House of Lords which overturned the child's conviction. In rebutting the presumption of *doli incapax*, the prosecution was required to prove beyond reasonable doubt that when a child defendant aged between 10–13 committed a criminal act the child knew that the act was seriously wrong as opposed to realising that it was merely naughty or a childish prank.

Young people aged 14 and over

Young people in this category are regarded as having the same mental capacity to commit a criminal offence as an adult.

The social dimension of juvenile crime

Each year about 7 million crimes, or a quarter of all offences are committed by juveniles. They steal or damage property worth £3 billion and the criminal justice system spends £1 billion in prosecuting and punishing them. It is estimated that 1:2 males and 1:3 females admit to having committed a criminal offence as a juvenile. The most common offence is theft and handling stolen goods. Approximately 60% of juveniles caught by the police are cautioned or warned about their future conduct which appears to have the desired result as the vast majority do not reoffend. Of the remaining 40%, 10% are discharged by the courts and 18% are given community service orders or put on probation. Five percent are given an attendance centre order and about 5,000 (7%) are given a custodial sentence, which in view of their age means serving time in either a young offender centre or local authority secure accommodation. The child's parents may also be punished. In 1996, 3,500 parents were bound over to control their children who had been convicted of an offence.

One problem with juvenile crime is the negative level of public perception. Many people confuse anti-social behaviour and criminal activity. For example, 25% of adults reported to the British Crime Survey that 'teenagers hanging about were a problem' and 20% of females reported that they were worried about being pestered or insulted by gangs of teenagers. Accurate figures about the true extent of juvenile crime are difficult to establish. Official statistics tend to show that the number of young offenders convicted or cautioned fell from around 200,000 10 years ago to 150,000 more recently. At the same time independent crime surveys show that juvenile crime has risen by 35% in the last decade.

A particularly disturbing trend is that a greater proportion of young men continue to reoffend beyond the age, where traditionally, they have given up a major criminal activity, got married and gained regular employment.

Whilst the trend towards juvenile crime and anti-social behaviour seems to be increasing, most crime at this level is not serious. In an average year, less than 400 juveniles are sentenced for very serious crimes.

The age of criminal responsibility – future developments

It is expected that the law relating to the age of criminal responsibility will be changed. The Home Secretary, Jack Straw has suggested that the present position 'defies common sense. Most young people aged 10–13 are clearly capable of knowing the difference between right and wrong ... This legal presumption makes it very difficult for youth courts to convict younger offenders and start the process of changing their offending behaviour'.

The government intends to introduce legislation reducing the age of criminal responsibility to 10 making England and Wales having one of the lowest ages of criminal responsibility in Europe. According to the Penal Affairs Consortium, that honour is presently shared by The Netherlands and Turkey where a juvenile becomes criminally responsible for their actions at 12. The age in other countries includes France at 13; Austria, Italy and Germany at 14; Norway and Sweden at 15; Poland, Spain and Portugal at 16; Belgium and Luxembourg have the highest at 18.

As well as lowering the age of criminal responsibility another discernible trend in combatting juvenile justice has been widening the court's powers against the offender's parents or guardian. This approach was advocated in the

Conservative government's proposals to combat juvenile crime contained in a Green Paper Preventing Children Offending, published in March 1997 and there is nothing to suggest that the Labour government will radically divert from this course of action. Under the proposals outlined in the Green Paper, parents could be ordered to pay compensation for acts of vandalism committed by their children and be required to keep them under curfew. Failure to comply would result in the parents being found guilty of a criminal offence and being fined up to £1,000. Further punishments could include the confiscation of a driving licence and/or electronic tagging. The parents would be subject to a 'parental control order'. The scheme's aim, which has its origins in the United States, is to 'nip' criminal behaviour in the bud by identifying children at risk and offering support to their families to divert them from crime. A national network of child crime teams, drawn from the police, probation officers, social workers and teachers would identify children likely to offend. The Green Paper states that 10 to 15 year olds make up 14% of known offenders and 10 to 17 year olds make up 26% of known offenders. Pilot programmes had already been established to test the effectiveness of three schemes.

- **Home Start** – A network of nearly 200 home-visiting schemes which uses experienced parents as trained volunteers to work alongside families with pre-school children, Families referred under the scheme may need help to assist with domestic violence, debt recovery, suspected abuse, children's behaviour or other problems. Research findings showed that 60% of mothers were very satisfied with the service.

- **Cities in School (UK)** – this is a 'bridge school' which allows teenagers excluded from mainstream education to pursue further education and work experience. Between 1994–97, 75 projects had been established with the result that one in three pupils went on to further education and one in four went on to youth training.

- **Fairbidge** – personal development programmes based on demanding out-door activities for those aged 14 to 25 at risk of truancy, school exclusion, long-term unemployment, drug misuse and crime. Research indicates that 81% of participants did not reoffend within 12 months.

Financing criminal litigation

Before leaving our overview of the criminal justice system this is a convenient point to consider the sources of funding available when advising a client who needs professional legal advice where he or she could be or has been charged with a criminal offence. You should be aware that state-funded advice and assistance may be available at the following stages of the police investigation and court prosecution process.

Client-funded advice and assistance

You should warn your client that privately funded advice is becoming increasingly common, even for people on relatively low incomes. In recent years the number of people entitled to free legal advice has been drastically reduced. At the very least, your client will be required to make a contribution to the legal aid order. Many solicitors will expect the client to pay a substantial sum on account before taking any action on their behalf in a criminal matter.

Advice under the Green Form Scheme

This can be given by a solicitor, in his or her office, on any matter of English law providing the client qualifies under the financial eligibility test. The client's financial eligibility is worked out by the 'key card', and if after taking into account certain deductions, the client is left with a maximum disposable income of £75 per week, assistance under the Green Form Scheme can be given, which will amount to approximately two hours work. During the course of this interview, a solicitor would take the client's statement; prepare an application for full legal aid and give general advice and guidance.

Advice at the police station under the duty solicitor scheme

Where your client is held at the police station either in custody after arrest or voluntarily helping the police with their enquiries, he or she is entitled to free legal advice and assistance up to £90 worth of work from the duty solicitor or his or her own solicitor. This scheme is not means tested. Therefore all clients, irrespective of their income and capital come within its provisions.

Advice at court under the duty solicitor scheme

The court duty solicitor will see your client before he or she appears in court for the first time. If the case goes beyond this preliminary stage, your client must apply for full legal aid. Assistance by way of representation (ABWOR) is where the court does not have a duty solicitor scheme, unrepresented defendants may obtain 'assistance by way of representation'. The representation is available only for the day in question and is free.

Legal aid

'Full' legal aid is administered under the substantive provisions of the Legal Aid Act 1988 and regulations issued under the Act. The application for legal aid is made to the court before whom your client appears, usually the magistrates' court (youth) or the Crown Court. The application is made on Form 1, together with a statement of means on Form 5. The application is usually dealt with expeditiously and the court decides whether your client is eligible for legal aid. The client's eligibility for legal aid will be assessed on two grounds under s 21 of the Legal Aid Act 1988: (i) the financial eligibility ground and (ii) the 'interests of justice' ground. The financial eligibility ground is determined by:

- your client providing evidence of his or her income and capital by completing the legal aid application form;

- 'evidence' includes most recent wage slips, building society account books, etc;

- your client may receive legal aid, without or without being required to make a contribution, depending on his or her financial means;

- the contribution can either be in the form of a lump sum; or an instalment out of capital and/or income;

- where your client fails to comply with the contribution order, the court can revoke the legal aid order.

Legal aid will only be granted where it is desirable in the 'interests of justice'. This is determined by the following criteria provided by s 22 of the Legal Aid Act 1988:

- the offence is such as might lead the defendant to losing his or her liberty or livelihood or suffering serious damage to his or her reputation; and/or

- the charge raises a substantial question of law; and/or

- the defendant has inadequate knowledge of English or suffers from mental illness or physical disability; and/or

- the defence will involve the tracing and interviewing of witnesses or the expert cross examination of a prosecution witness; and/or

- legal representation is desirable in the interests of someone other than the defendant.

Where your client is refused legal aid, there are several options available. Another application can be made to the court and/or an appeal can be made to the Legal Aid Area Committee, where your client is charged with an indictable offence triable at the Crown Court or with an either way offence which may be tried at the Crown Court.

Is your client likely to receive legal aid?

It is expected that many clients will satisfy the financial eligibility ground, although an increasing number may be required to make a contribution to the costs of their representation. In recent years there has been criticism of an inconsistent approach by the courts as to how they interpret the 'interests of justice' ground. As a result, the Legal Aid Board has published guidelines to encourage greater uniformity in applying the 'interests of justice' criteria.

Your client's application for legal aid will always satisfy the 'interests of justice' criteria where he or she is charged with the most serious type of offence, an indictable offence, including murder, rape, manslaughter, robbery, etc. Your client is unlikely to be eligible where he or she is charged with disorderly conduct; prostitution; television licence offences and most road traffic offences, unless there are exceptional circumstances.

Practice points

Social workers should:

- be aware of the wide range of roles you may be required to play in your professional dealings with the police and the criminal justice system;

- know the ways in which criminal offences are classified and their significance in the context of your social work practice;

- be aware of the criminal court system, the differing powers, procedures and personnel of each court;

- know the importance of the distinction between 'adults', 'young people' and 'juveniles' and be able to advise your clients accordingly;

- be aware of the different sources of advice and assistance available to your client and the ways in which the advice can be paid for.

Further reading

Sprack J, *Emmins on Criminal Procedure*, 1996, London: Blackstone Press.

11 Social workers and the police

It is expected that you will have dealings with the police in a number of ways. First, you will encounter the police as part of an inter-agency child protection team at case conferences and other formal and informal contacts. This is dealt with in detail in Chapter 5.

This chapter is concerned with your dealings with the police in the criminal justice system and includes the requirement that of maintaining formal channels of liaison with the police. Also, on the other side of the coin, in allowing you to give advice to a client who has been detained by the police in connection with his or her involvement in a criminal offence, we provide a general guide to police powers of stop and search, powers of arrest and the searching of premises. Chapter 11 should therefore be read in conjunction with Chapter 12, where the role of the social worker as the 'appropriate adult' is considered.

Liaison with the police

A social worker is required to maintain close formal and informal links with the police through a number of provisions. At a formal level, your relationship with the police is not legally defined but guidance can be obtained from a number of sources including:

- The Children Act 1989 emphasises the importance of liaison between social workers and the police and Schedule 2 places a duty on the social services agency to persuade children not to commit crime and to persuade the police not to charge them.

- Guidance issued by the DSS, the Home Office, the Department of Education and Employment and the Welsh Office, 'Juveniles: Cooperation between the Police and Other Agencies' (DHSS Circular LAC (78), recommends that in order to prevent juvenile offending, joint discussions should take place to consider the problems raised by juvenile crime in general and specific cases in particular.

Apart from the situations outlined above, which may be described as a constructive engagement with the police, your other dealings will either be where you are required to attend the police station to protect your client's interests where they have been classified as a 'vulnerable person' or where a client comes to you seeking advice after being detained by the police. To deal effectively with both of these situations it is necessary to have a working understanding of the most important of these powers. To this end the following chapters provide a detailed examination of the relevant areas.

Police powers

Police powers can be classified as 'general' powers in that they can be used in a wide variety of factual situations. Specific police powers can only be lawfully exercised to deal with the specified factual situations, for example to combat drugs, firearm or traffic offences.

The most important source of general powers are be found in the Police and Criminal Evidence Act 1984, which deals not only with the exercise of police powers on the street but also provides the legislative framework for a wide range of issues relating to the criminal justice system including the treatment of suspects detained at the police stations, the admissibility of confessions and the powers of the criminal courts to exclude illegally or improperly obtained evidence. The vast majority of police powers are now found in Acts of Parliament whilst a small minority remain common law powers, for example breach of the peace.

Whilst a detailed knowledge of police powers goes beyond not only the scope of this book but also beyond your professional duties and responsibilities, you should have a working knowledge of the most important provisions of the Police and Criminal Evidence Act 1984.

The Police and Criminal Evidence Act 1984 – a brief history

The Police and Criminal Evidence Act or PACE as it is universally referred to, came into force on 1 January 1986. The Act was based on the recommendations of the Royal Commission on Criminal Procedure (RCCP Report; Cmnd 8092, 1981) which reported in 1981. The Act attempted to achieve three things. First, it modernised the law relating to general police powers, much of which was archaic and outdated. Second, the police required a new legal framework to deal with increasingly common outbreaks of civil unrest. The late 1970s and early 1980s had seen inner city riots in many British cities; violent incidents of industrial unrest including the miners' strike in 1984, and football hooliganism. This had led many senior police officers to believe that existing police powers were inadequate to deal with the increasing social dislocation and unrest. Policing by consent, which had provided the legal foundation for existing police powers was no longer tenable. Coercive policing required a new legal regime which PACE and the Public Order Act 1996 were intended to provide. Third, public confidence in the police and the way in which they used, or in some cases abused, their legal powers have been highlighted by celebrated miscarriages of justice. The existing law, especially in relation to protection of suspect's rights at the police station known as the Judge's Rules, had proved to be inadequate. As a result, from 1 January 1986, PACE sought to achieve a delicate balance. On the one hand, the Act extended coercive police powers in a number of situations, especially with regard to police powers of stop and search in the street, whilst on the other hand, the Act provides a comprehensive framework for the protection of the civil liberties of those people detained by the police. In the context of your professional duties as an 'appropriate adult' and when giving advice to a client who has had dealings with the police, these provisions are discussed in detail below.

The Police and Criminal Evidence Act 1984 and the Codes of Practice

Before we consider how PACE 1984 works in practice, its necessary to consider the significance of the Codes of Practice issued by the Home Secretary under the Act.

By the nature of its powers and the wide factual circumstances in which the law is intended to be applied, the substantive provisions of PACE provide only an outline of the law. To assist in the day-to-day implementation of general police powers, the Codes of Practice provide practical guidance to both the police and those people being dealt with by the police of correct police practice and procedure to be followed in commonly encountered situations. In April 1995, five Codes of Practice were reissued under the Act: Code A deals with police powers to stop and search; Code B deals with the searching of premises and the seizing of property; Code C deals with the detention, treatment and questioning of suspects; Code D deals with identification procedures; Code E, the tape recording of police interviews.

In your role as an appropriate adult, you are advised to have a detailed working knowledge of Code C and outline knowledge of the other codes. When attending the police station you should certainly carry with you a practitioner's guide to the workings of PACE.

It is important to be aware that the Codes are not rules of law. Where an officer breaks one or more of a code provision, the officer will not be acting unlawfully. The codes are suggested examples of best police practice, which, when broken, may result in evidence obtained by the police being ruled inadmissible at any subsequent criminal trial. They are therefore of high evidential value in determining whether the police have acted lawfully in relation to your client. When attending the police station as an appropriate adult you need to go armed not only with a working knowledge of the codes but also be prepared to make representations on your client's behalf when the police fail to observe the provisions of the Act and its codes. It will become clear how the specific provisions operate as the chapter proceeds.

The exercise of police powers 'on the street'

Police powers to stop and search

The police have a wide range of powers to stop and search people in the street in specific situations, including for example, the Firearms Act 1968, the Misuse of Drugs Act 1971 and s 60 of the Criminal Justice and Public Order Act 1994. Section 1 of the PACE 1984 provides the police with powers to stop and search suspects and motor vehicles for 'stolen or prohibited' articles.

The use of stop and search powers have long been surrounded by controversy. The police regard stop and search powers as an effective weapon in controlling crime, whilst civil liberty groups often complain that the police use stop and search powers in a discriminatory way against ethnic minorities in the inner cities. On the basis of research published in the 'Operation of Certain Police Powers under PACE 1993' (HSOB 15/94) between 1986–93 the use of stop-searches dramatically increased from 109,800 to 442,000.

Section 1 of the PACE 1984 for the first time provided all police officers with a general power of stop and search. In practice, however, whilst more widely applied than other stop and search powers, s 1 can only be used lawfully when searching for 'stolen or prohibited' articles.

Section 1 provides that a police officer has the power to stop, search and detain any person or vehicle where he or she reasonably suspects he will find 'stolen or prohibited' articles. The following should be noted:

- the officer must justify the use of the power by proving reasonable grounds to suspect possession of 'stolen or prohibited' articles;

- the proof of 'reasonable grounds' is an objective test, determined by the specific circumstances of the exercise of the power. The test is satisfied where an impartial third party would have acted as the police officer acted in the circumstances;

- stereotypical factors, such as the suspect's ethnic origin, hairstyle, manner, style of dressing, or a criminal record, should never be the sole basis for the officer exercising powers under s 1 (para 1.7 Code A);

- 'stolen articles' means articles obtained by stealing, deception, etc;

- 'prohibited articles' fall into two categories: (i) offensive weapons, which is widely defined to include a knife, a cosh, telescopic truncheon, etc and articles adapted or intended to cause injury including a sharpened comb, a deliberately broken bottle, an article of clothing with razor blades embedded in it; (ii) articles carried for theft such as housebreaking implements, etc.

- When carrying out the stop and search the officer is required to comply with ss 2 and 3 and Code A of the PACE 1984. The officer should:

  give his or her name to the person to be searched or inform the person in charge of the vehicle to be searched;

  the object of the search; and

  the grounds for making the search;

  the conduct of the search should be based on co-operation not confrontation with the suspect;

  the officer is required to make a written record of the search which the suspect is entitled to a copy within one year of the search taking place.

- These powers have recently been supplemented by new provisions relating to stop and search under ss 60 and 81(1) of the Criminal Justice and Public Order Act 1994.

Answering police questions voluntarily

A distinction needs to be drawn between where the police can lawfully exercise their statutory or common law powers and where the person is asked to assist the police on a voluntary basis. Whilst the police have a statutory duty to investigate crime, the public have no equivalent duty to assist the police with their enquiries. The case of *Rice v Connolly* [1966] 2 All ER 649, is a well-known illustration of the principle. Two police-officers were on night-time patrol in an area where there had been a several break-ins. The officers observed Rice loitering about the streets. The officers asked him where he was going, where he had come from and for his name and address. Rice only gave his surname and the name of the street on which he lived. The police asked Rice to accompany them to a nearby police box so that his replies could be verified. Rice refused to move unless arrested. The officers arrested him. Rice appealed against his conviction for obstructing a police officer in the execution of his duty under s 51(3) of the Police Act 1964. His appeal was allowed, with Parker LJ making the instructive comment that: 'It seems to me quite clear that though every citizen has a moral duty, or if you like a social duty to assist the police, there is no legal duty to that effect.'

In practice however, when an officer seeks to exercise powers to stop and search under s 1 or voluntarily asks a member of the public for their assistance, there is very little the person can do other than co-operate. There is a very thin dividing line between insisting that the police act lawfully by recognising that a person should be free to walk down the street without having their civil liberties being interfered, and being arrested for obstruction. It is a subtle distinction that the courts do not recognise easily.

Powers of arrest

There is no legal definition of arrest. In practice an arrest involves the deprivation of liberty by seizing or touching a person's body with a view to restraining the person with the intention of communicating to the person that they are not free to go. An arrest therefore has both a physical and a psychological dimension. PACE provides the police with powers to make an arrest in a wide number of situations and also provides the grounds for a legally valid arrest to be made.

The requirements of a valid arrest

Section 28 PACE requires that each of the following elements must be present in order for a valid arrest to be made:

(1) there has to be an arrest warrant or a legal power to arrest without a warrant;

(2) the factual requirements of 'reasonable grounds' or 'reasonable suspicion' must be satisfied;

(3) the officer must inform the suspect they are under arrest either verbally and/or by physical means, for example by taking hold of the suspect's arm;

(4) the suspect must be informed of the fact of the arrest; and

(5) as soon as is reasonably practicable, the suspect must be informed of the ground of the arrest;

(6) the arrested person must be cautioned by the following words: 'You do not have to say anything. But it may harm your defence if you do not mention when questioned something which you later rely on in court. Anything you do say may be given in evidence.'

The law makes a basic distinction between a power of arrest with a warrant and the power of arrest without a warrant.

Power of arrest with a warrant

This form of arrest is used most commonly in respect of minor offences to be tried summarily in the magistrates' court. The power to arrest with a warrant is contained in s 1 of the Magistrates' Courts Act 1980, which gives powers to a justice of the peace either to issue a summons requiring the suspect to appear before a magistrates' court or to issue a warrant for the arrest of the suspect to bring him or her before a magistrates' court.

Powers of arrest without a warrant

The general powers to arrest without a warrant for 'arrestable offences' are contained in s 2 of the Criminal Law Act 1967. Also, Schedule 2 of the PACE 1984 provides a power of arrest without a warrant in respect of 42 offences. Included in this list are specific powers of arrest in relation to s 24(2) of the Immigration Act 1971; ss 18, 35(10), 36(8), 38(7), 136(1) and 138 of the Mental Health Act 1983; ss 3(6), 4(4), 5(4), 12(7), 13(10) and 14(7) of the Public Order Act 1986; and s 14 of the Prevention of Terrorism (Temporary Provisions) Act 1989.

Most importantly, the police have general powers of arrest under ss 24 and 25 of the PACE 1984. Section 24(4) provides that:

any person may arrest without a warrant –

(a)   anyone who is in the act of committing an arrestable offence;

(b)   anyone whom he has reasonable grounds for suspecting to be committing such an offence.

Section 24(5) provides that:

where an arrestable offence has been committed, any person may arrest without a warrant –

(a)   anyone who is guilty of the offence;

(b)   anyone whom he has reasonable grounds for suspecting to be guilty of it.

Section 24(6) provides that:

where a constable has reasonable grounds for suspecting an arrestable offence has been committed, he may arrest without a warrant anyone whom he has reasonable grounds for suspecting to be guilty of the offence.

Section 24(7) provides that:

a constable may arrest without a warrant –

(a)   anyone who is about to commit an arrestable offence;

(b)   anyone whom he has reasonable grounds for suspecting to be about to commit an arrestable offence.

It is important to note that the powers of arrest contained in s 24(4) and (5) can be exercised by anybody including a police officer. Powers under s 24(6) and (7) can only be exercised by police officers.

Section 25 allows a police officer, where he or she has reasonable grounds for suspecting that an offence that is not an arrestable offence has been committed or is being committed or has been attempted or is being attempted, he or she may arrest the person where it appears that the service of summons is impracticable or inappropriate for any one of the following reasons:

(a) the name of the relevant person is unknown and cannot be readily discovered by the officer;

(b) that the officer has reasonable grounds for doubting that the name provided by the relevant person as his name is his real name;

(c) (i) the relevant person has failed to provide a satisfactory address for service; or

    (ii) the officer has reasonable grounds for doubting whether an address furnished by the relevant person is a satisfactory address for service;

(d) the officer has reasonable grounds for believing that arrest is necessary to prevent the relevant person from –

    (i)   causing physical injury to himself or another person,

    (ii) suffering physical injury,

    (iii) causing loss or damage to property,

    (iv) committing an offence against public decency, or

    (v)   causing an unlawful obstruction of the highway,

(e) that the officer has reasonable grounds for believing that arrest is necessary to protect a child or another vulnerable person from the relevant person.

Removing the arrested person to the police station

Where your client has been arrested at any place other than the police station, he or she must be taken to the police station as soon as practicable after arrest (s 30 of the PACE 1984). On arrival at the police station your client should be taken before the custody officer, who, according to Code C para 16.1, is required to:

> ... determine whether he has sufficient evidence before him to charge that person with the offence for which he was arrested and may detain him at the police station for such period as is necessary to enable him to do so.

In most investigations it unlikely that the police will have sufficient evidence to charge your client at this stage. The custody officer to open and maintain your client's custody record. The grounds for his or her detention without charge must be recorded in the custody record and a chronological record of the suspect's detention must be kept.

As the appropriate adult, along with your client's legal adviser, you are entitled to inspect the custody record as is your client's legal representative. Your client will also be entitled to have a copy of the custody record when he or she appears before a court and on release. The police are required to keep the relevant documentation for 12 months after the detention has ended to enable your client to obtain a written record of the detention.

Police powers to search people and property

At various stages of a criminal investigation, the police are given wide powers to search the suspect for dangerous and/or incriminating articles and to search the suspect's property.

The police have the following powers:

- to enter and search any premises with the written permission of the occupier;

- to enter and search any premises:

  (i) where they have a warrant of arrest or commitment to prison;

  (ii) to arrest a person for an arrestable offence;

  (iii) to save life or limb or prevent serious damage to property;

- after a suspect's arrest to search premises to look for evidence in connection with the offence for which the arrest has been made (s 32 of the PACE 1984);

- where the suspect has been arrested in respect of an arrestable offence, to search premises controlled or owned by the arrested person, to search for evidence relating to that offence or connected or similar arrestable offences;

- where the police have obtained a search warrant from a magistrate.

Search of the suspect away from the police station

The police have the following powers:

(1) Section 32 of the PACE 1984 provides that an arrested person may be searched away from the police station where the officer:

- has reasonable grounds for believing that the arrested person may present a danger to himself or others; or

- has reasonable grounds for believing that a person might have concealed on him anything which might:

(a) be used to assist him to escape from lawful custody; or

(b) be evidence relating to an offence.

(2) Section 54 of the PACE 1984 provides that a custody officer may search an arrested person where he or she considers it necessary to ascertain or record property that the person has in his or her possession when brought to the police station.

Practice points

Social workers should:

- be aware of the formal and informal contacts required with the police;

- know in outline general police powers such as: stop and search; arrest; powers of detention at the police station; and the rights of suspects and be able to apply this knowledge to your social work practice.

Further reading

Card and English, *Butterworths Police Laws*, 1994, London: Butterworths.

Lidstone, K and Palmer, C, *Bevan and Lidstone's Investigation of Crime – A Guide to Police Powers*, 1996, London: Butterworths.

12   Social workers at the police station

The legal protection of your client's civil liberties at the police station is to be found in both the substantive provisions of the Act and the Codes of Practice issued under the Act.

In attending a client at the police station you will need a working knowledge of the following provisions: Code C relating to the treatment and detention of suspect at the police station; Code D which deals with identification procedures adopted by the police and Code E the tape recording of interviews. In addition to the Codes you should also be familiar with the following substantive provisions including: s 56 of the PACE 1984 which provides that the suspect is entitled to inform someone of their arrest, subject to certain conditions under which the right can be suspended; s 58 of the PACE 1984 which provides that the suspect is entitled to receive legal advice, subject to certain conditions under which the right can be suspended and s 77 which deals with the procedure to be adopted by the police in relation to a suspect whom they believe to be mentally handicapped. These will be discussed in more detail below but first it is necessary to consider the role of the custody officer.

The custody officer

Part IV of the PACE 1984 creates the post of the custody officer who has responsibility for ensuring that both the interests of the police and your client are protected whilst the suspect is in police detention. Most significantly, the custody officer plays a central role in ensuring that the police do not abuse your client's rights and take advantage of his or her vulnerability. The following should be noted on the role of the custody officer:

- the custody officer has to be at least the rank of sergeant;

- he or she is required to remain independent and impartial from the investigation;

- he or she is responsible for keeping a 'custody record' which details all aspects of the suspect's detention and interrogation;

- after release the suspect is entitled to a copy of the custody record;

- where the suspect is brought to the police station, he or she must be brought before the custody officer who is required to decide whether there is sufficient evidence to charge the suspect or to release the suspect on police bail or otherwise or to keep the suspect in police detention.

Voluntarily attending the police station

Where your client voluntarily attends the police station to 'help the police with their enquiries', s 29 of the PACE 1984 provides that:

• the person shall be entitled to leave at will unless he or she is placed under arrest; and

• the person shall be informed at once that he or she is under arrest.

Your client in police detention

You will normally be required to attend a police station to protect the interests of two types of 'vulnerable' clients: a 'juvenile' or a mentally handicapped person. In either case to be lawfully held, they will have been arrested or attending voluntarily. As we saw above where your client is voluntarily assisting the police with their enquiries they are free to leave the police station at any time. If the police want to continue to question them, they will have to arrest your client.

In relation to young clients, the police can only lawfully arrest a juvenile aged between 10–17 years in connection with the investigation of a criminal offence, subject to the comments made in s about the criminal responsibility in respect of children under 10 years and aged between 10–13 years.

An arrested juvenile for the purpose of the detention is defined as 'a person arrested with or without a warrant who appears to be under the age of 17'. The following detention provisions apply therefore to juveniles who are aged 10 and yet appear to be 17.

Attending the juvenile aged between 10–17 at the police station

Research by Brown in 1992 found that 17% of all those detained at the police station were aged 17 or under. In some inner city areas this figure will be considerably higher. Where the juvenile has been arrested the custody officer must take all practicable steps to identify his or her parent, guardian or local authority (where it is relevant to do so), to inform that person or body of the juvenile's arrest and the juvenile's whereabouts. The person responsible for the juvenile's welfare will be asked to attend the police station to be the appropriate adult.

When a juvenile is kept at the police station, the Codes of Practice require (Code C, para 1.7; Code D, para 1.6) that an 'appropriate adult' should be present. Code C, Annex B, Note B1 requires that as soon as reasonably practicable after a juvenile's detention, the appropriate adult is informed of the reasons for the detention and the juvenile's whereabouts and ask the appropriate adult to attend the police station as soon as possible. It is important that the juvenile is not questioned until the appropriate adult arrives.

The 'appropriate adult' is required to act as an impartial observer to ensure the child's rights are respected by the police. In the case of a juvenile this means:

(i)   a parent or guardian or, if he is in care, a representative of the care authority or voluntary organisation under the Children Act 1989; or

(ii) a social worker; or

(iii) failing either of the above, a responsible adult aged 18 or over who is not a police officer or employed by the police.

The background to the role of the 'appropriate adult'

The Royal Commission on Criminal Procedure which reported in 1981 considered that it was essential that a juvenile and other vulnerable people being interviewed should have an adult other than a police officer present and that:

> ... the adult should be someone in whom the juvenile has confidence, his parents or guardian or someone else he knows, a social worker or school teacher. Juveniles may not as readily understand the significance of the questions or of what they themselves say and are likely to be more suggestible than adults. They may need the support of an adult presence; of someone to befriend, advise and assist them to make their decisions (para 4.103).

As a result, Code C para 11.16 requires the 'appropriate adult' where he or she is present at the interview to be aware that:

> ... he should be informed that he is not expected to act simply as an observer; and also that the purposes of his presence are, first, to advise the person being questioned and to observe whether or not the interview is being conducted properly and fairly, and, secondly, to facilitate communication with the person being interviewed.

The role of the 'appropriate adult'

Note the following considerations:

• The law requires the 'appropriate adult' to be independent of the police investigation.

- Deciding who is best suited to acting as an 'appropriate adult' is not always clear.

- The 'appropriate adult' is required to be suitable and competent to protect the child's interests.

- The choice of the wrong person might invalidate any evidence obtained against the child during the police interviews. A good illustration of this point is *R v Blake* (1989). The accused, who was a juvenile, did not want her father to be the 'appropriate adult' but requested the presence of her social worker. The police ignored her request and proceeded with her father present. As a result, the juvenile's confession was excluded. Similarly, the person chosen must be able to make a realistic contribution in protecting the child. In *R v Morse* [1991] Crim LR 195, the juvenile's father who had a low IQ was nominated and was regarded by the court as being incompetent to act.

- The wishes of the juvenile must therefore be taken into consideration as should the wishes of the parent or guardian.

- There is no legal requirement that the juvenile's parent or guardian should act as the appropriate adult.

It is quite common therefore in these situations for the custody officer to contact social services. Whether the social worker is prepared and/or qualified to act is dependent upon a number of circumstances including the availability of resources and realistic alternatives to you attending.

In most cases, when asked to do so, it will be presumed that you will attend the police station. However, as a matter of good professional practice you should agree to act as the 'appropriate adult' where the juvenile has previously admitted the offence to you, or had admitted the offence in your presence. In these circumstances, in the 'interests of fairness' you should not attend the police station. You should also not attend where other circumstances might adversely affect your role. An important lesson in this respect is provided by the case of *DPP v Morris* (1990) (unreported) in which it was held that a social worker who had called the police and who would have been seen by the police as being on the side of the police should not be the person to act as the appropriate adult.

Interviews with vulnerable people under PACE

A 'vulnerable person' for the purposes of PACE is a juvenile or a mentally disordered or handicapped person. A person may also be classified as potentially vulnerable where they are under a disability relating to sight, hearing or speech difficulties.

Most importantly Code C para 11.14 provides that a vulnerable person: '... must not be interviewed or asked to provide or sign a written statement in the absence of an appropriate adult ...'

The attitude of the court adopts the rationale of Code C in holding the attendance of an appropriate adult as an essential prerequisite for a lawful interview. In practice, when interviewing vulnerable people, the police are required to proceed with caution. Code C, Guidance para 11B provides that:

> It is important to bear in mind that, although juveniles or young people who are mentally disordered or mentally handicapped are often capable of providing reliable evidence, they may, without knowing or wishing to do so, be particularly prone in certain circumstances to provide information which is unreliable, misleading or self-incriminating. Special care should therefore always be exercised in questioning such a person, and the appropriate adult should be involved, if there is any doubt about a person's age, mental state or capacity. Because of the risk of unreliable evidence it is also important to obtain corroboration of any facts admitted whenever possible.

At the end of the interview Code C, Guidance 11D gives the following advice:

> When a suspect agrees to read records of interviews and of other comments and sign them as correct, he should be asked to endorse the record with words such as 'I agree that this is a record of what was said' and add his signature. Where the suspect does not agree with the record, the officer should record the details of any disagreement and then ask the suspect to read these details and sign them to the effect that they accurately reflect his disagreement. Any refusal to sign when asked to do so shall be recorded.

Special considerations in relation to interviews with juveniles include:

- The importance of establishing a rapport with the juvenile.

- Remember that your role is to provide support, encouragement and friendship.

- Where necessary, adjust your language to meet his or her needs.

- Where appropriate provide sweets and/or cigarettes – it is an obvious way of breaking down barriers and building rapport.

- The juvenile may be particularly nervous and/or fail to understand the seriousness of his or her position. It is your responsibility to reduce the trauma of the police interview.

- You are required to assume a proactive role especially in relation to unfair, inappropriate or oppressive questioning.

169

- Wherever possible juveniles should be interviewed at the police station.

- Code C para 11.15 provides that juveniles may only be interviewed in their places of education in 'exceptional circumstances'.

- Your client must be cautioned in your presence.

Special considerations in relation to interviews with mentally handicapped and mentally disordered people include:

- The person's mental capacity at the time of police detention, not at the commission of the alleged crime, determines whether he or she is suffering from mental incapacity.

- Where the officer has any suspicion, or is told in good faith, that a person of any age, may be mentally disordered or mentally handicapped, or mentally incapable of understanding the significance of the questions put to him, or his replies, then that person shall be treated as mentally disordered or mentally handicapped for the purposes of this code.

- It is important that a mentally disordered or mentally handicapped person who has been detained under s 136 of the Mental Health Act 1983 should be assessed as soon as possible. If that assessment is to take place at the police station, you, as an approved social worker, and a registered medical practitioner should be called to the police station as soon as possible to interview in order to interview and examine the person. Once the person has been interviewed and examined and suitable arrangements have been made for this treatment or care, he can no longer be detained under s 136. The person should not be released until he has been seen by both you and the registered medical practitioner.

- Your client must be cautioned in your presence.

- Your client must not generally be interviewed or asked to provide a written statement in your absence.

- During the police interview, you are expected to take a proactive role in protecting your client's interests and not simply act as a passive observer.

- The law recognises that whilst your client can give relevant and useful evidence, he or she may also exhibit a tendency to give information that is misleading, unreliable and self-incriminating and both the police, the appropriate adult and legal adviser is required to take these factors into account.

- Where your client's detention is reviewed, you should be available to make representations on your client's behalf.

170

- Where your client is charged with a criminal offence, it must be done in your presence and you are entitled to receive written notice which provides details of the charge.

- At any time your client should be free to consult privately with his or her legal representative.

Confidentiality and the 'appropriate adult'

It is important to remember that when dealing with confidential information given to you by your client, you do not enjoy the same legal privilege as a lawyer in that you may be required to disclose information told to you in confidence by your client. Both the British Association of Social Workers and the Association of the Directors of Social Services believe that social workers have a duty to assist in the prevention and detection of crime, and that when asked, are required to pass on relevant information to the police.

Because of this you may be excluded from the initial consultation between the legal adviser and your client. Whether you will be invited to attend later consultations depends on a number of factors, including the lawyer's assessment of the risk of you being required to disclose confidential information and the wishes of your client. Alternatively, you may be giving an undertaking not to pass on to the police any information divulged during interviews with your client's lawyer. This approach is unsatisfactory, however for two reasons. First, it undermines your status as a reliable and concerned professional and second, the undertaking is not legally enforceable and as a result, it might lead to you being put into a compromised position.

The appropriate adult – an evaluation of the role

The role of the appropriate adult is not an easy one to effectively discharge. You are required to provide support whilst at the same time not interfere with the proper conduct of the investigation or interfere with the equally important role of your client's solicitor or paralegal. Research into police interviews with juveniles, funded by the Royal Commission on Criminal Justice, found that approximately 75% of all appropriate adults (parents, social workers and other individuals) made 'no contribution whatsoever'. It is easy for the appropriate adult to be as intimidated by the institutionalised pressures which exist at a police station.

Thomas in 1994 suggested that juveniles do not get much of a better deal when a social worker is the appropriate adult. The reasons for this are clear to see: lack of effective training; uncertainty about the role they are expected to play and a lack of awareness about the rights of the juvenile and the powers of the police. Without the proper training how can they assess whether the police are conducting the interview fairly: whether the police are abusing the suspect's rights. These deficiencies can only be remedied by clear guidelines, advice and an improved system of training.

The length of detention at the police station

The custody officer has a duty under PACE to ensure that the suspect's continued detention at the police station is lawful. In practice this means that the custody officer has to decide whether there is sufficient evidence to charge the suspect. Where there is not sufficient evidence to charge, the suspect should be released from police custody unless:

- the suspect's detention is necessary to secure or preserve evidence relating to an offence for which he is under arrest or to obtain such evidence by questioning him (s 37 of the PACE 1984);

- a review officer, who is independent of the investigation, is required to review the suspect's detention to ensure that it continues to be justified six hours after the suspect arrived at the police station and every nine hours thereafter;

- most suspects should be detained for no longer than 24 hours after which they must either be charged or allowed to leave police custody;

- in exceptional circumstances the suspect can be held for longer than 24 hours where the suspect has been arrested in connection with a serious arrestable offence;

- a serious arrestable offence will always include murder, manslaughter, rape, robbery and other crimes where the offence has led to 'serious consequences' as defined by s 116(7) of the PACE 1984;

- in the case of serious arrestable offences, the police have additional powers to detain the suspect without charge for up to 36 hours, ie the basic 24 plus 12 where:

- at the end of 36 hours, the police are required to apply to a magistrates' court on oath for a warrant of further detention;

- the suspect is present in court and can be legally represented;

- the police are required to justify the grounds of further detention;

- the period of detention can be extended by the magistrates' to 96 hours from the time the suspect arrived at the police station, ie 24 hours plus 12 plus 60;

- at the end of the 96 hours, the suspect should either be charged or released.

Police powers and responsibilities at the police station

PACE provides the police with certain powers and responsibilities under ss 56 and 58 and Code C in relation to a suspect held in police detention. In addition to the role of the custody officer and the requirement for a review of detention, these include:

- where there are grounds to suspect a person of an offence the right to be cautioned;

- the right to be cautioned where an interview recommences after break;

- the right to read a copy of the relevant Codes of Practice;

- to be informed of their rights under PACE and the Codes of Practice;

- the right to refreshment and meal breaks at appropriate times in compliance with Code C to include eight hours rest within a 24-hour period;

- an overriding duty on the police to charge an individual as soon as there is sufficient evidence to justify a charge;

- s 56 allows a suspect who has been arrested to contact a friend or relative informing them of his or her arrest and the police station at which he or she is being held;

- s 58 allows a suspect who has been arrested to obtain legal advice at any time;

- the consultation should be in private, in person or by telephone;

- the consultation can be with the suspect's own solicitor or where he or she is not available with the duty solicitor;

- where a request for legal advice has been made, the suspect should be asked no further questions by the police until after the suspect has received the legal advice;

- where a suspect has exercised his or her rights under s 56 and/or s 58 the matter should be noted in the custody record.

The suspension of a suspect's rights under s 56 and/or s 58

In the following circumstances a suspects right to inform someone of their arrest under s 56 and the right to legal advice under s 58 can be suspended:

- where the suspect has been arrested in respect of a serious arrestable offence; and

- an officer of at least the rank of superintendent authorises the delay; and

- the officer has reasonable grounds for believing that if the suspect exercises his or her right under s 56 and/or s 58 it would:

  (i) lead to interference with evidence of an offence or to interference with, or physical injury to, some third person;

  (ii) lead to persons suspected of an offence being warned that the police are looking for them; or

  (iii) hinder the recovery of the proceeds of the offence.

What is an 'interview'

According to Code C para 11.1A, an interview is the questioning of a person regarding his involvement in a criminal offence where there are grounds to suspect him of such an offence.

Some police questions and comments made by the suspect will not amount to an 'interview'. Where this occurs, the police are required to make a written record of the accused's comments which should be signed and verified by him or her and to indicate which parts of the record (if any) are inaccurate.

The tape recording of interviews

Interviews between the police and your client in connection with serious and middle-ranking offences will be tape recorded. The appropriate adult and the your client's legal adviser will be also be present along with the suspect and the interviewing officers. The tape recording of interviews is dealt with in Code E of PACE. The important provisions of Code E are as follows:

- tape recorded interviews are required to be made in respect of all indictable and 'either way' offences;

- the tape recording should be done with the full knowledge of the person to be interviewed;

- the interview is recorded on two tapes, one is a working copy; the other tape is sealed at the completion of the interview;

- a transcript of the interview is produced from the working tape;

- the transcript is required to be a 'balanced' version of the interview;

- the tape and the transcript must record where the interview took place; the identity of those people present and the time the interview commenced, the time of any breaks and the time the interview finished;

- written transcript;

- where there is argument about the accuracy of the written transcript, the tape can be replayed to resolve any difficulties.

At the time of writing a limited number of police forces are experimenting with the videotaping of interviews. If the pilot schemes prove to be successful, it is likely that other forces will adopt the practice at least in relation to the interviewing of suspects accused of committing serious offences.

Non-taped interviews

Not all interviews will be taped. An interview between the police and the suspect outside the police station will not be taped nor will all interviews relating to summary offences. In these situations the police are under an obligation to make an accurate record of the interview and that in most cases, the person being interviewed is required to read the record and sign it as correct, where the suspect agrees with its contents.

The role of the interviewing officer

Home Office Circular 7/1993 introduced a national training package for interviewing suspects, known as the 'PEACE approach', which has been adopted by all police forces in England and Wales. Under PEACE, the interviewing officer has the following responsibilities:

(a) to obtain accurate and reliable information from suspects, witnesses and victims to discover the truth of matters under investigation;

(b) to approach the interview with an open mind;

(c) to act fairly in the circumstances of each individual case;

(d) not to accept the first answer given by the suspect. Questioning will not be unfair where it is persistent;

(e) even where the suspect remains silent, the officer has the right to put questions to the suspect;

(f) to ask any question in order to establish the truth except for interviews with child victims of sexual or violent abuse;

(g) vulnerable people, whether victims, witnesses or suspects must be treated with particular consideration at all times.

The interviewing officer is responsible for the welfare of the detained person during the interview and must apply to the senior officer where it is intended to suspend the suspect's rights under ss 56 and/or 58; and must account to the custody officer for the treatment the suspect has received during the interview.

The right to silence

Historically, a person detained by the police in connection with a criminal offence has enjoyed two fundamental rights. First, the freedom from being compelled to answer questions which might incriminate him or her or their spouse in relation to a criminal offence. Second, the right not to allow the court to draw adverse inferences from his or her silence. The first right is commonly known as the privilege against self-incrimination. The second right, commonly known as the right to silence, is dealt with below and in Chapter 18 on the cross examination of witnesses.

The meaning of the right to silence

The right to silence was an inaccurate description. More properly, a suspect enjoyed several rights which included the following:

- a suspect was under no legal obligation to assist the police with their enquiries;

- a suspect was not required to give advance notice to the prosecution of evidence in support of his defence;

- adverse comments could not be made by the court or the prosecution by the suspect's silence during police questioning or refusal to answer specific questions or failed to reveal his or her defence;

- adverse comments could not be made in relation to the suspect's refusal to give evidence.

Many of these historic rights have been curtailed by ss 34–38 of the Criminal Justice and Public Order Act 1994, the effect of which is discussed in the following section.

The Criminal Procedure and Public Order Act 1994

The provisions of the Criminal Procedure and Public Order Act (CPPOA) 1994 relating to the right to remain silent came into effect on 10 April 1995 with the following important consequences:

Failure to mention facts when questioned or charged – s 34

Where in any proceedings against a person for an offence, evidence is given that the accused:

(a) at any time before he was charged with the offence, on being questioned under caution by a constable trying to discover whether or by whom the offence has been committed, failed to mention any fact relied on in his defence in those proceedings; or

(b) on being charged with the offence or officially informed that he might be prosecuted for it, failed to mention any such fact,

being a fact which in the circumstances existing at the time the accused could reasonably have been expected to mention when so questioned, charged or informed, as the case may be ... the court or jury may draw such inferences from the failure as appear proper.

Its important to be aware that inferences may only be drawn under s 34 from an accused's failure to mention a fact relied on in his defence. The section does not take away the suspect's right to remain silent. The court will only be allowed to make adverse inferences from his decision to remain silent where it would have been reasonable for the accused to have mentioned the facts which he or she later relies on in support of their defence.

Failure or refusal to account for objects, substances and marks – s 36

Section 36 provides:

Where:

(a) a person is arrested by a constable and there is:

    (i)   on his person; or

    (ii) in or on his clothing or footwear; or

    (iii) otherwise in his possession; or

    (iv) in any place in which he is at the time of his arrest, any object, substance or mark, or there is any mark on any such object; and

(b) that or another constable investigating the case reasonably believes that the presence of the object, mark or substance may be attributed to the participation of the person arrested in the commission of an offence specified by the constable; and

(c) the constable informs the person arrested that he so believes, and requests him to account for the presence of the object, substance or mark; and

(d) the person fails or refuses to do so then ... the court or jury ... may draw such inferences from the failure or refusal as appear proper.

Unlike s 34, s 36 operates irrespective of whether the accused raises a defence or not. Under s 34, the court will be allowed to draw inferences only where it considers it appropriate to do so – it is not a mandatory requirement. The accused must be told in ordinary language the effect of failing to account for the object, substance or mark, etc and only applies to interviews at the police station.

Failure to account for presence at a particular place – s 37

Section 37 provides:

Where:

(a) a person arrested by a constable was found by him at a place at or about the time the offence for which he was arrested is alleged to have been committed; and

(b) that or another constable investigating the offence reasonably believes that the presence of the accused at that place and at that time may be attributed to his participation in the commission of the offence; and

(c) the constable informs the person that he so believes, and requests him to account for that presence; and

(d) the person fails or refuses to do so,

then ... the court or jury ... may draw such inferences from the failure or refusal as appear proper.

Section 37 operates irrespective of whether a defence is put forward and only applies to interviews at the police station.

The taking of samples

In recent years, the scientific examination of body samples based on an analysis of a person's DNA has become an integral part of the criminal investigations. In recognition of these significant scientific developments, the law has developed procedures for the taking of intimate and non-intimate samples from people suspected of involvement in a criminal offence.

Intimate samples where the suspect is in custody

Under s 62 of the PACE 1984 the police may take an intimate sample from a person in police custody where:

• an officer of at least the rank of superintendent authorises the sample to be taken; and

• the suspect consents to the sample being taken.

Intimate samples where the suspect is not in police custody

Under s 62(1A) an intimate sample may be taken from a person not in police custody but from whom in the course of an investigation for an offence, two or more non-intimate samples have been taken for the same analysis which have proved insufficient. The sample may be taken where:

- if a police officer of at least the rank of superintendent authorises it to be taken; and

- the suspect consents.

By s 65 an intimate sample can be a sample of:

- blood;

- semen;

- any other tissue fluid;

- urine;

- pubic hair;

- a dental impression;

- a swab taken from the person's body orifice other than the mouth.

An officer can only give authorisation under s 62(1) or (1A) where he or she has reasonable grounds for believing:

- the involvement of the suspect in a recordable offence; and

- the sample will tend to confirm or disprove the suspect's involvement.

A recordable offence is an offence, where on conviction will be recorded in national police records.

Inferences that can be drawn from a refusal to give an intimate sample

Section 62(10) provides that where the suspect refuses without good cause to give his or her consent to the taking of an intimate sample, the court when determining whether the suspect has a case to answer or is guilty of the offence charged, may draw such inferences as appear proper.

It is worth noting that before a person is asked to provide an intimate sample, the suspect must be warned that if he or she refuses without good cause, the refusal may harm his or her case if the matter comes to court. In determining whether refusal was given with good cause is a matter of fact. The suspect's physical or mental bodily condition may amount to a good cause, including for example a Jehovah's Witness refusal to give a blood sample.

The taking of a non-intimate sample

Under s 63(3), a non-intimate sample can taken without the suspect's consent when the suspect is:

- in police detention; or

- in custody on the authority of the court; and

- an officer of at least the rank of superintendent authorises it to be taken without the appropriate consent.

Under s 63(3A), an non-intimate sample may be taken from a suspect without the suspect's consent where:

- he or she has been charged with a recordable offence; or

- reported that he or she will be reported for such an offence; and

- he or she has not had a non-intimate sample taken during the investigation of the offence; or

- a non-intimate sample has been taken but it was not suitable; or

- the sample proved insufficient.

Under s 63(3B) a non-intimate sample may be taken without the suspect's consent where he or she has been convicted of a recordable offence and where the conditions of s 63(4) apply.

Under s 63(4) an officer may only give authorisation under s 63(3B) if he or she has reasonable grounds:

- for suspecting the involvement of the person from whom the sample is to be taken in a recordable offence; and

- for believing that the sample will tend to confirm or disprove his involvement.

Under s 65 a non-intimate sample means a sample:

- of hair other than pubic hair;

- taken from the suspect's nail or from under a nail;

- a swab taken from any part of the suspect's body including the mouth but not any other body orifice;

- saliva;

- a footprint or other similar impression of any part of the suspect's body apart from the hand.

Identification procedures

The police are entitled to use a variety of methods under PACE and Code D to either ascertain or confirm the identity of an accused. The methods and law relating to these identification methods are as follows.

Identification parades

An identification parade provides an opportunity for a witness to see the suspect as soon as possible after the crime and to test the witness's ability to pick the suspect out from a group of similar appearance. The guidelines include:

- an ID parade should be held where the police have a suspect in mind and the evidence against that suspect depends on identification evidence;

- the suspect must consent to taking part in an ID parade;

- the suspect must be given certain information in writing before the start of the parade;

- the suspect may have a solicitor or a friend present during the parade;

- the parade must be conducted by a uniformed officer of least the rank of inspector who is independent of the investigation;

- the parade must consist of at least eight people who, as far as possible, must be of a similar age, height, general appearance and position in life of the suspect;

- the suspect may choose his or her own position in the line;

- any witness must be segregated from the parade;

- the witness should not be shown a photograph or description or in any other way be prompted towards identifying the suspect.

The parade may be held in a room where the witness is required to walk along the line. Increasingly likely, however, many police stations are now equipped with an identification suite equipped with a 'one-way' screen which allows the witness to see the people in the parade but not be seen by them. Immediately before the inspection takes place, the identification officer is required to inform the witness that the suspect may or may not be present. The witness may ask a member of the parade to speak, move or adopt any posture. Once the witness has carefully looked at the parade the identification officer will ask whether the person he or she saw earlier is present in the parade. Where appropriate, the witness is then required to make the identification by indicating the number of the person concerned.

Where the suspect refuses to attend an ID parade

As indicated above, the police may only hold an ID parade where the suspect consents. Where consent is withheld, the following consequences apply:

• the refusal may be referred to in evidence at the trial and may be subject to comment;

• the police will use an alternative, and in some cases, a less satisfactory form (as far as the suspect is concerned) of identification such as a group identification, video identification or a confrontation.

In most cases, your client should be strongly advised to take part in a parade. A refusal to participate does not preclude the police from obtaining identification evidence, but as the following sections indicate, alternative methods of identification may prove to be more prejudicial to your client's interests.

Identification by photographs

Photographs should not be used where a suspect is already available. A witness should be shown at least 12 photographs, which as far as possible, resemble the suspect. Where the witness makes a positive identification, the witness should not be shown any more photographs.

Group identification

There is no set format but it will usually involve the suspect being in a group of people, for example in a room, at a railway or bus station or in a busy shopping area. The suspect is asked to stand or walk through the group. The witness will be asked whether he or she can identify the suspect in the group.

Video identification

A video film is made of the suspect and at least eight other people of similar height, age, etc. All participants should be filmed in the same position carrying out the same task. Only one witness may see the film at a time. The film may be frozen and there is no limit to the number of times the witness may see the film.

Confrontation

A confrontation involves taking the witness to the suspect and asking whether the suspect is the person in question. A confrontation is only permitted where none of the other procedures are practicable.

Fingerprints

The police may take your client's fingerprints whether he or she gives consent or not. Where your client agrees, the consent must be in writing. Where your client does not consent, s 62 of the PACE 1984, allows the police to take fingerprints before charge where:

- an officer of at least the rank of superintendent provides authorisation; and

- it is believed that fingerprints will tend to confirm or disprove his or her involvement in the commission of a particular offence.

After charge, the power can be exercised where:

- an officer of at least the rank of superintendent provides authorisation; and

- your client has been charged in respect of a recordable offence.

A recordable offence is an offence where on conviction it will be recorded in the national police records.

Releasing your client: bail or custody?

There are two stages of the criminal process where the question of whether the suspect should be released on bail or kept in custody arises. The first stage is when the suspect is at the police station having been interviewed by the police and either police enquiries are continuing without charge or where your client has been charged with an offence(s). The second stage is where the case has proceeded to court and the hearing is adjourned. The court has to decide whether the defendant should be released on bail under the Bail Act 1974 or kept in custody.

At the first stage, where your client has been charged, the custody officer has to decide whether to release the suspect on bail or to keep him or her in custody until he or she can be brought before the magistrates' court.

Under s 38(1) of the PACE 1984, the custody officer must release the suspect unless the custody officer has a belief, based on reasonable grounds that one or more of the following conditions will apply:

- the name and address of the suspect cannot be ascertained or the custody officer has reasonable grounds for believing that the information provided by the suspect is not his or her real name and address; or

- the custody officer has reasonable grounds for believing that the person arrested will fail to appear in court to answer bail; or

- where the person has been arrested in respect of an imprisonable offence, the custody officer has reasonable grounds for believing that the detention of the arrested person is necessary to prevent him or her from committing an offence; or

- in the case of a person arrested for an offence which is not an imprisonable offence, the custody officer has reasonable grounds for believing that the detention of the person arrested is necessary for him or her from causing physical injury to any person or from causing loss or damage to property; or

- the custody officer has reasonable grounds for believing that the detention of the arrested person is necessary to prevent him or her from interfering with the investigation of offences or of particular offence; or

- the custody officer has reasonable grounds for believing that the continued detention of the suspect is necessary for his or her own protection.

In relation to a juvenile, bail can be refused on the additional ground that 'it is not in the juvenile's interest' to be released. Section 38 does not give guidance as to what kind of circumstances are envisaged when it is not in the juveniles interest but we can all envisage circumstances where it will be in the juvenile's interests to be in secure accommodation as opposed to going home.

Having made the decision to release the accused on bail, the custody officer is then required to consider whether to impose any bail conditions. Section 27 of the Criminal Justice and Public Order Act 1994 allows the custody officer to impose the conditions. A person released on bail under s 38 may therefore be required to comply with a very wide range of conditions, including for example:

- reporting to a designated police station;

- imposing a curfew;

- condition of residence.

Where conditions are imposed, the custody officer is required to:

- inform the person bailed of the conditions;

- record the conditions and the reasons in the custody record;

- justify the imposition of conditions.

Where your client has not been charged, the custody officer is required to take the following steps:

- if the custody officer is satisfied there is not sufficient evidence to charge a suspect and is not prepared to authorise a further period of detention for questioning, the suspect must be released either:

    ◦ unconditionally; or

    ◦ on bail (s 37(2) of the PACE 1984).

Where bail is granted to the suspect, it will be on the condition that he or she returns to the police station on a specified future date for further questioning.

Detention after refusal of bail

As we have seen, after your client has been charged, the police are required to grant bail unless one of the grounds in s 38(1) applies. In relation to a juvenile client, s 39(6) requires the custody officer to make arrangements for the child or young person to be sent to local authority secure accommodation. Exceptionally in the case of a young person, s 36(8) provides that the custody officer can refuse to send the person to secure accommodation where:

- the young person is at least 15 years old; and

- the custody officer regards the young person is a danger to the public; and

- the local authority lacks adequate secure accommodation; or

- it is not practical to make arrangements for a transfer.

It would not be 'practical', where, for example, the road to be used for travelling is hazardous due to bad weather. Where the custody officer exercises discretion under s 38(6), he or she must certify the reason for not sending the young person to secure accommodation. The juvenile will then be remanded in custody in the same way as an adult until the court appearance.

Practice points

Checklist for appropriate adult attending at the police station

Stage 1: you are contacted by the police:

- Request name, address, date of birth, telephone number of vulnerable person.

- Why has your authority or agency been contacted?

- What is the suspect's vulnerability or impairment?

- What grounds are available to substantiate the description of the suspect as 'vulnerable'?

- Obtain the suspect's address. Who does the suspect live with?

- Have these people been told of the suspect's arrest?

- Why have you been contacted?

- Have the suspect's parent/guardian or any other relevant person been contacted to attend the police station?

- What is the suspect's gender/racial/ethnic origin?

- Do they speak or understand English?

- Do they require an interpreter?

- What is the suspect's current medical/mental condition?

- Have they seen or do they need to see a doctor?

- Is the suspect known to the police/social services/other recognised agencies/ probation service.

- Why was the suspect arrested? Obtain reasons and location of arrest.

- What time was the suspect arrested?

- What time did he or she arrive at the police station?

- Has the suspect been interviewed?

- Has the suspect asked for legal advice?

- Do the police intend to interview the suspect? Obtain time, place, etc.

- Is the suspect's solicitor to be called or will he or she use the duty solicitor?

- Is your presence required? Get full instructions about the location, etc of the police station.

Stage 2: the appropriate adult arrives at the police station

- Request a private interview with the vulnerable person.

- Introduce yourself to the suspect, speak in plain, ordinary language.

- Try to gain the suspect's confidence by telling him or her that:
  - ◦ you are the appropriate adult;
  - ◦ that you are at the police station to help him or her;
  - ◦ explain plainly your role as the appropriate adult.

In relation to the alleged offence(s) for which the suspect has been arrested its important that you follow these guidelines:

- Explain that you do not want to hear anything about the alleged offence(s) for which the suspect has been arrested.

- Explain that if the suspect requires further information about the offence you will arrange for a solicitor to attend free of charge.

- Avoid speaking of the police evidence in the case and the suspect's reaction to the allegations.

- Ensure that the suspect understands the effect of the caution.

- Remember that as a social worker you do not enjoy the same confidential privileges as a solicitor with the suspect.

- Does the suspect need an interpreter?

- Where the suspect appears to be confused and/or distressed. Where he or she is confused/distressed ensure that this is noted by the custody officer on the custody record and that the interview is suspended.

Stage 3: the interview

- When you enter the interview room ensure that the seating arrangements allow you to give the necessary support and advice to the suspect.

- Where the seating arrangements are inadequate, move the furniture to ensure that you can give the necessary support to the suspect.

- Does the suspect understand the significance of being cautioned? This should be explained in ordinary language. Where the suspect does not seem to understand the caution this fact should be recorded on the tape recording of the interview.

- As the appropriate adult you can request that the interview should be stopped so that the suspect can seek legal advice.

- As the appropriate adult you can request that the interview should be stopped where the suspect is distressed and confused.

- Provide the necessary support as required in the circumstances.

Stage 4: after the interview

- Explain to the suspect the next stage in the procedure, ie that they may either be released unconditionally, released on bail, kept at the police station and/or charged with an offence(s).

- Ask the custody officer what action the police intend to take next.

- Where the suspect is to be detained, is it time for a review to be made of the suspect's detention. Note the previous time of review on the custody record.

- Where the suspect is to be charged explain the procedure and try to allay any fears and concerns the suspect may have.

- Where the suspect is refused police bail and kept in custody, explain what this means.

- Where the suspect is refused bail make contact with the Probation Service Bail Information Officer with any relevant information.

- Where the police grant the suspect bail is it going to be conditional or unconditional?

- Where conditional bail is proposed:
  - does the suspect understand the conditions?
  - can the suspect meet the conditions?
  - is there any assistance the social services agency can give to help the suspect meet the bail conditions?

Further reading

Cape, E and Luqmani, I, *Defending Suspects at Police Stations*, 1995, Legal Action Group.

13 The criminal process

Criminal procedure flow chart

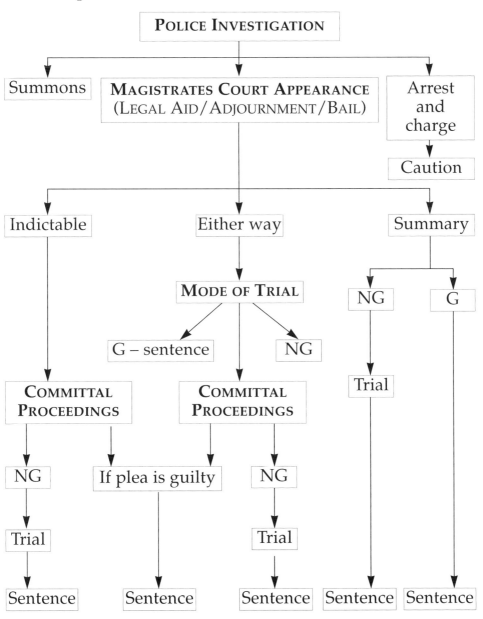

In this chapter we consider the procedural steps that follow the completion of the police investigation. The main point for consideration at this stage is whether the matter will proceed to prosecution in court or whether the case can be diverted from the prosecution process by the police administering a caution.

Your client and cautioning

At the conclusion of the police investigation, subject to the matter being referred to the Crown Prosecution Service (CPS) for advice, it may be decided not to the take the matter any further or that the case against your client should be prosecuted through the courts or alternatively your client might be dealt with by way of caution. Cautioning is an important way of keeping minor offences out of the courts, and in relation to young offenders, it attempts to reduce the risks of them reoffending. Cautioning may also be appropriate for the elderly and infirm who admit having committed a minor offence and it is not in the public interest to proceed with the prosecution.

Two Home Office Circulars No 14/1985 and No 59/1990 provide the police with guidance on cautioning offenders as an alternative to prosecution. It recommended that all juvenile offenders should be cautioned for all but the most serious offences. A second caution should be given where there is a time lapse between the commission of offences. In general, forces were advised to keep juveniles away from the criminal courts unless prosecution was the last resort open to them.

A caution can be given in respect of any criminal offence, and is regarded as a serious and formal step. It should not be seen as an easy alternative to prosecution and may be taken into account when deciding whether to prosecute your client if he or she reoffends. The caution does not formally count as a conviction and does not have to be disclosed on job applications. A caution will be appropriate where:

- your client has admitted the offence; and

- agrees to be cautioned; and

- it is in the public interest for the your client to be cautioned.

The factors to be taken into account in terms of the 'public interest' include your client's: age, previous criminal history, state of health and attitude towards the offence. It is becoming increasingly common for the victim's views to be taken into account. As the offender's social worker, your views will often be taken into consideration as well.

Negotiating with the police

As well as giving your advice it may also be your responsibility to negotiate with the police on your client's behalf for him or her to be cautioned. This is especially appropriate for juvenile clients. The police will administer a caution to a juvenile where he or she admits the offence and, as required by the National Standards for Cautioning (HO Circular 18/1994), the juvenile's parents or guardian are also required to give their consent. In theory it may be possible for a caution to be administered where the juvenile does not consent but his or her parents do consent, but in practice this is most unlikely to happen as a major reason for administering a caution is to encourage the offender to recognise their wrongdoing and undertake not to commit further offences.

Alternatively, where the police charge the juvenile and report it for a summons to be issued, the case may be referred to a juvenile or young offender's bureau. In many police forces the decision whether to caution the offender or deal with the matter in another way is left to the bureau. In making its decision the bureau will consult widely with the child's lawyer, social worker and parents or guardian. Once again you may be required to apply your negotiating skills in arguing with the bureau on your client's behalf.

Commencing a criminal prosecution

Where it is decided to proceed with the prosecution the case against an adult offender, the matter will be listed for its first hearing in the magistrates' court. With very few exceptions all criminal prosecutions begin in the magistrates' court and will be commenced either by laying an information or by charging the accused.

Laying an information

The information is the document containing the charge to which the accused in summary trails pleads guilty or not guilty.

Each information should allege only one offence, to be written in ordinary language and cite any statutory provision as the basis of the charge. It can be brought about in one of three ways:

- by the prosecutor delivering to the court a written, signed allegation against the accused; or

- the prosecutor dictates the allegation and the charge to the magistrates' clerk who writes the details down; or

- where the accused has been arrested by the police, the charge sheet will serve as the information. The accused is given a copy of the charge sheet.

The summons

Following the laying of an information, the magistrates will issue a summons which will be served by post to the defendant's last known address. The summons is required to set out the following:

- the name and address of the accused;

- the name and address of the court where the accused is required to appear;

- the day and time of the appearance;

- the content of the information(s);

- the name and address of the informant;

- the signature of the magistrate or magistrates' clerk who signed the summons.

The indictment

Where the accused is charged with a serious offence, known as an indictable offence(s) and the case has been committed to the Crown Court for trial or where the accused is charged with an offence triable either way and it has been decided that the case should be tried in the Crown Court, a formal document known as the indictment must be prepared which contains the charge(s) alleged against the accused. It is against the indictment that the accused is required to plead guilty or not guilty at the Crown Court trial.

Restrictions to commencing criminal prosecutions

There may be two restrictions on the prosecuting party when it decides to commence a prosecution – time limits and geographical location. We shall consider each in turn.

Time limits

The general rule is that there is no time limit within which a criminal prosecution must be commenced. In the case of serious offences, heard on indictment, and either way offences, this principle is generally observed. The more serious the alleged offence(s), the more likely it will be that it will be tried many years after the crime was committed where it is in the public interest to prosecute the offence and where important witnesses are available and capable of giving cogent evidence. In recent years the prosecution of alleged war criminals and some murderers have been started many years after the offences were alleged to have taken place.

In respect of minor offences, however, those which are to be tried summarily in the magistrates' court, the information must normally be laid within six months of the offence being committed, unless the statute creating the offence, otherwise directs.

Geographical restrictions

Magistrates' courts only have jurisdiction to try summary offences which have been allegedly committed within their area. In addition a magistrates' court can try a case not committed in their area where:

- the accused has allegedly committed one or more additional summary offences outside the magistrates' area, s 2(6) of the Magistrates' Courts Act 1980; or

- where it is necessary and/or expedient that the accused should be charged with another person in the same place as the other person, s 2(2) of the Magistrates' Courts Act 1980; or

- where the offence was allegedly committed within 500 yards of the court's area.

Geographical limitations do not exist in relation to offences which are triable either way. The prosecution have the choice of which court to commence the proceedings in.

Court procedure

Summary trial in a magistrates' court

The case will be heard in a magistrates' court where one of two circumstances apply:

- the suspect is charged with a summary offence; or

- the suspect is charged with an offence triable either way and at the mode of trial hearing, your client elected to be tried in the magistrates' court.

Where the accused pleads not guilty

The court clerk will read the charge(s) to the accused. The accused will reply 'not guilty' and the prosecution will make an opening speech. The prosecution put their evidence to the court, this can be done in a number of ways by either:

- calling witnesses to give oral evidence through examination-in-chief, cross examination by the defence and where appropriate re- examination by the prosecution; or

- tendering statements made under s 9 of the Criminal Justice Act 1967; or

- tendering statements or documentary evidence under ss 23 and 24 Criminal Justice Act 1988.

At the close of the prosecution case, the defence may make a submission of no case to answer where either:

- the prosecution have failed to prove an essential element of the offence; or

- the prosecution evidence has been so discredited.

The defence will then call its witnesses. The accused normally gives evidence first. The defence presents its case by the same methods as the prosecution above, and then will proceed to making the closing speech. The magistrates make their decision, advised by the clerk on matters of law and evidence only. Where no matter of law or evidence arises, the clerk should not retire with the magistrates. Where the magistrates decides the accused is not guilty, the accused is discharged and will be able to make an application for costs.

Where the accused pleads guilty

Where the accused pleads guilt to a summary offence or an offence triable either way in the magistrates' court, the procedure will be as follows:

- the prosecution will read a statement of how the offence(s) occurred;

- the defence will make a submission in mitigation;

- the court may adjourn to obtain reports and then proceed to sentence the accused;

- where the accused is convicted, the court will proceed to sentence the accused after dealing with other matters including the defence submission in mitigation.

It is also possible for the accused to plead guilty by post without attending court. Pleading guilty by post is dealt with by s 12 of the Magistrates' Courts Act 1980 and relates to an offence where the maximum penalty does not exceed three months imprisonment.

The prosecution of 'either way' offences

For those offences in the middle range of seriousness, such as theft and unlawful wounding, they can be tried in either the magistrates' court or the Crown Court. The decision as to where they are tried is made at the 'mode of trial' hearing by the magistrates, which is dealt with by ss 18–21 of the Magistrates' Courts Act 1980. The 'mode of trial' hearing will take the following course:

- The charge will be read to the accused.

- The accused is not required to answer guilty or not guilty but under s 49 of the Criminal Procedure and Investigations Act 1996, the clerk is required to explain the charge to the accused in ordinary language so that he or she may indicate if the case was to proceed to trial whether they would plead guilty or not guilty. Where the accused indicates that he or she would plead guilty, the matter then proceeds to summary trial.

- Where the accused indicates that he or she will plead not guilty the court proceeds to determine mode of trial.

- The prosecution will explain to the court the background to the offence and indicate whether they consider the case should be heard by the magistrates or before a judge and jury at the Crown Court.

- The defence will then make representations as to where the case should be heard.

- The magistrates then make their decision on the following criteria:
    ○ the 'statutory factors' provided by s 19 of the Magistrates' Courts Act 1980 to include:
    ○ the nature of the case;
    ○ the seriousness of the offences;
    ○ whether the magistrates have adequate powers of punishment; and
    ○ any other relevant circumstances.

The magistrates will also be guided by the National Mode of Trial Guidelines contained in the *Practice Direction (Mode of Trial Guidelines)* [1990] 1 WLR 1439, which set out relevant mitigating and aggravating factors relating to each offence.

After hearing prosecution and defence submissions and applying the above criteria the magistrates make their decision. Where the magistrates consider that the case should be heard in the Crown Court, the accused is told of the decision and the matter proceeds at a later date to a committal hearing. Where the magistrates consider that the case should be heard in the magistrates' court the accused is then given the choice of where the case should be heard. Where the accused elects trial in the magistrates' court, he or she will be informed that if he or she is found guilty and where the magistrates consider their powers of sentencing are inadequate, he or she can be committed to the Crown Court to be sentenced. Where the accused elects trial at the Crown Court the case proceeds to a committal hearing.

Factors in choosing the court

It is generally submitted that the following factors are relevant in deciding which court an accused should be tried in:

Factors in favour of being tried at the Crown Court:

- higher acquittal rate;

- much better at dealing with contested areas of law and evidence;

- guaranteed to know the prosecution case through advance disclosure.

Factors in favour of being tried in the magistrates' court

The case will be heard much sooner than in the Crown Court. It is more convenient, less stressful, and there will be less publicity surrounding the magistrates' court. Further, there will be less draconian powers of sentencing and the costs will not be as high.

Indictable offences to be heard in the Crown Court

The court process to determine the most serious criminal offences, known as indictable offences and including murder, rape, manslaughter and robbery, takes place in two stages. Stage 1 is known as the committal stage. Committal proceedings are held in the magistrates' court and their purpose is to act as a filter to prevent any unnecessary and hopeless cases going forward to the very expensive forum of the Crown Court. Where a case successfully encounters the committal stage, this is not taken as conclusive evidence of the defendant's guilt in the Crown Court. The threshold for a case to be committed to the Crown Court is very low, and the prosecution only have to prove that there is a case to be answered at the Crown Court. The result is that the vast majority of cases are committed to the Crown Court for trial.

The procedure dealing with committal proceedings has recently been revised by ss 44, 47 and Schedule I of the Criminal Procedure and Investigations Act 1996. Until the 1996 Act there were two forms of committal: under s 6(1) of the Magistrates' Courts Act 1980: committals with consideration of the evidence where the prosecution was required to call its witnesses to be examined and cross examined by the parties and committals without consideration of the evidence under s 6(2) of the Magistrates' Courts Act 1980.

With effect from 1 April 1997, the Criminal Procedure and Investigations Act abolished committals with consideration of the evidence under s 6(1).

Under the modified system the procedure is that:

- the charge is read to the accused but no plea is taken;

- the court clerk will ask the defence whether they wish reporting restrictions to be lifted;

- the clerk will ask the prosecution to confirm that all their evidence is in the form of statements made under s 102 of the Magistrates' Courts Act 1980 and that copies have been served on the defence and that the accused is legally represented;

- evidence will be limited to documentary evidence and exhibits tendered by the prosecution;

- oral evidence will no longer be permitted;

- evidence from the defence will no longer be permitted;

- the prosecution and defence are entitled to make representations to the court about the issues arising out of the evidence and whether there is an issue to be tried in the Crown Court;

- the magistrates decide whether the case should be committed to the Crown Court for trial;

- where the case is committed the following matters will also be addressed:

  - the defence are informed that if they are to rely on an alibi at the trial they are required to serve notice of this fact on the prosecution within the next seven days;

  - full or conditional witness orders are made in respect of witnesses required to attend at the trial;

  - where appropriate the court is required to decide whether to remand the accused in custody or to release him or her on bail;

○ an application for legal aid in respect of the Crown Court trial can be made to the magistrates' court.

Committals under s 6(2)

The provisions of s 6(2) allows the accused to agree to be committed for trial without consideration of the evidence. The procedure under s 6(2) would be appropriate where for example the accused intended to plead guilty at the Crown Court, or he or she accepts that the prosecution have a prima facie case to be tried on indictment. The procedure will be as follows:

• the charge is read to the accused;

• the accused is not required to plead guilty or not guilty;

• the prosecution confirm that all their evidence in the form required by s 102 Magistrates' Courts Act 1980 have been served on the defence;

• the defence are asked whether they have received the prosecution material and whether they object to anything contained in the statements;

• in the vast majority of cases, the magistrates will announce that the matter has been committed for trial at the Crown Court;

• after the decision to commit, the court will deal with other matters including the notice of any defence alibi; witness orders are made requiring the attendance of witnesses at the Crown Court trial; an application for the accused to be released on bail and where appropriate, the accused will make an application for legal aid.

The advanced disclosure of evidence

Where your client is charged with an indictable offence or an offence triable either way, he or she is entitled under the Magistrates' Court (Advance Information) Rules 1985 to advance disclosure of the prosecution case. This will usually include copies of all the written prosecution witness statements. From 1 April 1997, these rules are supplemented by the provisions of Part I of the Criminal Procedure and Investigations Act 1986 for cases to be heard in the Crown Court. Under Part I, the prosecution are required to disclose to the defence all material which might undermine their case. Having received full details of the prosecution case, the defence is then required to set out in general terms the nature of the accused's defence and indicate the matters on which the accused takes issue with the prosecution case and give details of any alibi upon which the defendant intends to rely. Where the defence make inadequate disclosure, adverse inferences can be drawn by the court and the prosecution.

In summary trials in the magistrates' courts, the above principles relate to prosecution evidence only, where your client pleads not guilty. Where it is in their interests to do so, the defence may voluntarily disclose the details of their case.

Preparatory hearings

From 15 April 1997, Part III of the Criminal Procedure and Investigations Act 1996 provides that in long or complex hearings in the Crown Court there should be preparatory hearings involving the parties and the judge which will be required to identify the key issues in the case, expedite proceedings at the full trial and assist in the management of the case by the judge.

Trial procedure in the Crown Court

Where the accused pleads not guilty the course of the trial will be as follows:

- The jury – usually composed of 12 people – is chosen, sworn in and informed of the charge(s) to which the accused has pleaded not guilty.

- When being empanelled jurors may be challenged by the defence for cause where it is alleged they are biased; the prosecution may ask a juror to stand by, in that they object to the person being a juror, but in practice this power is rarely used. Wherever possible, it is desirable that juries should be sexually and/or racially balanced reflecting the community they are drawn from. The judge has the right to remove a juror where there is suspicion of bias or other impropriatory.

- The prosecuting barrister (counsel) will summarise the facts and law in the case and the evidence he or she proposes to call.

- Prosecution witnesses will then be called to be examined-in-chief, cross-examined by the defence and where appropriate, re-examined by the prosecution.

- Prosecution evidence may also be put before the court in statement form where it is not necessary or possible for the witness to attend court under: ss 9 and 10 of the Criminal Justice Act 1967, or ss 23 and 24 of the Criminal Justice Act 1988.

- At the end of the prosecution case, the defence are entitled to make a submission of no case to answer where the prosecution have failed to adduce evidence in respect of an essential element of the offence or prosecution evidence has been so discredited by cross examination.

- If there is a case to answer, the defence then call its evidence in examination-in-chief, cross examination by the prosecution and where necessary, re-examination. Evidence can also be presented under ss 9 and 10 of the Criminal Justice Act 1967 and ss 23 and 24 of the Criminal Justice Act 1988.

- It is usual that the accused should be called as the first defence witness.

- The prosecuting barrister may make a closing speech.

- The defence barrister makes a closing speech.

- The judge sums the case up and directs the jury on important points of law and evidence.

- The jury are directed and invited to retire to consider their verdict.

- The jury will be told that the court requires a unanimous verdict.

- Where a verdict has not been reached after a minimum of two hours 10 minutes, the jury will be told by the judge that the court will accept a majority verdict of no less than 10:2.

- Where the jury's verdict is guilty, the judge will sentence the accused having heard a plea in mitigation and where necessary, pre-sentence reports.

- Where the jury decides the accused is not guilty, the accused will be discharged and the defence barrister will ask for the costs of defending the case to be met out of public funds including the remission of legal aid contributions.

The right to bail under the Bail Act 1976

Bail is the release of a person who is under a duty to surrender to custody at the date of the next court hearing or where the date is not known of the next court is not known, bail can be open-ended. The question of bail in criminal cases arises when the magistrates or the Crown Court adjourns the proceedings – even in principle overnight or for the lunch period!

Under s 4 of the Bail Act 1976, there is a general presumption that every offender has a right to be released by the court on bail. This principle will not apply in the following circumstances:

(1) Where the offence is punishable with imprisonment, the accused will not be granted bail where

- the court is satisfied that there are substantial grounds for believing that if released on bail the accused would fail to surrender to custody, or commit an offence while on bail, or interfere with witnesses or otherwise obstruct the course of justice, whether in relation to himself or herself or some other person; or

- the court is satisfied that he or she should be kept in custody for his or her own protection, or where a juvenile for his or her own welfare; or

- he or she is already serving a custodial sentence for some other reason; or

- the court is satisfied that it has not been practicable to obtain sufficient information for the purpose of taking decisions required by the Bail Act 1976 due to the lack of time since the commencement of the proceedings; or

- having been released on bail in connection with the proceedings for the same offence, he or she has been arrested for absconding; or

- where the case has been adjourned for enquiries or a report, it appears to the court that it would be impracticable to complete the inquiries or the report without keeping the defendant in custody; or

- the offence is an indictable offence or triable either way; and it appears to the court that he or she was on bail in criminal proceedings on the date of the offence.

With the exception of the final ground, these provisions are contained in Part I Schedule 1 of the Bail Act 1976. The final ground is found in Schedule 1 para 2A of the Bail Act 1976.

Where the offence is not punishable with imprisonment

Where the offence with which the defendant is charged is a minor offence and does not attract a sentence of imprisonment, for example breach of the peace, the court is required to apply different conditions when deciding whether the defendant should be granted bail. The defendant need not be granted bail where:

- it appears to the court that having been previously granted bail he or she has failed to surrender to custody as required and the court believes, in view of that failure, that the defendant if released on bail would fail to surrender to custody; or

- the court is satisfied that he or she should be kept in custody for his or her own welfare; or

- he or she is already in custody in serving another sentence of the court; or

- having been released on bail in connection with proceedings for the present offence, he or she has been arrested for absconding.

These conditions are contained in Part II, Schedule 1 to the Bail Act 1976.

Remanded in custody

Where your client is refused bail, he or she will be remanded in custody either in the police station or to a prison, until the next court appearance. The court's decision to refuse bail can be appealed against by your client in the following ways.

Appeals against being refused bail

Where your client is refused bail there are two ways in which the application can be pursued. First, where bail was refused in the magistrates' court, the defendant may apply to a Crown Court judge in chambers. Second, an application can be made to the High Court.

Appeal to the Crown Court

The hearing takes place in the judge's chambers at the Crown Court. The case will normally be listed before the day's business starts at 10am. Your client will be represented by his or her solicitor and where the prosecution have no objection to bail being granted they will either not attend or send in written representations. Where the prosecution object to bail a solicitor or barrister will attend. Both parties will address the judge and can use the same arguments presented at the original hearing and any new additional evidence.

Appeals to the High Court

Where your client has been denied bail by either the magistrates and/or a Crown Court judge in chambers, your client can make an application to the High Court. The application will be by a summons and a sworn statement in support known as an affidavit. The hearing will take place in judge's chambers at the High Court and your client should be represented by a solicitor.

Appeals by the prosecution

Its important to be aware that since 1993 the prosecution have had a right to appeal against the decision to grant the accused bail under the Bail (Amendment) Act 1993. Section 5B of the Bail Act 1976 permits the prosecution to apply to the magistrates' court requesting that the decision to grant the accused bail should be reconsidered. The section applies where the accused is charged with a non-summary offence and that new information has come into the prosecutor's possession since the decision to grant bail was made.

Practice points

Social workers should:

- be prepared to negotiate with the police to protect your client's interests;

- consider whether it is in your juvenile client's interests to be cautioned for an offence rather than prosecuted;

- be aware in outline the ways in which a criminal prosecution can be commenced;

- be aware in outline the differing ways in which each court deals with cases and be prepared to advise your client where necessary;

- know in outline your client's right to receive bail and the circumstances in which the right can be denied or conditions imposed on your client;

- be aware of how the appeals system operates where your client has been refused bail and be prepared to advise.

Further reading

Burton, F and Clore, J, *Criminal Litigation and Sentencing*, 1997, London: Cavendish Publishing.

Seabrooke, S and Sprack, J, *Criminal Evidence and Procedure – The Statutory Framework,* 1996, London: Blackstone Press.

14 Sentencing adult offenders

A conviction will follow where the magistrates or the jury have found the accused guilty or where the accused pleaded guilty. In many cases the court will not proceed to sentence the accused at this time, and in some circumstances the court is required to adjourn the matter in order for post-conviction reports should be prepared. Where this occurs the accused can either be remanded in custody or released on conditional or unconditional bail.

The factors influencing sentence

In deciding what sentence to impose the judge or magistrates will consider a number of factors, including:

(1) The particular circumstances of the offence(s) for which the accused has been found guilty or pleaded guilty. This relates to any mitigating and/or aggravating factors surrounding the offence. Magistrates are required to follow sentencing guidelines prepared by the Magistrates Association. Judges sitting in the Crown Court are obliged to follow sentencing guidelines laid down by the Court of Appeal. Courts are also required to give general consideration to the sentencing factors provided by the Criminal Justice Act 1991 in that sentences imposed on an offender must be:

- proportional with the offence(s);
- provide a deterrence against further offending;
- prevent the offender committing more crimes; and
- contribute towards the offender's rehabilitation.

To supplement these provisions, sentences are divided into four broad divisions in order of seriousness:

- custodial sentences for the most serious offences;
- community sentences for the less serious offences;
- fines; and
- discharges, conditional or absolute for trivial offences.

(2) The accused's character and any previous convictions (known as antecedents) which are presented to the court by the police or the Crown Prosecutor. This will include details of the offender's age, education, upbringing, employment record and domestic circumstances.

(3) Offences taken into consideration is an informal but long-recognised convention where the offender is not formally charged with the offences but they can be taken into account when the offender is sentenced for those offences he or she has been found guilty of committing.

(4) Sentencing powers imposed by law involves considerations of two issues. First, a court can only impose a sentence which is allowed either by the statute creating that sentence, for example and/or by the jurisdiction of the court sentencing the offender. The magistrates' court therefore can only imprison an offender for a maximum of six months for a single offence or a maximum of 12 months where the offender is found guilty of two or more offences. Second, the court is required to consider the provisions of the Criminal Justice Act 1991. Under s 1, a court cannot impose a custodial sentence unless where one or more of the following conditions applies:

The 'seriousness' test

A court may impose a custodial sentence where it considers the offence, or combination of offences, is so serious that only a custodial sentence can be justified. In determining whether the seriousness test applies, the court is entitled by s 29 to take into account the previous convictions of the offender or his or her failure to respond to previous sentences.

The offence is a violent or sexual offence

Where the offender has been convicted of a serious sexual or violent offence, a custodial can be imposed where where it is necessary to protect the public from serious harm from the defendant.

Criteria for deciding the length of the sentence

Section 2 of the Criminal Justice Act 1991 requires that the custodial sentence must be:

- for such a term as the court considers is commensurate with the seriousness of the offence or the combination of offences; or

- where the offence is a violent or a sexual offence, for such longer term as the court considers necessary to protect the public from serious harm from the defendant;

- the Crime Sentences Act 1997 introduces minimum sentences for those people who repeatedly commit serious offences such as rape and robbery.

Pre-sentence reports

Pre-sentence reports are prepared by the probation service or social services, compiled by interviews between the officer and offender. Matters covered include the circumstances of the offence, the offender's social background, education, employment history and future prospects. Under s 3(1) of the Criminal Justice Act 1988 a pre-sentence is usually required before the imposition of either a custodial sentence or a community sentence and:

- the report will often conclude which type of sentence is appropriate;

- it is common practice for the offender to be released on bail to enable the report to be carried out, although where the court considers it appropriate, it will remand the offender in custody.

The sentences available in respect of adult offenders

Imprisonment

A person over 21 may be sentenced to prison:

- by the Crown Court up to the maximum period fixed by the statute creating the offence; or

- by the magistrates' court up to a maximum of six months for any one offence or up to a maximum of 12 months when dealing with two or more offences.

Time spent in custody before and during the trial is taken as part of the term of imprisonment. The Criminal Justice Act 1991 provides that a custodial sentence should only be imposed where the offence is so serious that only a custodial sentence can be imposed, or where there is a need to protect the public from a sexual or violent offender. The court is required to explain to the offender why it is passing a custodial sentence.

Suspended sentence

The court can pass a suspended sentence under s 22 of the Powers of the Criminal Courts Act 1973 where the offender has been sentenced to a term of imprisonment for a maximum of two years.

The court can order the suspended period, also known as the 'operational period', to be between one and two years. Whilst the power to impose suspended sentence is available to both the Crown Court and magistrates' court, given the limited period that the magistrates' court can impose, the sentence is of little practical value in the magistrates court. Where the offender commits an offence within the 'operational period', the offender can be sentenced for both the new and original offence(s).

Fines

About 80% of adult offenders are punished with a fine. The power to impose fines are as follows:

- a magistrates' court may impose a maximum fine of £5,000 for each offence;

- depending on the statute creating the offence, can either be the only sentence that can be imposed or whether it can be imposed in combination with other sentences;

- the Crown Court can fine an offender any amount unless the statute creating the offence prescribes a maximum;

- under s 18 of the Criminal Justice Act 1988, when deciding to fine an offender the court must take into account the financial circumstances of the offender and the seriousness of the offence.

Community sentences

A community sentence involves one or more of the following orders: probation order; community service order; curfew order; supervision order; attendance centre order. Supervision orders and attendance centre orders are dealt with below as non-custodial sentences, in respect of offenders aged 17–20.

A probation order

A probation order involves the following:

- a court probation order can last between six months and three years;

- special conditions such as a residence order or a requirement to attend a drug rehabilitation course can be attached to the probation order;

- where the offender fails to comply with the probation order or the conditions, he or she will be brought before the court to be sentenced for the original offence;

- whilst a probation order is a sentence in its right, it can be combined with other penalties such as a suspended sentence, a fine or a community service order;

- a probation order requires the offender to maintain regular contact with the probation officer, who is expected to confront the offender with the consequences of his or her conduct;

- a probation order is regarded as a punishment for an offender who will benefit from a period of probation and which will enable the offender to reassess his life to reduce further offending.

Community service order

Where an offender is aged 16 and over and convicted of an imprisonable offence, they may with the offender's consent, be given a community service order (CSO). A CSO will require the offender to:

- do community service for a period of between 40 and 240 hours;

- to be completed within 12 months.

Typical examples of community service activities will include decorating the houses of the elderly or disabled, gardening and building adventure playgrounds. Where the CSO is combined with a probation order the maximum term for the probation element is the same as for a period of probation and the maximum period of community service is 100 hours. This is known as a combination order.

Curfew order

A curfew order requires an offender to remain at a particular place, which is usually his/her home, for between two and 12 hours on any specified days over a period which must not exceed six months from the date of the sentence. The order was introduced by s 12 of the Criminal Justice Act 1991, and is a punishment aimed at preventing certain types of criminal behaviour such as theft from cars and public order offences outside pubs and night clubs. It may also be imposed to keep an offender away from a particular place. The order must be preceded by pre-sentence report.

The refusal of a community sentence

A custodial sentence can be imposed where the defendant refuses to consent to a community sentence.

Absolute and conditional discharge

The sentences will be imposed for relatively trivial offences, or where the court does not want to impose another type of sentence because of the mitigating circumstances surrounding the offence and/or the offender. The offender will not be punished further for the offences where he or she does not commit a further offence(s) during the operational period, which can last for a period of up to three years, ie that is the condition of the offender's discharge from the court. An absolute discharge allows the accused to walk free from the court.

Binding over

Binding over to keep the peace is contained in s 115 of the Magistrates' Courts Act 1980. A binding over order will be imposed where an accused has led the court to believe that a breach of the peace may arise from his or her future conduct. The accused will be bound over to keep the peace and be of good behaviour in a given sum of money. The sentence is appropriate to prevent any minor public order situation from developing including domestic disputes and quarrels between neighbours.

Hospital order

The Crown Court or the magistrates' court dealing with an offender for an imprisonable offence may make a 'hospital order' that the defendant be sent to a hospital to receive treatment for a mental disorder. The Crown Court can make a direction that the defendant can only be released upon the direction of the Home Secretary or a Mental Health Review Tribunal. The preconditions for the making of a hospital order are provided by s 37 of the Mental Health Act 1983.

Custodial sentences in respect of offenders aged between 17–20

Where an offender is aged between 17–20 the court has the full range of sentences available as detailed above, with the exception of imprisonment. An offender under the age of 21 who is given a custodial sentence cannot be sent to an adult prison. A custodial sentence imposed on an offender in this age group will be served in a young offender's institution.

Young offender's institution

An offender aged between 17–20 will serve a custodial sentence in a young offender's institution. The length of the sentence will be determined either by:

- **if in the Crown Court** – by the statute creating the offences which will specify a maximum; or

- **if in the magistrates' court** – they may impose detention for up to six months for each offence up to a maximum of 12 months.

The minimum terms that may be prescribed are 21 days for an offender of 18 or more or two months for an offender aged 17. Where the court imposes a custodial sentence it is required to give reasons why the defendant qualifies for the order and explain to the defendant in ordinary language that a detention order is being imposed. There is no power to suspend a detention centre order.

The following non-custodial sentences can also be imposed

Supervision order

A supervision order is available in respect of offenders up to the age of 17 and can be imposed for a maximum of three years. The offender is supervised by a local authority social worker for the area in which the offender lives or the supervision can be by a probation officer. The supervisor is required to 'advise, assist and befriend' the offender. Conditions may be attached to the order, for example that the offender should live away from home for a specified period to attend a course of training.

Attendance centre order

An attendance centre order can be imposed where the offender is aged under 21 and convicted of an imprisonable offence. There must be an appropriate attendance centre place available for the offender and the offender has not previously received a custodial sentence. The court is required to fix the number of hours the suspect is required to attend the centre, attendance can be for a minimum of 12 hours and a maximum of 36 hours. Attendance centres are supposed to provide the offender with a degree of discipline, encourage physical activities and the development of practical skills.

Practice points

Social workers should:

- be aware of the practice and procedure of sentencing, in particular, the purpose of the pre-sentence report;

- understand the principles which guide the court in the sentencing process;

- the available sentences in respect of adult offenders and offenders aged between 17–20 and be able to advise your client accordingly.

Further reading

Burton, F and Clore, J, *Criminal Litigation and Sentencing*, 1997, London: Cavendish Publishing.

Sprack J, *Emmins on Criminal Procedure*, 1996, London: Blackstone Press.

15   Juvenile justice

Where the police or the CPS have decided that this is not a case where administering a caution would be the appropriate course of action, and the case proceeds to the prosecution stage, the matter will be heard either in the youth court, or the adult magistrates' court or the Crown Court depending on the circumstances of the offender and/or the offence.

The general rule is that defendants under the age of 18 must be dealt with in the youth court.

The Youth Court

The vast majority of cases taken against juveniles will be heard in a special type of magistrates' court known as the Youth Court. It was formerly known as the Juvenile Court. The Youth Court was established to ensure that children and young people are tried in their own court, where procedure is less formal and less intimidating than in the adult court or the Crown Court. The Youth Court has the following characteristics:

- it should be held in a room which has not been used as an adult court within the last hour to ensure that juveniles do not mix with adult offenders (s 47 of the Children and Young Persons Act 1933);

- proceedings should not be open to the public (s 47(2) of the Children and Young Persons Act 1933);

- only those people directly involved in the case can attend, including the magistrates, court officials, parties, lawyers, social workers and probation officers;

- the press have the right to attend but their reports must not identify the accused;

- magistrates who sit in the Youth Court will be drawn from a special panel who are qualified to deal with cases involving juveniles;

- the bench must consist of not more than three magistrates and must include a man and a woman;

- the course of trial in the Youth Court is essentially the same as in the adults magistrates' court.

The lay out of the court is, however, different from an adult court to create a less intimidating and more informal environment:

• there is no dock;

• the juvenile will sit at a desk in front of the magistrates, with a parent, guardian or social worker sitting close by;

• the magistrates sit at a table and not on a raised dais;

• the juvenile will be addressed by his or her first name;

• the court will explain to the juvenile, in ordinary language, the substance of the charge;

• the juvenile will not be asked to plead guilty or not guilty;

• witnesses are required to promise and not swear;

• the magistrates will find the case proven or not proven;

• there will not be a 'finding of guilt against him';

• the juvenile will not be sentenced but the magistrates will 'make an order upon a finding of guilt' (s 59 of the Children and Young Person Act 1933).

In exceptional circumstances, a juvenile will be tried in the Crown Court where:

• he or she is charged with homicide, where the case must be committed to the Crown Court;

• the juvenile is jointly charged with an adult and the court considers it necessary in the interests of justice for both to be tried in the Crown Court;

• the defendant is aged 10–17 (inclusive) and is charged with an offence which carries a maximum penalty of 14 years or more for an adult and the court considers that, if he or she is convicted, no disposal would be appropriate other than a term of detention under s 53 of the Children and Young Person Act 1933, in which case the matter should be sent to the Crown Court.

In the following exceptional circumstances a juvenile will be tried in the adult magistrates' court where:

• the juvenile is charged jointly with an adult; or

• the juvenile appears before the magistrates' together with an adult, and has been charged separately but the charges allege that he aided and abetted in the commission of the offence alleged against the adult or vice versa; or

- the juvenile appears before the magistrates' charged with an adult and the charge arises out of the same or connected circumstances as the adult; or

- the trial has started against the youth in the erroneous belief that the youth was an adult.

Sentencing juvenile offenders

The Youth Court's sentencing powers

Where the juvenile is found guilty of the offence or offences charged, the Youth Court has a number of sentencing options depending on the age of the offender, the statutory powers of punishment that can be imposed for that offence.

A juvenile for the purpose of sentencing is a person aged 10 to 16 years inclusive. Different considerations apply to sentencing where the offender is aged 17 years and above. In relation to the sentencing of juvenile offenders, each court has the following powers.

The Crown Court

Where those very exceptional circumstances apply: where the juvenile is tried and convicted in the Crown Court, under s 56 of the Children and Young Persons Act 1933, the Crown Court is required to send back the case to the Youth Court for the juvenile to be sentenced. This requirement must be followed unless the juvenile has been convicted of homicide or it would be 'undesirable' to send back the case to the Youth Court.

It appears that it would be 'undesirable' to do so where sending the case back would cause delay or an unnecessary duplication of the proceedings or unnecessary expense. Common practice appears to be therefore that in most cases, the Crown Court judge will sentence the juvenile.

Secure training order

A secure training order is introduced by ss 1–4 of the Criminal Justice and Public Order Act 1994 and is available in respect of offenders aged 12–14 at the date of the offence and not the date of the sentence.

It is available where the offender has been convicted of an offence punishable with imprisonment (except murder) and has been convicted of three or more imprisonable offences and previously, or in relation to the present offence, has breached a supervision order or has committed an imprisonable offence while being subject to a supervision order.

A secure training order is regarded as a custodial sentence and when deciding whether to impose the sentence the court is required to consider the custody threshold criteria, including:

- the seriousness of the offence; and

- where relevant to do so, the combination of the offences; and

- the offender's previous convictions.

The sentence can be imposed for:

- a minimum of six months and a maximum of two years;

- the sentence can only be imposed after a pre-sentence report has been obtained;

- the secure training order comprises of a period of detention followed by a period of detention;

- the supervision will be undertaken by a social worker or probation officer.

The adult magistrates' court

The general rule is that the adult magistrates' court is required to send the case of a juvenile back to the Youth Court for sentence (s 7 of the Children and Young Persons Act 1969) apart from where the court:

- imposes a fine on the juvenile; or

- imposes a disqualification and/or endorsement on the juvenile after conviction of a motoring offence(s).

The Youth Court

The Youth Court has a wide range of powers to sentence juvenile offenders. These include:

Detention in a young offender's institution

- a sentence of detention can be imposed for a maximum of six months for any one offence where the defendant is aged 15–16 years;

- a sentence of detention can be imposed for up to six months on conviction of any two or more summary offences;

- a sentence of detention can be imposed for up to 12 months for two or more 'either way' offences.

Fine

- a fine up to a maximum of £1,000 may be imposed in respect of offenders aged 15–17 inclusive;

- a fine may be imposed up to a maximum of £250 in respect of an offender aged 10–14 inclusive;

- for obvious reasons, the Youth Court rarely imposes a fine on the offender.

In addition, the Youth Court may impose the following sentences, where appropriate:

- a conditional and absolute discharge;

- an order binding over the juvenile;

- a fine up to a maximum of £1,000 in respect of an offender aged 14–17 years; and a maximum of £250 in respect of an offender aged 10–13 years;

- a compensation order is available up to a maximum £5,000 for each offence;

- an attendance centre order is available where the offender is aged under 21;

- a supervision order is available where the offender is aged under 18;

- a probation order is available where the offender is aged 16 years and over;

- a community service order is available where the offender is aged 16 years and over;

- a combination order is available where the offender is aged 16 years and over.

Detention in a young offender institution can be imposed on those aged 15 and 16 up to six months for any one offence and up to 12 months for two or more either way offences. A secure training order can be imposed under ss 1–4 of the Criminal Justice and Public Order Act 1994. This is the most recent sentence that can be imposed on juvenile offenders. It is available in respect of those offenders who are aged 12–14 at the date of the offence and not the date of the sentence. Three conditions have to be satisfied before a secure training order can be imposed, where the juvenile:

(1) has been convicted of an imprisonable offence;

(2) has been convicted of three or more imprisonable offences;

(3) has previously, or in relation to the present offence, has breached a supervision order or has committed an offence while subject to such an order.

The order can be imposed for a minimum of six months up to a maximum of two years which will be determined by a number of factors including the seriousness of the offence or offences and the previous findings of guilt made against the juvenile.

Where the juvenile has been convicted of a motoring offence, the court has power to impose the endorsement of the licence (or future endorsement when the accused is old enough to hold a licence) and/or to disqualify the juvenile from driving.

The juvenile's parent or guardian is required to attend court when the juvenile appears. The parent or guardian can be required to enter into an agreement with the court to take proper care and control over the juvenile. Where the recognisance is breached they can be ordered to pay up to £1,000. Parents or guardians may also be required to pay or make a contribution to fines, costs or compensation orders imposed by the courts.

The Youth Court's powers to deal with serious offences

- Where the juvenile is aged between 15–17 (inclusive) is found guilty of an indictable offence(s); and

- the Youth Court considers that its powers to imprison the juvenile for a maximum of six months is inadequate, the Youth Court can commit the juvenile to the Crown Court to be sentenced.

- the Crown Court can pass a sentence of up to 24 months for the offence; or

- the Crown Court can impose on the juvenile any sentence which the Youth Court could have imposed.

Practice points

Social workers should:

- be aware of the practice and procedure in the Youth Court and be able to advise your client accordingly;

- know, in outline, the court's sentencing powers and be able to advise your client.

Further reading

Burton, F and Clore, J, *Criminal Litigation and Sentencing*, 1997, London: Cavendish Publishing Ltd.

Seabrooke, S and Sprack, J, *Criminal Evidence and Procedure – The Statutory Framework*, 1996, London: Blackstone Press.

16 Criminal justice appeals and police accountability

At various stages of the criminal justice system both the accused and the prosecution can appeal against a decision. 'Appeal' is given its broad meaning to include not only traditional areas of appeal but also judicial review and the influence of the European Convention on Human Rights 1950. This chapter will look at issues relating to police accountability, the avenues open to your client where he or she has been the victim of unlawful police conduct.

Seeking a retrial in the magistrates' court – s 142 of the Magistrates' Courts Act 1980

A person convicted by a magistrates' court may apply to that court that in the 'interests of justice' the case should be heard by different magistrates. Where the application is successful, the court will order a retrial. An application under s 142 will be appropriate where new evidence is found or a crucial defence witness failed to turn up for the original hearing.

Appeal from the magistrates' court to the Crown Court against conviction and/or sentence – ss 108–10 of the Magistrates' Courts Act 1980

Where an accused pleads not guilty in the magistrates' court he or she may appeal to the Crown Court against conviction and/or sentence.

Appealing against conviction

- The notice of appeal should be in writing and sent to the magistrates' clerk of the court concerned and to the prosecution within 21 days of the sentence being passed.

- An appeal against conviction will be heard by a judge or recorder sitting with two lay magistrates.

- There will be no jury.

- The court will completely rehear the case.

- The parties will present the same evidence as in the first hearing and are also entitled to call new evidence.

The Crown Court on making its decision can confirm the conviction or overturn the conviction.

Appealing against sentence

The accused may appeal against sentence where they have pleaded not guilty in the magistrates' court and have subsequently been found guilty or where they have pleaded guilty. On hearing the appeal against sentence the Crown Court may impose any sentence, whether heavier or lighter, which the magistrates could have imposed.

Where your client wishes to appeal to the Crown Court, their sentence could be increased to the maximum which the magistrates' court could have imposed.

Appeal from the magistrates' court to the High Court – s 111(1) of the Magistrates' Courts Act 1980

This avenue of appeal is open to both prosecution and the defence. In technical terms it is known as 'appealing by way of case stated' to the Queens Bench Division, Divisional Court of the High Court. It is a suitable avenue of appeal where either party alleges that the magistrates' court in making a decision during the trial have misinterpreted a point of law or evidence, or has acted outside its powers. Evidence is not called before the three judges hearing the appeal. Legal argument is presented on the written submissions. On deciding the issues, the Divisional Court may:

- reverse the magistrates' decision;

- confirm the decision;

- amend the decision; or

- remit the case back to the magistrates.

Application for judicial review to the Queen's Bench Division of the High Court

Judicial review should not come strictly within the section on criminal appeals because the court in deciding whether to grant judicial review acts is fulfilling a different purpose than an appeal court. Judicial review is concerned with examining the way in which the magistrates' court has exercised its legal powers lawfully. Where the Queen's Bench Division concludes that magistrates have exercised its powers unlawfully, it can order that the magistrates decision can be quashed (by making an order for *certiorari*) and/or an order that the magistrates exercise their powers in a lawful way (by making an order for mandamus). The case can then be remitted back to the magistrates requiring them to exercise their powers lawfully and, where the whole decision is unlawful, both the conviction and sentence can be overturned. The most common reason for seeking judicial review is where the magistrates have either exercised a legal power or made a decision that they cannot, in law make or where the court has acted in breach of the rules of natural justice, for example where the court has not given the defence sufficient time to prepare its defence.

Appeals from the Crown Court to the Court of Appeal (Criminal Division) – the Criminal Appeal Act 1968

An accused can appeal from the Crown Court to the Court of Appeal against conviction and/or sentence.

Criminal Cases Review Commission

From April 1997 the Criminal Cases Review Commission, based in Birmingham, took over responsibility from the Home Office into the investigation of alleged miscarriages of justice. The Commission has wide powers to reopen police investigations and can order cases to be referred to the Crown Court or the Court of Appeal.

Appeal against conviction

An appeal against conviction can only be made where:

- the Court of Appeal grants (ic gives its consent) for the appeal; or

- the trial judge in the Crown Court grants a certificate that the case is fit for appeal.

The Court of Appeal can only overturn a conviction where it considers the conviction is 'unsafe'.

In most cases, the procedure will be as follows:

- Within 28 days of conviction the appellant must serve on the Registrar of Criminal Appeals a notice of application for leave to appeal accompanied by the draft grounds of appeal.

- The papers, including a transcript of the trial or the relevant part of the transcript will be considered by a single judge.

- Where the single judge gives leave to appeal, the case proceeds to the hearing.

- Where the single judge does not give leave, the appellant can appeal that his or her application should be heard by the full court.

- Where the single judge refuses leave to appeal and the application proceeds to the full court, the full court will in most cases give a 'direction for loss of time', which means that the period spent in jail by the accused between the single judge refusing the application for leave and the decision of the full court will not count as part of his or her custodial sentence unless the accused decision to appeal was supported by his or her barrister.

Hearing the appeal

At the hearing of an appeal against conviction the court will listen to oral argument of the party's barristers and may receive fresh evidence where the evidence is credible and would have been admissible at the trial on indictment and there is a reasonable explanation as to why the evidence was not presented at the original trial.

Powers of the Court of Appeal

On the hearing the evidence, the court may:

- quash the conviction and enter the verdict of an acquittal; or

- quash the conviction and order a retrial; or

- dismiss the appeal.

Appeals against sentence

An appeal against sentence will follow largely the same procedure as appeals against conviction. In order to successfully appeal against sentence, the appellant has to successfully argue that the trial judge made an error in that the sentence is manifestly excessive or that the sentence was wrong in law.

The Court of Appeal does not have the power to increase the sentence imposed. However, the Attorney General has the power under s 36 of the Criminal Justice Act 1988, where it is believed the offender has been dealt with too leniently, to refer the sentence for review to the Court of Appeal. In this situation the Court of Appeal does have the power to increase the sentence.

Appeals to the House of Lords

An appeal can be made to the House of Lords by either the prosecution or the defence from a decision of the Court of Appeal, where:

- the Court of Appeal certifies that the decision involves a point of law of general public importance; and

- either the Court of Appeal or the House of Lords gives leave to appeal.

The European Convention on Human Rights 1950

In May 1997 the Labour government announced that the European Convention on Human Rights would be incorporated into UK law by an Act of Parliament. This means that litigants would be able to directly rely on the Convention's provisions in English court proceedings. For the foreseeable future, however, if your client wishes to pursue a case under the Convention it will be necessary for them to take the matter to the European Court of Human Rights in Strasbourg. A prospective litigant has no direct right of access to the court. The Convention's Commission will first vet the case to ensure that there is no further assistance to be gained from a UK national court and that issue relates to a right guaranteed by the Convention.

Where the case is accepted by the Commission and where it has not been possible to reach a friendly settlement between the litigant and the signatory state against whom the complaint is made, the case proceeds to be heard by the Court of Human Rights. The court is made up of a judge from each signatory state, and each judge gives a separate decision.

Where the state is found to be in breach of the Convention, financial compensation may be paid to the aggrieved party. The bad news is however that the process is painfully slow. In spite of attempting to speed up the number of cases heard, your client could be waiting at least two years and perhaps longer before the case is decided.

As indicated in Chapter 2, the Convention covers a wide range of civil and political rights. In relation to criminal matters, however, most applications under the Convention are made under Article 5, the right to liberty and security of the person and Article 6, the right to a fair trial.

Police accountability

Where your client has been the 'victim' of unlawful or unfair conduct police, he or she can pursue the matter in one or more of the following ways.

The Police Complaints Authority

The Police and Criminal Evidence Act 1984 established the Police Complaints Authority, which is a semi-independent body charged with the investigation of complaints against the police. The complaints can be made from either members of the public or internally from the police itself. Most significantly, a breach of any provision of the Code of Practice is a breach of discipline and can be referred for investigation to the Authority.

Criminal prosecution

Certain actions by police officers, for example assault or giving false evidence, may give rise to criminal liability. If the Crown Prosecution Service (CPS) decide that it is not in the public interest to prosecute the officer, it might be possible for your client to bring a private prosecution against the officer – subject to taking into account the considerable financial obstacle that he or she would face if the prosecution was unsuccessful.

Civil actions

An action in the county court or High Court could be commenced against the individual officer and his or her chief officer for trespass, assault, false imprisonment, negligence or breach of statutory duty. This course of action is becoming increasingly popular, not least because the standard of proof, on the balance of probabilities, is lower than the criminal standard and that when successful, damages awarded against the police for misconduct can be high.

Practice points

Social workers should:

- be able to advise your client about the options available to him or her after conviction and/or sentence;

- understand in outline, the practice and procedure of the Police Complaints Authority and be able to advise your client accordingly.

Further reading

Bloy, D, and Parry, P, *Criminal Law*, 3rd edn, 1997, London: Cavendish Publishing.

Hungerford-Welch, P, *Criminal Litigation and Sentencing*, 3rd edn, 1996, London: Cavendish Publishing.

Seabrooke, S and Sprack, J, *Criminal Evidence and Procedure – The Statutory Framework*, 1996, London: Blackstone Press.

PART IV

SOCIAL WORKERS IN THE COURTS

17   Court attendance and giving evidence

In 1794 at the trial of Warren Hastings, Edmund Burke suggested that he knew a parrot who could learn the rules of evidence in half an hour and repeat them in five minutes. Today, for social workers and other professional witnesses, it takes considerably longer than 30 minutes to acquire an understanding of this complex subject.

As more of the professional work of a social worker requires an involvement with both civil and criminal courts, an acquaintance with the law of evidence in the following situations will be necessary. First, when appearing as a witness in criminal or civil case including proceedings under the Children Act 1989; second, when providing support to child witnesses testifying in cases involving alleged incidents of sexual and/or physical abuse; third, when acting as a guardian ad litem in 'specified' proceedings under the Children Act.

Therefore, this section aims to be an introduction to the basic principles of evidence; the procedure of giving evidence; identify the procedure and practice of child testimony and finally highlight the special evidential considerations that apply to proceedings under the Children Act.

Evidence – the legal background

In the context of how the English legal system works, the law of evidence provides a good example of the partnership between Parliament and the courts working together to make and apply the law on a day-to-day basis. In recent years, Parliament has introduced important changes to the law of evidence which have required the courts to interpret and apply the new law on a day-to-day basis. Indeed, whilst most, but not all, important evidential principles are to be found in statutes, the detailed application of the law is left to the courts. The law of evidence therefore remains a subject heavily reliant on court decisions and the best way to understand how the principles affect your professional role is to be acquainted with the important decisions.

What role does evidence play in the legal system?

The law of evidence has the following functions:

- it provides the body of rules which allows a party to legal proceedings to prove their case;

- it seeks to protect the defendant in criminal proceedings against injustice;

- it establishes the ground rules of the court process so the parties know exactly what they have to establish in order to successfully prove their case.

Evidence and the adversarial process

The English criminal and civil trial is based on the adversarial principle as opposed to the inquisitorial system that applies in many European legal systems. The judge in the inquisitorial system is a public official who plays a proactive role in both the pre-trial investigation of the case and in the court proceedings by calling and questioning witnesses. The European judge plays the prominent role in ascertaining the truth.

By contrast in the English adversarial system, the judge or magistrate is not involved at all at the investigation stage nor does he or she normally call and question witnesses. The English judge or magistrate is a neutral umpire, deciding the case or directing the jury on the evidence the party's lawyers have presented to the court. Their overriding purpose is not to ascertain the truth but to ensure a fair trial is conducted in the interests of justice (whatever that means). Consequentially the English adversarial system has the following characteristics:

- in criminal cases the ultimate issue of the accused's guilt or innocence is determined by lay people – in the Crown Court by a randomly selected jury and in the Youth Court or magistrates' court by people drawn from the community;

- the issue of liability in civil proceedings is determined in the vast majority of cases by a judge;

- evidence should normally be given by a witness orally in court, so that the truthfulness and credibility of the witness can be tested by the parties, the judge and the jury or magistrates;

- whilst the lawyer must not mislead the court his or her primary duty is to represent the client's case in the most advantageous way.

It is important to note that many of these principles do not apply in proceedings under the Children Act, which because of the Act's overriding purpose of promoting and protecting the child's welfare, has developed many of the characteristics of inquisitorial system in that the judge plays a proactive role in case management, identifying the key issues in the case and controlling the number of witnesses to be called.

These matters are further dealt with in Chapter 21 in Evidence under the Children Act 1989.

The terminology of evidence

The law of evidence has developed a terminology all of its own. In this section we introduce you to the most important terms:

Admissibility

This is the most basic of all evidential concepts. Evidence will only be accepted by the court where it is admissible. Admissible evidence is evidence which, as a matter of law, is capable of being put before the court. Questions about the admissibility of evidence are questions of law to be decided by the judge in the Crown Court and by the bench in the magistrates' court after taking advice from the magistrates' clerk and by the judge in the High Court and county court.

The rules relating to admissibility of evidence in proceedings under the Children Act are considerably relaxed in comparison with the general principles outlined in this section.

Categories of excluded evidence

Even where evidence is relevant and probative of a fact in issue, it might be excluded on the ground that to allow the evidence to be put before the court would be unfair to the defendant. These are known as the rules of exclusion, which apply mostly to criminal cases. There are few rules of exclusion in civil trials and proceedings under the Children Act. The reason is that virtually all cases are heard by a judge sitting alone, who can deal with and give appropriate weight to what might be relevant but prejudicial evidence. In criminal trials, however, where the issues of guilt and innocence are decided by people without formal legal training, such as jurors and lay magistrates, certain types of relevant but highly prejudicial evidence, are, as a general rule, excluded to ensure the defendant receives a fair trial. The most notable rules of exclusion in criminal trials are the rules relating to evidence of the defendant's bad character and previous convictions and the rules regarding hearsay evidence, which are admitted only where the exceptional circumstances provided for by statute or the common law, arise.

Types of evidence

Admissible evidence may take one of several forms as listed below. It is important to be conversant with these classifications, as the type of evidence adduced can have a bearing on the weight to be attached to it. Collectively, the following varieties of evidence are known as 'judicial evidence'.

Oral evidence

This is evidence given by a witness in court of what he has directly perceived or has personal or first-hand knowledge about, eg 'I saw the defendant stab Mr Jones in the stomach'. In the adversarial system of the English trial, direct oral testimony is the preferred way for evidence to be put before the court. It is usual in childcare cases for the court to require to hear oral evidence, although not at every stage of the proceedings. In some situations, it is enough that the witness's written statement is read to the court, provided the witness is available for cross-examination.

Hearsay

Any statement, other than one made by a witness in the course of giving evidence, where the statement is represented to be the truth of its contents. The general rule is that hearsay evidence is inadmissible in criminal proceedings unless it falls within one of the recognised exceptions such as confessions or documentary evidence admitted under the Criminal Justice Act 1988.

In recent times, the exceptions to the hearsay rule have become more significant than the operation of the rule itself. Therefore, in criminal cases, hearsay evidence contained in a written statement may be put before the court under s 23 of the Criminal Justice Act 1988 where the maker of the statement is unable to attend to court to give oral evidence because he or she has died; or is unfit to attend court; or is outside the UK; or the witness cannot be found; or, of increasing importance, where the witness does not give oral evidence through fear or because he is kept out of the way because of the problem of witness intimidation. Evidence in documentary form including, local authority files, memoranda, receipts, etc are admissible under s 24 of the Criminal Justice Act 1988. Other important legislation includes statements in public documents such as birth, marriage and death certificates; statements made to police under s 9 of the Criminal Justice Act 1967 for trials in the Crown Court and the magistrates' court, and under s 102 of the Magistrates' Courts Act 1980 in committal proceedings.

In civil cases under the Civil Evidence Act 1995, and proceedings under the Children Act, the rule against excluding hearsay evidence has virtually been abolished.

In addition to oral testimony and hearsay, evidence put before the court can take a variety of forms.

Real evidence

This usually takes the form of an object produced for inspection by the court. Examples of real evidence would be a child's drawing; an X-ray of an injury; photographs; an audio tape or a video recording. The purpose of putting such objects in evidence is to allow the court to draw such inferences from the object or to make observations about it. In practice, however, objects of real evidence will invariably be accompanied by the oral evidence of a witness who will testify to its authenticity and significance in the case.

Documentary evidence

This can include photographs, maps, plans, blueprints, a witness's written or recorded statement, local authority records, expert reports, health trust records, video cassettes, etc. The document may be adduced in evidence because its content, or merely its existence, is relevant. The original document constitutes 'primary' evidence, a copy 'secondary' evidence (but increasingly the law of evidence provides for the admissibility of copies of documents).

Circumstantial evidence

Circumstantial evidence comprises evidence of a fact from which the court may draw inferences as to a fact in issue, eg fingerprints of the defendant at the scene of the crime; or evidence given by a witness as to a vendetta between the defendant and the homicide victim.

Primary evidence

Evidence of the best kind, for example the original of a document.

Secondary evidence

Evidence of an inferior kind, for example the copy of a document. Note that it is important to be aware that evidence may fall into more than one category; for example, documentary evidence may also be real evidence, circumstantial evidence, hearsay evidence, in addition to its classification as documentary evidence. Into which category evidence falls depends very much on the purpose for which it is put before the court.

Opinion evidence

The general rule is that where a witness gives opinion evidence it will be inadmissible. A witness may only speak of those facts which he has personally perceived, and not of inferences drawn from those facts. There are two exceptions to this general rule.

First, a non-expert witness may state his opinion on matters not requiring expertise as a way of conveying facts which he has personally perceived. Second, given the complex nature of modern civil and criminal litigation, it is becoming increasingly common for the court to determine issues that are so far removed from its experience that evidence from an expert in that field is required to assist the court in determining the issue in question. In these circumstances, opinion evidence from the expert will be admissible.

The list of matters upon which expert evidence has been required in both civil, criminal cases and proceedings under the Children Act is not exhaustive and continues to grow to include accident investigation; ballistics; blood tests; breath tests; blood-alcohol levels; facial mappings; facial identification; insanity and a wide range of medical, scientific, architectural, technical, forensic and professional matters.

Expert evidence, medical, psychiatric and psychological is widely used in child abuse cases. As we consider in detail in Chapter 19, the court, in cases involving children, has specific powers to control the use of expert evidence and the judges are anxious to move away from the general trend in recent years, to have trial by experts. This said, there will be many cases where the court will require expert evidence on matters which go beyond its normal competence and expertise.

Who is an expert?

A witness is competent to give expert evidence only if, in the opinion of the judge, he is properly qualified in the subject calling for expertise. The expertise may have been acquired through study, training, or experience. You may be asked to produce proof of your qualifications; asked whether you are a member of a recognised professional body and how much experience you have had in the matters about you which you will be asked to testify. The courts generally presume that following the decision in *F v Suffolk County* [1981] Fam LR 208, a qualified social worker is competent to give expert evidence on matters of general child care. This important matter is dealt with in further detail in Chapter 21 Evidence in proceedings under the Children Act.

Crown Court trials: functions of judge and jury

In the relatively small number of criminal cases which are tried in the Crown Court, there is a strict division of responsibilities between the judge and the jury. It is for the judge to determine matters of law and evidence, and for the jury to decide issues of fact – most significantly whether the defendant is guilty or not guilty. The judge rules on the admissibility of evidence; the jury determines how much significance should be attached to that evidence. The judge instructs the jury on what matters must be proved by the prosecution, and where it arises, what matters must be proved by the defence and indicates the required standard of proof. Issues of evidence are decided in a procedure known as the voire dire or trial within a trial. During the *voir dire*, the jury are absent from the court and will not hear legal arguments submitted by counsel. The judge has a discretion to exclude any prosecution evidence under s 78 of the Police and Criminal Evidence Act 1984, where it would be unfair to allow the evidence to be put before the court, or evidence can be excluded where its probative value is excluded by its prejudicial effect.

Where the evidence is ruled inadmissible, the jury's verdict about the accused's guilt or innocence will not be tainted by having heard potentially highly prejudicial but unfair evidence.

The magistrates' court

The vast majority of criminal cases (about 96%), are heard in the magistrates' court by magistrates, who are not legally qualified, assisted by a court clerk who is usually a solicitor or barrister. Unlike trials in the Crown Court issues of law, including evidential matters, are decided by the magistrates following proper guidance and advice from the clerk.

The Youth Court

As in the adult magistrates' court, evidential issues are decided by the magistrates on the advice of the court clerk.

The Children Act courts

In courts hearing cases brought under the Children Act, questions of evidence are decided by the judge who must ensure that the proceedings reflect the underlying purpose of the Act, in that the court's and the party's primary concern should be the child's welfare.

The burden of proof

The general rule in criminal cases, is that where a defendant pleads guilty, it is for the prosecuting authority, the Crown Prosecution Service or the social services authority, to prove the accused's guilt and not for the defence to prove the accused's innocence. This fundamental principle is known as the legal burden of proof as stated in the famous case of *Woolmington v DPP* [1935] AC 463.

Where the prosecution has the legal burden, it will also have an evidential burden. The matters which make up the legal burden can be ascertained by reference to the substantive law. The evidential burden is simply the way in which the prosecution discharges its legal burden by adducing evidence before the court: calling witnesses, producing documents and real evidence. It is through this fact-finding process and by applying the law to the facts the case, that the court will make its decision.

Although beyond the scope of this book and not directly relevant to the professional involvement in the legal process of a social worker, there are exceptional circumstances where the defence have the legal and/or evidential burden of proving certain issues to the court.

The *Woolmington* principle described above also applies in civil cases. It is for the party, either the plaintiff or the defendant, who is required to prove those matters upon which are essential to proving their case.

The standard of proof

The general rule in criminal proceedings is that where the prosecution have the legal burden of proving the essential issues in the case, they must do so beyond reasonable doubt. This does not mean that in order to find the defendant guilty of the offence, the jury or magistrates have to be certain but in their minds there must be a high degree of probability about the accused's guilt.

Where the defence in criminal cases, and the plaintiff and defendant in civil cases have the burden, they must prove their case 'on the balance of probabilities', ie that it was more likely than not that there version of the facts was correct.

Over the years, as a matter of public policy, the courts have developed different principles in relation to the formula that satisfies the standard of proof in cases involving family law in general and children in particular, which as we shall see in proceedings under the Children Act is 'on the balance of probabilities'.

Practice points

Social workers should:

- be aware of the types of evidence that are presented to courts enabling a party to prove its case;

- remember the general rule: in the vast majority of criminal proceedings it is for the prosecution to prove the accused's guilt beyond reasonable doubt. In civil cases, the plaintiff or defendant who alleges certain relevant facts must prove those facts to the court on the balance of probabilities.

Further reading

Murphy, P, *A Practical Approach to Evidence*, 1997, London: Blackstone Press.

Murphy, P, *Evidence and Advocacy*, 4th edn, 1994, London: Blackstone Press.

18 The social worker as a professional witness

In this chapter, you will be taken through the practice and procedure when giving evidence in criminal proceedings. You may be required to appear as a witness in the magistrates' court or Crown Court where your client has been the alleged victim of sexual and/or physical abuse and you may be required to give oral evidence about your involvement in the case. This chapter will also be useful where you are required to give support and advice to a child or other vulnerable witness who are required to testify in court.

Whilst there are common elements in the practice of giving evidence between the criminal and civil courts, appearing as a professional witness in Children Act cases is dealt with in Chapter 21.

Before going into court

Your Crown Prosecution Service (CPS) lawyer should have taken you through the preparatory steps of giving evidence. In a criminal prosecution your witness statement will most likely be the signed statement you made to the police. As a witness you will not be allowed to hear the proceedings before giving evidence. You will wait outside the courtroom until you are called by the prosecution or defence. For many witnesses this can be a nervous time although it might be an opportunity for you to make good use of your time. You are allowed to refresh your memory from your statement before going into the witness box.

The examination of witnesses

Unless your evidence is uncontroversial or has been agreed by the prosecution and the defence or is presented to the court in your absence, the examination of your evidence is likely to be in three stages: first, examination by the side calling 'Examination-in-chief'; second, examination by the opposing side 'cross examination'; third, examination again by the party calling him, to repair any damage done by the other side's questions, known as 're-examination'.

Examination-in-chief

Examination-in-chief is when you will be called and questioned by the lawyer for the party calling you. You will be led by the court usher to the witness box, where first, you will be required to take the oath or affirm. If you choose to take the oath you will be given the Bible and a card with the words of the oath printed as following:

> I swear by Almighty God that the evidence I shall give shall be the truth, the whole truth and nothing but the truth.

If you object to swearing on the Bible you affirm:

> I, [full name], do solemnly, sincerely, and truly declare and affirm that the evidence I shall give shall be the truth, the whole truth and nothing but the truth.

The general rule during examination-in-chief is that your lawyer will not be allowed to ask you the leading questions – that is a question which suggests the answer to be given or which assumes facts which have yet to be established or asserted. For example, in prosecution for a physical assault on a child, your advocate will not be permitted to put the question in the following way: 'When you last saw Sarah, she was covered with bruises wasn't she?' It would be permissible for the question to be asked in this way: 'When you last Sarah, what was her physical condition?'

Whilst giving evidence you will be able to refresh your memory from your witness statement document provided that the document was made or verified by the witness while the events were still fresh in your mind. You will be required to produce the document for inspection by the other side and the judge or magistrate. Where the original is not available you may use a copy.

Cross examination of witnesses

At the conclusion of the examination-in-chief, the opposing side will have the opportunity to cross examine you. Occasionally this right will not be exercised, but in the vast majority of cases it will: so be prepared!

The defence lawyer will already have a copy of your proof of evidence through a pre-trial procedure known as advance disclosure, so he or she should be well prepared to question you about the matters arising out of your statement and any further matters brought out during the examination-in-chief.

The object of cross examination is to reduce the effectiveness of your evidence, and to elicit evidence from you which is favourable to the case of the party undertaking the cross examination. It is also permissible for a cross examination to include questions aimed at challenging your credibility as a witness, which you will be required to answer.

Whilst the judge or magistrates should ensure that the cross examination should be kept within the limits and fairness and confined to relevant issues before the court, the going can get quite tough! The other sides advocate might suggest that you are biased, mistaken or seek to impugn your professional judgment. You have to stand firm, not to be intimidated or roused, answer the questions honestly upholding your professional integrity.

Re-examination

Re-examination merits little discussion. It is available as the third stage in examination of witnesses. If your evidence or your credibility as a witness has been discredited in cross examination, or it is considered that some points need to be clarified, then the examiner-in-chief may decide to re-examine his witness.

The accused's failure to testify – s 35 of the Criminal Justice and Public Order Act 1994

This is a convenient point to consider what will happen where the accused does not given evidence. In these circumstances his silence may be the subject of adverse comment by the court unless it was undesirable for him to give evidence. The court will approach the matter in this way:

(2) ... the court shall at the conclusion of the evidence for the prosecution satisfy itself ... that the accused is aware that the stage has been reached at which evidence can be given for the defence and that he can, if he wishes, give evidence, or having been sworn, without good cause refuses to answer any question, it will be permissible for the court or jury to draw such inferences as appear proper from his failure to give evidence or his refusal, without good cause, to answer any question.

(3) ... the court or jury in determining whether the accused is guilty of the offence charged, may draw such inferences as appear proper from the failure of the accused to give evidence or his refusal, without good cause, to answer any question.

Section 35 does not apply in the following circumstances:

- where the accused is aged under 14; or

- where the accused pleads guilty; or

- where the accused's physical or mental state makes it undesirable for him or her to give evidence;

- the suspect cannot be convicted solely on the ground that he or she has not given evidence (s 35(3)).

Section 35 will apply where the prosecution evidence has raised issues which call for an explanation from the defendant and he fails to give evidence, a court will be entitled to infer guilt from that failure.

In *R v Cowan* [1995] 4 All ER 939, the Court of Appeal provided the following guidance to the courts as to how they should approach s 35:

- the judge must direct the jury that the burden remains on the prosecution to prove the accused's guilt;

- the judge should make it clear that the accused can remain silent and this right remains;

- the jury must be satisfied the prosecution have satisfactorily established their case before drawing inferences from the accused's silence.

Practice points

Social workers should:

- when appearing as a professional witness, carefully read over your statement before be called to give evidence;

- remember that you are entitled to refresh your memory in the witness box whilst you give evidence;

- remember that the purpose of the other side cross-examining you is to test the accuracy of your version of events and to undermine your credibility as a witness in the jurors or magistrates' minds;

- remember that under cross examination you should not lose your temper or rise to rebut allegations put to you by the other side. You are in the witness box to tell the court honestly and accurately your version of the events not to engage in a tit-for-tat argument with the other sides advocate.

Further reading

Murphy, P, *A Practical Approach to Evidence*, 1997, London: Blackstone Press.

Murphy, P, *Evidence and Advocacy*, 4th edn, 1994, Blackstone Press.

19 Children giving evidence

The trauma experienced by children when giving evidence in court, either as the victim of a serious sexual or physical assault, or as a witness to an offence, has been belatedly recognised in recent years. Children are the most vulnerable victims of the adversarial nature of English criminal proceedings, from the initial investigation, to the conclusion at the trial.

As the victim of sexual or physical abuse, the child will invariably have had their home life disrupted and be required to relive their experiences during successive interviews with the police and social service agencies. In *Re E* (1990)*The Times*, 2 April, the child had been questioned by parents, social workers and then, on seven separate occasions, by a child protection officer. This practice continues to be widespread in spite of a recommendation in the Cleveland Report (1988, Cmnd 412, para 12.34), that a child should be subjected to no more than two interviews.

Having experienced the trauma of the investigation, the child then faces the full horrors of the adversarial trial – the imposing courtroom, the requirement to talk about embarrassing and intimate experiences in front of strangers and the imposing formality of the occasion.

The child's competency

The first matter to be considered is whether the child will be allowed (competent) to give evidence. As a general rule, all witnesses are competent. The only exceptions to the general rule are witnesses who are mentally ill and very young children.

Children

In determining whether a child or young person is competent to give evidence in criminal proceedings, a distinction is drawn between a witness who is aged below 14 years and a witness who is aged 14 years and above.

Where the child is under 14 years of age, s 33A of the Criminal Justice Act 1988 provides that a child can give unsworn evidence only unless it appears that they are incapable of giving 'intelligible testimony' – in practice this means whether the child understands the questions put to him or her, the ability to communicate, to give a coherent and comprehensible account of his evidence and the ability to distinguish between fact and fantasy, for further details see *R v D* (1995) *The Times*, 15 November. The child will be presumed capable of giving evidence unless the issue is raised by the court or one of the parties. For the procedure to be adopted see *R v Hampshire* [1995] 3 WLR 260. Where the child is competent to give unsworn evidence he or she is also compellable, ie as a matter of law can be made to give evidence.

There is no minimum age at which a child is considered competent to give 'intelligible testimony'. In *R v Wallwork* (1958) 42 Cr App R 153 the judge called as a witness the five-year-old complainant to give unsworn evidence against her father who was accused of having had incest with her. The girl was terror stricken, and therefore unable to give evidence. Lord Goddard CJ stated that the judge was wrong in calling her, as at five she was too young to give unsworn evidence. The position in *Wallwork* no longer applies. The decision as to whether the child is competent to give evidence is a matter left entirely with the court to determine the child's age, maturity, understanding of the proceedings and involvement in the case.

Young people in criminal proceedings

For the purpose of giving evidence in criminal proceedings, a young person will be aged 14–17 years. The court will assume that the young person is competent to give sworn evidence unless the issue of competence is raised by the court, the defence or the prosecution. Where the issue is raised, the procedure in Hampshire will be followed and the test in *R v Hayes* [1977] 1 WLR 234 applied. The witness will be asked whether he or she understands the nature of the oath, the importance of telling the truth and has sufficient understanding of the solemnity of the occasion to give sworn evidence. Where the young person fails the *Hayes* test, he will be incompetent.

Methods of giving evidence

Historically, the English trial, based on the adversarial system, has long recognised that the best and most reliable evidence comes from a witness giving oral testimony in open court through examination-in-chief by the party calling him, and then being cross-examined by the other party or parties; and where necessary, by re-examination. However, it goes without saying that an appearance as a witness in court is daunting enough for an adult, but in the case of child witnesses it has often been so traumatic that the child has been unable to withstand cross-examination, or so terrified as to become hysterical and be incapable of giving any evidence at all. Particularly terrifying is the situation where a child complainant in a case of sexual or physical abuse is required to give evidence against the accused who, in most cases, will be facing the victim across the courtroom.

In recognition of these difficulties, in recent years, the legal system has introduced provisions to allow child witnesses to give evidence by a number of alternative methods where it is in the interests of justice for them to do so.

Evidence by live TV link

In certain circumstances, a child's evidence may be given by a live television link s 32(1), (1A) and (2) of the Criminal Justice Act 1988 makes provision for a 'child', with leave of the court, to give evidence through a live TV link where the accusation is of injury, assault, or threat of injury; or is of cruelty to a child under 16, or of a sexual offence as defined. If the offence alleged is a sexual offence, then a 'child' is a person under the age of 17; if it is of physical abuse, but not a sexual offence, a 'child' is a person under the age of 14. (In addition, any witness, of whatever age, if unavailable to give direct oral testimony because he is outside the UK, may be allowed to give evidence, on oath, by a live TV link.)

As regards a 'child', the provision applies whether the evidence is being given by the complainant witness, or by a witness to any such offence committed against any person, regardless of age. The complainant, therefore, may be a child or adult, and could be a sibling or the parent of the 'child' witness, or could be any other person. The most compelling reason for this form of giving evidence must be when it is a very young child giving evidence against a parent, as in *Wallwork* above.

The aim of s 32 is to remove the need for a child to give evidence in open court where it might be intimidating or embarrassing for them to do so. The child is not entitled to give evidence in this way as a matter of right – the leave the court must obtain.

Where leave is granted, the child will be watching a TV monitor in an adjacent room. The screen will show the head of the lawyers and the judge, but the witness will not see the accused. You will be allowed to sit with the child to provide comfort and support but must not prompt the witness when answering questions.

The provision does not apply to trials in the magistrates' court and only about 40 Crown Court trial centres have facilities which can provide live TV links.

In this type of case there is, obviously, the facility of cross-examination of the child witness, but that under s 34A of the Criminal Justice Act 1988, the cross-examination of the child witness can never be by the accused himself, but only by his legal representative.

Evidence by videotaped interview

In addition to the facility of a live television link, there is also the facility under s 32A of the Criminal Justice Act 1988, where the same type of allegation is made, ie children under 14 violent offence and under 17 in respect of a sexual offence for the child witness (whether complainant or other witness to the incident) to be interviewed by an adult and for that interview to be videotaped and the video recording be adduced in evidence as, the examination-in-chief of that child. s 50 of the Criminal Justice and Public Order Act 1994, allows a further examination-in-chief of any matter not adequately dealt with in the video recorded evidence of the child. The same upper ages apply as for television links.

Such a video recording, however, is not admissible as evidence if the child will not be available for cross-examination (by live television link); or the rules requiring details of how the video recording was made have not been followed; or the court considers that it would not be in the interests of justice to admit the recording.

The interviewer of the 'child' must be an adult, but not necessarily a lawyer; in practice, it will probably be a social worker or some other person who is sympathetic to the child's problems. In addition, the accused cannot cross-examine in person, even when the evidence-in-chief is given by way of video-recorded interview. Obviously, child abusers must be prosecuted to conviction, and it is unthinkable that they should escape punishment because the victim is too frightened to give direct oral evidence in court. But there is potentially the risk of justice to the accused person being subjugated by these methods of adducing evidence from complainant and child witnesses. No doubt judges will exercise the discretion to exclude given to them by the Criminal Justice Act 1988 itself, and by s 78 of the Police and Criminal Evidence Act 1984.

For the video-recording of a child's evidence-in-chief to be accepted by the court, it will need to comply with the Memorandum of Good Practice on Video-recorded Interviews with Child Witnesses for Criminal Proceedings issued by the Home Office in 1992.

Some recent important cases have provided useful guidance to the courts as to how they should treat a child's videotaped interview. In *R v Atkinson* [1995] Crim LR 490, the Court of Appeal held that it was not inappropriate for a jury in retirement to see videos of police interviews with the child victim of a sexual offence where the defendant had made the issue of inconsistencies in the witness's evidence. The judge made it clear that the video itself is not evidence but is to enable the jury to compare the evidence with any previous statement on video to assess their consistency and to consider how the evidence was obtained.

In two later cases, the procedure that the courts should follow was made clearer by the Court of Appeal. In *R v Rawlings*; *R v Broadbent* [1995] Crim LR 335, the jury saw for a second time, the video containing the evidence-in-chief of a child complainant in a trial for buggery. The Court of Appeal held this practice was acceptable provided: (i) the replaying of the video was done in open court in the presence of the judge, the jury and counsel; (ii) the judge warned against disproportionate weight being accorded to the evidence that was being reheard; and (iii) the judge reminded the jury of the evidence that was obtained as a result of the cross examination and re-examination of the witness.

A case which fell foul of the rules was *R v M* [1995] Crim LR 336, where an appeal against conviction for indecent assault on the accused's daughter aged 10 was allowed, because the video of her evidence had been replayed in court at the trial with the judge, jury and counsel present but without the necessary warnings and reminders from the judge.

Evidence from behind a screen

As indicated above, it is not possible for a child to give evidence by a live TV link in trials held in an adult magistrates' court. Where the 'interests of justice' require it, and the court exercises its discretion, witnesses (including children) may give evidence from behind a screen erected in the court.

The social worker's role

It does not matter by which method the child gives evidence, whilst you should provide comfort and support to a child witness you should not talk to the child whilst he or she is giving evidence. If you do more than whisper a consoling word, the suspicion is aroused that you are saying something about the evidence or prompting the child's answers. Where the suspicion is aroused, the court may refuse to hear the child's testimony, which given the importance of the child's evidence in these cases, may lead to the prosecution being discontinued and perhaps a child abuser escaping conviction.

The mentally handicapped in criminal proceedings

The same rules apply in determining the issue of the competence of a mentally handicapped witness as to other witnesses. Where the witness is under 14 the test of 'intelligible testimony' will apply and the evidence will be given unsworn. Where the witness is over 14, the court will refer to the Hayes test. In *R v Bellamy* (1985) 82 Cr App R 222, a case dealing with a witness who was mentally handicapped, the Court of Appeal stated that the *Hayes* test is of general application and that it is unnecessary for the court to embark on an inquiry into the witness's appreciation of the effect of taking the oath unless doubts are raised about his competency to give sworn evidence.

It may sometimes be necessary to determine the issue of competency by calling expert evidence to give a medical opinion about the witness's state of mind. Where this occurs the expert's evidence should be given in the absence of the jury (see *R v Deakin* [1994] 4 All ER 769).

Evidence of corroboration

There may be occasions where it will be necessary for the judge to give a warning to the jury about the dangers of convicting the accused on the unsupported evidence of a child witness and the victim of a sexual offence. This is known as the rule relating to corroboration. Corroborative evidence is independent evidence which supports the testimony of the child or the alleged victim of a sexual offence in a relevant way.

Corroborative evidence, therefore, could be the testimony of another witness. Or documentary, circumstantial, or real evidence.

Under s 32 of the Criminal Justice and Public Order Act 1994, the judge has a discretion whether to give a warning about the dangers of convicting on the uncorroborated evidence of of a child witness or the alleged victim of a sexual offence. Whether that discretion is exercised will depend on the particular circumstances of the particular case. For further consideration of how the courts are required to approach corroborative evidence, see *R v Makanjuola; R v Easton* (1995) *The Times*, 17 May.

Practice points

Social workers should:

- be aware that the test to determine a child's competency in criminal cases is whether he or she is capable of giving 'intelligible testimony';

- a 'child' is a person aged under 14 years;

- remember there is not a minimum age at which a child is competent to give evidence. The decision will be taken on the basis of the child's maturity and understanding;

- remember that a child's evidence can only be given unsworn ie without the child taking the oath or affirming;

- be aware that young people aged 14–17 years can give sworn evidence in criminal cases provided he or she understands the nature of the oath and the importance of telling the truth;

- be aware that children and young people may give evidence in a number of ways: orally in court like any other witness; or by a live tv link; or by a videotaped interview; or from behind a screen;

- remember that your role is to provide comfort and support to the witness. You should not talk to the child or young person whilst he or she is giving evidence nor in any way appear to prompt the witness.

Further reading

Murphy, P, *A Practical Approach to Evidence*, 1997, London: Blackstone Press.

Murphy, P, *Evidence and Advocacy*, 4th edn, 1994, London: Blackstone Press.

20 Public interest immunity, confidentiality and privilege

In this chapter, we look at three separate, but related, issues as to the obligations the law imposes on social service agencies and the NSPCC to make available 'confidential' and sensitive information contained in their files and other documents as evidence in court proceedings. As we have seen, the general rule in most litigation is that all evidence which is relevant to the matter before the court and which may assist the court in reaching its decision must be disclosed. An important exception to this general rule is where the law recognises that there may be situations where it would not be in the wider public interest for information, documents, files, etc to be disclosed, as this may compromise a confidential source of information or interfere with the proper discharge of the organisation's responsibilities. Would delegates at a case conference speak with full honesty if they were aware that the records of the case conference might be produced as evidence in court open to full public scrutiny and cross-examination? Would an informant who made allegations about an alleged abuse of a child come forward with that information if he or she knew that their identity would be disclosed?

These questions are typical of the kind of dilemmas that you will frequently encounter in practice. In this chapter we will be examining the operation of public interest immunity; the doctrine of privilege and the rights and obligations you owe as a social worker when dealing with unofficial 'confidential' information – or 'tip-offs'.

Public interest immunity

As a general rule in criminal and civil cases and in proceedings under the Children Act 1989, to enable the court to be appraised of all the relevant facts and evidence in the case, the parties are required to disclose to the court and other sides all the relevant documentation in their possession. In criminal proceedings the procedure is referred to as advance disclosure. In civil proceedings and under the Children Act the procedure is known as the discovery stage. As an exception to the general rule, public interest immunity covers evidence which may be relevant to an issue before the court, but as a matter of public policy does not have to be disclosed to the other parties because it is of a confidential or sensitive nature. The decision as to whether a document needs to be disclosed lies with the court, which will examine the material weight of two 'public interest' arguments. On the one hand it is clearly in the public interest that a court should decide issues between the parties in cases by being in possession of all the relevant material, whilst on the other hand it is also in the public interest that certain confidential and sensitive information, documents and other evidence should not be disclosed – even in court proceedings!

In the social work context this involves considering whether the public interest in protecting the social work records, case conference notes, medical records should override the public interest of the person who is a party to the proceedings seeking the information required to obtain legal redress. Let us therefore consider how the principles work in practice.

Public interest immunity and social service files

Two propositions arise from the court decisions. First, the good news. As a general rule, social work files will be confidential, and protected from disclosure. The bad news, however, is that there are no 'hard and fast rules' as to how the courts decide these matters. Whether a document or a file should be disclosed depends on the particular circumstances of the case. Lawyers say that the categories of public interest immunity (PII) are not closed, and on this occasion they are right. The categories are not closed. So let us consider some practical examples.

A good example of the principles involved in this area is the case of *Re D (infants)* [1970] 1 All ER 1088. The case concerned two children, a four-year-old girl and a boy aged three. In the preceding two years, the children had been cared for by foster parents and been made wards of court. The children's mother wanted to look after the children herself and at the court hearing, her barrister asked the court to order that Cheshire County Council should disclose all the case notes and reports compiled by its child care officers. The Court of Appeal decided that the notes and reports were privileged documents and should not be disclosed, other than in exceptional circumstances. Unhelpfully, the court did not elaborate on what amounted to 'exceptional circumstances'.

In *R v City of Birmingham DC ex p O* [1982] 2 All ER 356, a councillor who was not directly involved with the social services department requested access to foster parent's file for a reason unconnected with social services, the council was right not to permit access.

An influential case dealing with the position in proceedings under the Children Act is to be found in *Re M (A Minor) (Disclosure of Material)* [1990] 2 Fam LR 36. The Court of Appeal concluded that although social work records and case conference minutes should be protected from disclosure, but this protection would be waived where it would be in the 'interests of justice' to do so.

It is worth noting that these provisions have no application to a guardian *ad litem*, who is entitled to gain full access to all 'relevant, material'.

Local authority records

The general proposition is that the records and files will be protected from disclosure. But, where it is in the interests of justice to do so, you could be compelled to attend court and produce your files, records and notes from case conferences.

Medical records

The same principles apply to medical records. As a general proposition they are protected against disclosure but public interest immunity is not absolute and the court does have the power to order disclosure, where it is in the interests of justice to do so.

Procedure

Where the social services agency considers that it might hold relevant evidence in the proceedings it is required to:

- consider which documents it holds in its possession;

- disclose documents which not only support its case but also cast doubt upon its case;

- where documents may be protected by public interest immunity it should write to the parties legal advisers drawing attention to the documents and inviting them to apply to the court;

- write to the guardian *ad litem* drawing attention to the documents and inviting her/him to apply to the court;

- the file or documents should be made available to the court, with the relevant material highlighted and a short written account of the information contained in the file or document;

- in a disputed case documents which establish facts should be disclosed;

- generally, documents which contain opinions, including case conference records, should not be disclosed;

- where it is in the child's interests disclosure may be limited to specified proceedings.

Local authority records in criminal proceedings

A defendant in a criminal trial may apply to the social services agency to disclose information from social services files which may be relevant to the criminal prosecution.

Where the documents are confidential the social services agency is required to claim that the documents cannot be produced because they are subject to PII. Where PII is claimed, the defence should obtain a witness summons requiring the material to be produced to the court. The defence will have to prove to the court the need for the material to be disclosed. Where the judge concludes that non-disclosure will lead to miscarriage of justice, the material must be disclosed.

Access to information

In addition to the requirement that all but the most confidential documents should be disclosed, members of the public may also gain access to information held by the social services agency under a number of related provisions which provide for general access to information held by local authorities.

Data Protection Act 1984

The law relating to the disclosure of personal information contained on a computer is provided for by the Data Protection Act 1984. The Act has no application to information contained in paper files.

The Data Protection Registrar and Data Protection Tribunal were created to administer the provisions of the Act, the significant provisions of which are as follows:

* an individual has the right to be informed of the data held by the local authority concerning him; and

* the right to be supplied with a copy of the data.

Procedure

The applicant is required to make a request in writing and pay the fee. The local authority is required to supply the information within 40 days of the request.

The disclosure of data held for social work purposes is governed by the Data Protection (Subject Access Modification) (Social Work) Order 1987 which includes data held by local authorities, designated organisations such as the NSPCC, guardian *ad litems* and reporting officers, education welfare officers, health authorities and family practitioner committees.

Exempt information

There are four categories of information which are exempt from disclosure under the Data Protection Act 1984:

- the data should not be disclosed where social work practice would be prejudiced in that it would result in serious harm to the person requesting the data or some other person;

- the data should not be disclosed where it would lead to the identification of another person to whom the information relates or identify some other person as the source of the information;

- adoption records and reports; and

- a statement of a child's educational needs.

Local Government (Access to Information) Act 1985

The 1985 Act adds ss 100A–K to the Local Government Act 1972 and allows the public greater access to local government documents and meetings. However, because of its confidential nature, a considerable amount of information held by social service will be exempt from inspection and scrutiny. This includes:

- information relating to the adoption, care, fostering and education of any specified person;

- information relating to particulars of any service and/or accommodation provided for by the local authority to any specified person;

- information in respect to the discharge of a local authority's duties and obligations under the Children Act 1989.

Access to Personal Files Act 1987

The 1987 Act and its attendant regulations allows a social service's client and anyone living with the client, access to local authority files containing personal information about the client. The information which can be disclosed is defined by the Act as 'accessible personal information'. Where a composite file is maintained including information about the client and others, for example in the case a family file, the client is not entitled to receive personal information about the other people in the file, without the consent of those other people.

Included in the category of accessible personal information which the local authority is required to make available is material held in files, card indexes and day books.

The procedure for obtaining information is contained in the Access to Personal Files (Social Services) Regulations 1989 which states that:

- the request should be in writing;

- identify the person about whom the information is sought; and

- pay a fee.

Where the request has been made the local authority is required, within 40 days, to reply indicating whether it has any accessible personal information and where it has it in its possession, the information requested.

Exempt information

There are six categories of information which are exempt from disclosure:

- the disclosure of information which would prejudice the functions of social services in that it is likely to result in another person suffering serious harm to his physical, mental or emotional health;

- where the information would lead to the identity of another person being disclosed;

- where the information is held for crime prevention, detection or the apprehension or prosecution of offenders;

- where the information is contained in a court report;

- where the information is prohibited from disclosure;

- where the information is protected from disclosure by legal professional privilege.

Where the request for information is made by a child, the local authority is required to make sure that the child has sufficient understanding to make the application. Where the application is made on behalf of the child by a person exercising parental responsibility, the local authority is required to ensure that the application is in the interests of the child.

Unofficial confidential information

So far, this chapter has been concerned with information contained in official files. What is your legal responsibility disclose information or 'tip-offs' told to you in confidence? The general rule is that such information is confidential and should not be disclosed. This principle was established by the landmark decision of *D v NSPCC* [1978] AC 236. The plaintiff was a mother who was confronted by a uniformed NSPCC officer at her door who stated that he was investigating a report that she was abusing her child. D suffered nervous shock – the allegation was totally without foundation. She brought an action in negligence against the NSPCC alleging that they had not exercised reasonable care in properly investigating the complaint before accusing her. To pursue her action she sought discovery of the source of the complaint, and on this issue the case eventually reached the House of Lords, where it was accepted that exclusion on the ground of public policy extends beyond the working of government departments to any organisation including a voluntary one such as the NSPCC which discharges a public duty. It was stated that confidentiality itself would not be a sufficient ground for non-disclosure, but in the NSPCC case the confidentiality of informants must be protected if the organisation were to function properly in protecting children who may be at risk of abuse or neglect. Since most of their information derives from members of the public, the public must be certain that their identity will not be revealed. Consequently, the identity of even a potentially malicious informant must be protected, and that outweighed D's interest in discovering the source of the baseless, or even malicious, report.

Whilst there is no requirement for you to disclose your sources, you are under a duty under s 47 of the Children Act 1989 to take some positive action to safeguard and promote the welfare of the child. Where the allegations prove to be true, it might not be possible for you to keep the source of your suspicions from disclosure. The courts have given guidance on this difficult professional dilemma in two cases. In *Re M and Another (Minors)* [1990] 1 All ER 205

Private privilege

As well as public bodies not being required to disclose otherwise admissible and relevant evidence, individuals are also granted equivalent rights by the doctrine of private privilege. But whereas in public interest immunity the conflicting interests are the proper administration of justice and the efficient functioning of various bodies or agencies, in the area of private privilege the competing interests are those of the proper administration of justice and the protection of confidential relationships or the encouragement to settle disputes without the need to take up the precious time of the courts.

For social workers there are two types of privilege which you need to be aware of: the privilege against self-incrimination and legal professional privilege.

The privilege against self-incrimination

The privilege against self-incrimination has been recognised by the courts since at least 1847. In criminal proceedings, the accused may be asked questions about the offence for which he is being tried, but he or she is entitled to refuse to answer any question if his answer would tend to expose him to a criminal charge other than the one currently being tried. In a similar way in civil proceedings, a witness may claim self-incrimination privilege if his or her answer would tend to expose him or her or their spouse to a criminal charge.

Legal professional privilege

Any communication between a legal adviser and his client, for the purpose of legal advice, is privileged – the privilege being that of the client not the adviser, so that if the client waives the privilege the legal adviser could be compelled in criminal or civil proceedings to reveal the content of such a communication. The legal profession is the only profession regarding which this privilege exists, ie there is no similar provision as regards doctor and patient, priest and penitent, and most significantly between you and your client.

Practice points

Social workers should:

- be aware of how the principles of public interest immunity applies to social work files;

- remember that access to local authority information is controlled by number of statutory provisions including the Data Protection Act;

- be aware that unofficial confidential information does not as a general rule have to be disclosed;

- remember that the relationship with your client does not enjoy the same privileges against the disclosure of confidential information as the lawyer/client relationship.

Further reading

Murphy, P, *A Practical Approach to Evidence,* 1997, London: Blackstone Press.

Murphy, P, *Evidence and Advocacy,* 4th edn, 1994, London: Blackstone Press.

21 Evidence and the Children Act 1989

The general rules of evidence apply to proceedings under the Children Act 1989 subject to some modifications in important areas. These modifications arise for two reasons. First, proceedings under the Children Act are inquisitorial rather than adversarial in nature. Second, in most proceedings under the Act, the court is required to act in compliance with the 'child welfare' principle as defined in s 1(1). Therefore, many of the evidential rules which apply in other proceedings would be out of place in the Children Act.

It is worth noting that the rules of evidence under the Act are to be found in a number of places including: the substantive provisions of the Act, court decisions and important pieces of secondary legislation such as the regulations issued under the Act, for example, the Children (Admissibility of Hearsay Evidence) Order 1993 which provides for the relaxation of the rules of hearsay evidence in proceedings involving children.

This chapter will guide you through the important evidential exceptions that apply in proceedings under the Children Act.

The application procedure

Its important to recall that one of the changes introduced by the Children Act was to unify the system of courts and procedures dealing with cases under the Act creating a three tier court system based on the High Court, county court and family proceedings court. Most public law cases involving children are commenced in the family proceedings court, apart from when a local authority is applying for a care or supervision order, where the court has directed that a local authority investigation should be carried out under s 37. In these circumstances the application should be made to the court ordering the investigation.

The result of establishing a unified system of courts and procedure is that the traditional distinction in the rules of evidence between civil and criminal cases has largely been abolished in proceedings under the 1989 Act.

The burden of proof

The general rule in both criminal and civil cases is that the party bringing the proceedings has the legal burden of proving its case to the required standard in order to be successful. This is known as the legal burden of proof. In simple terms, the legal burden means no more than the legal responsibility of the party bringing the case to prove the allegations that it is making. The matters which constitute the legal burden are known as the 'facts in issue' and are determined by reference to the section of the Act creating the order.

The legal burden of proof in proceedings under the Children Act follows this general principle. Therefore, when a local authority applies to the court for a care order, as the party bringing the case (ie the applicant), it has the legal burden of proving the facts in issue defined in s 31(2) of the 1989 Act that:

- the child concerned is suffering; or

- is likely to suffer significant harm; and

- that the harm or likelihood of harm is attributable to the care given to the child; or

- likely to be given to the child if the order was not made, not being what it would be reasonable to expect a parent to give to the child; or

- the child is beyond parental control.

The same principles apply where the local authority as the applicant applies for a child assessment order under s 43(1)(a). The local authority is required to prove the following facts in issue:

- that the applicant has reasonable cause to suspect that the child is suffering, or is likely to suffer, significant harm;

- an assessment of the state of the child's health or development, or the way in which the child has been treated, is required to enable the applicant to determine whether or not the child is suffering, or is likely to suffer, significant harm; and

- it is unlikely that such an assessment will be made, or be satisfactory, in the absence of an order under this section.

The evidential burden

The evidential burden describes the way in which the party which has the legal burden, proves its case is by producing evidence to the court.

Therefore when applying for a care order under s 31, the local authority will discharge its evidential burden by calling witnesses, expert's reports, local authority records, health records, other relevant documents, X-rays, photographs, video and audio tapes to prove to the court that the child is suffering or likely to suffer significant harm because the child is beyond parental control.

Where the applicant has successfully discharged its legal and evidential burden by proving the conditions in s 31(2) applies, the respondents, where they oppose the making of a care order, have an evidential burden of proving to the court that the child is not suffering or likely to suffer significant harm or because the child is beyond parental control, etc. In order to discharge this burden, it will be necessary for the respondents to put relevant evidence before the court by oral and documentary evidence.

The court will decide the issues on the basis of these two conflicting interpretations of the law and facts.

The standard of proof

Both applicants and respondents are not only required to put evidence before the court to substantiate their case, but in order to be successful, must also convince the court to the required standard – this is known as the standard of proof.

In proceedings involving the 'welfare of children' the applicant must prove its case to the civil standard, ie on the balance of probabilities. In *Re H and Others (Minors)(Sexual Abuse: Standard of Proof)* [1996] 1 All ER, the House of Lords defined the balance of probability as it is applied to children's cases. Lord Nicholls in the leading speech suggested the following approach:

> The balance or probability standard means that a court is satisfied an event has occurred if the court considers that on the evidence, the occurrence of the event was more likely than.

In cases involving allegations of sexual abuse, grievous bodily harm and other serious matters, the courts will require strong and cogent evidence to prove the case on the balance of probabilities.

According to the case of *Re H; Re K* [1989] 2 Fam LR, in determining whether the requisite legal burden and standard of proof has been satisfied, the court will look searchingly at the evidence and apply a two-stage approach. Stage 1 will involve the courts evaluating the evidence in relation to the facts already in existence and frequently expert opinion as to future advantages and risks of possible decisions as to the child's future. Stage 2 will involve the judge exercising her/his discretion with the test of the welfare of the child paramount and weighs in the balance all the relevant factors and assesses the relevant factors and assesses the advantages and risks to a child of each possible course of action. Where after assessing the risks, the judge concludes that there is a real possibility that the child is at risk, he or she will take the appropriate steps to safeguard the child.

In *Re W (Minors) (Sexual Abuse: Standard of Proof)* [1994] 1 Fam LR 419, Sir Stephen Brown, President of the Family Division (the most senior specialist judge dealing with family law cases) stated in *Newham London Borough Council v Attorney General* [1993] 1 Fam LR 281 that:

> I very much hope that in approaching cases under the Children Act 1989 courts will not be invited to perform in every case a strict legalistic analysis of the statutory meaning of s 31. Of course, the words of the statute must be considered, but I do not believe that Parliament intended them to be unduly restrictive when the evidence clearly indicates that a certain course should be taken in order to protect the child.

Giving evidence under the Children Act 1989

The order of procedure and the oral tradition of the English trial is preserved in proceedings under the Children Act. If you are required to give evidence, for example in a care proceedings application, on behalf of your agency, the applicant's case will be heard first. Unlike in criminal cases, the court has a discretion to allow you, as the social service agency's representative to sit in court before giving evidence (see *R v Willesden Justices ex p London Borough of Brent* [1988] Fam LR 341).

In outline, the procedure will follow the same course as giving evidence in criminal proceedings. However, there will be a much greater reliance on written evidence, so that often, after taking the oath or affirming, examination-in-chief may be by-passed because the parties will have read your statement. The practice of cross-examination will again follow the same lines as already discussed but in consideration of s 98 of the Children Act, you cannot refuse to answer any question. If necessary you will be able to refer to your case notes or file to refresh your memory whilst you are giving evidence, although the respondent's advocate will be entitled to examine its contents.

Sometimes you will be giving evidence as an expert, see *F v Suffolk County Council* [1981] 2 Fam LR 208, in that the courts presume that a qualified social worker is an expert on child care issues. In other areas you will be regarded as an ordinary witness giving evidence on matters of which you have personal knowledge.

Whilst there is a much greater reliance on evidence given in written statements, the case of *H v H and C* [1969] 1 All ER 240, stated the court should not decide an issue concerning the future of a child without hearing the oral evidence of the parties. That is not to say however that documentary and real evidence will not play a significant part in assisting the court to come to a decision.

The evidence of children and young people

In proceedings under the Children Act the following provisions apply:

- the court will not normally hear the child's evidence directly, as it will be given by the guardian *ad litem*;

- there is a presumption against hearing the evidence from the child and the court will have to be persuaded by the guardian as to why the child him- or herself should give evidence;

- where the court considers it necessary for a child to give evidence, the child's competency will be determined by whether, in relation to witnesses' aged under 14 years, they are capable of giving 'intelligible testimony';

- a child aged under 14 years can only give unsworn evidence;

- where the witness is aged 14 years and over, they will be competent where they understand the nature of the oath and the importance of telling the truth, the so-called *Hayes* test;

- a witness aged 14 years and over can only give sworn evidence;

- where the court decides to hear a child or young person's evidence, the guardian *ad litem* will be required to give reasoned advice as to whether the evidence shall be given in court like any other witness, or from behind a screen or through a live television link;

- doctors can also be compelled to give evidence about matters ordinarily covered by medical privilege where ordered to do so by the court;

Evidence in child sexual abuse cases

Evidence in cases alleging the sexual abuse of a child can be given in a number of ways:

- the child may give oral evidence directly to the court;

- the child's evidence may be reported to the court by another person;

- other witnesses may give oral evidence directly to the court;

- expert psychiatric, psychological or medical evidence can be given to the court orally, or in documentary form or a combination of the two.

In practice the court will base its decisions on a number of the ways described above.

As a field social worker you should be aware of the main recommendations of the Report of the Inquiry into Child Abuse in Cleveland in 1987.

In deciding whether the social services agency or NSPCC have proved their case, the court will take the two-stage approach advocated by the court in *Re H; Re K* discussed above. At stage 1, the court will ask itself whether there is any evidence of sexual abuse. Where stage 1 is answered affirmatively, the court will proceed to stage 2: is there evidence of the identity of the abuser?

Interviews with children

Interviews with children who are suspected to be the victims of sexual abuse should always be videotaped. Where the abuse is disputed the court will require to see the videotape of the childs' account of the events.

Where video recording facilities are not available the interview should be recorded on audio-tape or a manuscript note of the essential parts.

It is desirable that interviews with young children should be recorded as soon as possible after the allegations have been made.

Where the child is interviewed on a number of occasions, the court is likely to place less importance on the evidence arising out of the later interviews. It is normally not necessary for the child's parents to be present during the interview. The responses which the child gives should not be prompted.

In the case of *Re A and Others (Minors) (Child Abuse Guidelines)* [1992] 1 Fam LR 214, the court highlighted common faults of interviews with young children:

- the widespread use of untrained and inexperienced interviewers;

- a failure to approach the interview with an open mind;

- each child subjected to too many interviews;

- interviews conducted at a pace suitable for adults not children;

- lack of adequate video and audiotaping facilities;

- lack of background information in the interviewer's possession;

- interviews conducted by too many people;

- telling the child what another child has said;

- the interviewers showing too much anxiety to obtain a result.

The videotaping of interviews with children should follow the Memorandum of Good Practice (1992) issued by the Home Office and can be admitted as evidence as an exception to the hearsay rule.

Privilege and the Children Act 1989

The privilege against self-incrimination

In proceedings under Parts IV and V of the Children Act 1989, no person can be excused from giving evidence or answer questions on the basis that the answer may incriminate them in a criminal charge in respect of themselves or their spouse (s 98). The privilege against incrimination does not apply to proceedings in relation to care and supervision orders and cases involving the protection of children. However, where a witness does make an incriminating statement, it cannot be used in other proceedings other than a prosecution for perjury. Under s 98(2) the court can give leave that a document or statement used in these proceedings can be disclosed to the police.

Litigation privilege

The general principles of litigation privilege are suspended in proceedings under the Children Act. As a result where the court gives leave for the disclosure of specified papers to an expert, the expert's report must be disclosed to the court and the other parties. This practice has recently been endorsed by the House of Lords in *Re L (A Minor) (Police Investigation: Privilege)* [1996] 2 All ER 78. Not to allow a full and open disclosure of all evidence, including expert's reports, would be inconsistent with the philosophy and purpose of the 1989 Act.

The requirement for the full disclosure of expert reports is extended to cover all relevant evidence. In *Essex County Council v R* [1993] 2 Fam LR 826, the court decided that all parties to proceedings under the Children Act are required to make a full and frank disclosure of any material which was relevant to the decision in the case, even where the material was adverse to the party's cause.

Legal professional privilege

The privilege of the solicitor/client relationship cannot be broken in proceedings under the Act unless voluntarily surrendered by the parties involved.

Disclosure and the guardian *ad litem*

The privilege against disclosing confidential material does not extend to the guardian *ad litem*. Under s 42 of the Children Act 1989, a guardian has the right to examine and take copies of the following:

- any records held by the social services agency or NSPCC compiled or held in connection with any application under the Children Act 1989;

- any records compiled or held by a social services agency in respect of any matter covered by the social services committee and concerns the child in question.

Copies of the documents taken by the guardian will be admissible in any court proceedings.

Hearsay evidence

The Children (Admissibility of Hearsay Evidence) Order 1993 which came into force on 5 April 1993 has had a significant effect on the admissibility of hearsay evidence in proceedings under the Children Act. The effect of the order is that:

- in civil proceedings before the High Court or county court and in family proceedings in a magistrates' court, evidence given in connection with the upbringing, maintenance or welfare of a child will be admissible, even though it might be hearsay;

- included in the ambit of the order is an application for a secure accommodation order.

The effect of the order is significant for the following reasons:

- for the first time there is a common approach to the admission of hearsay evidence in all civil cases dealing with children;

- the rule against hearsay does not apply to court hearings connected with the child's upbringing, maintenance or welfare, either in the public law or private law fields;

- a party to the proceedings no longer has the right to challenge the admissibility of evidence connected with the child on the ground that it is hearsay.

Other evidential exceptions under the Children Act 1989

Be aware that the following are also important modifications on the normal rules of evidence in proceedings under the 1989 Act, including:

- the court may take account of any statement contained in the report of the guardian *ad litem* (s 41(11)(a) of the Children Act 1989);

- the court may take account of any evidence given in respect of matters referred to in the guardian *ad litem's* report (s 41(11)(b) of the Children Act 1989);

- local authority records produced or referred to in the guardian *ad litem's* report (s 42(2) of the Children Act 1989).

The court has the power to consider and rely on any statement which is contained in the guardian ad litem's report without the need for the statement to be proven in any other. The same rule applies to local authority records contained in the guardian's report and any statement contained in a welfare report.

Expert evidence

In proceedings under the Children Act, expert evidence plays a vital role. It can relate either to the witness giving his or her opinion on specific matters, such as the stage of a child's psychological development or a medical diagnosis as the cause of an injury. From this evidence, the court will be entitled to draw inferences from the expert. Also, an expert may be called upon to give an opinion on the ultimate issue before the court, for example the applicant or a respondent or even the court may ask the expert whether in his or her opinion a child has been physically or sexually abused.

Generally, expert witnesses are called to give evidence on those relevant matters which go beyond the normal competence of the court. In proceedings under the Children Act, expert evidence is a common requirement and may be used by either the applicant or a respondent in the following areas of professional competence:

- psychiatric assessment of the child;

- psychiatric assessment of the family structure and functioning and the relationship between each of the relevant family members and/or the child;

- assessment of contact between the child and a parent or another relevant adult;

- paediatric examination of the child;

- developmental assessment of the child;

- specific assessments of the child's social skills;

- expert assessment in any other relevant matters.

The above list is neither prescriptive nor exhaustive but includes a wide range of expertise including psychiatrists, psychologists, specialist child psychiatrists and psychologists, social worker and doctor or teams consisting of specialism. An expert's report will normally be made up of one or more of the following components:

- admissible evidence of facts observed by the expert;

- an interpretation of those facts or an interpretation of the evidence of facts provided by another witness;

- opinion evidence on the basis of those facts.

A doctor will therefore be allowed to give evidence of the physical injuries that he or she has observed on a child; indicate to the court the possible cause of the injuries and provide an opinion as to what extent the child will recover from the injuries.

It is important to be aware that when choosing an expert witness, consideration should be given to the child's religion, ethnic background, gender, language and any other special needs. In relation to expert evidence in proceedings under the Children Act, the general rule is that the court exercises close control over the expert assessment of the child, see *Re G (minors) (expert witnesses)* [1994] 2 Fam LR 291. As a result, the following points should be noted:

- rules of the court require that a child should not be examined or assessed for the preparation of an expert's report for use in the proceedings without the leave of the court;

- where a child is examined by an expert without the court's consent, evidence from the expert will not be heard without the court's consent;

- leave of the court is required even if the papers in a Children Act case are to be shown to an expert irrespective of whether the child is to be examined or assessed;

- as in other legal proceedings, the court has power to limit the number of experts a party to a case under the Children Act can consult.

A useful case to be aware of is *Re C (Expert Evidence: Disclosure Practice)* in which the court gave guidance on directions that should be given when seeking expert evidence:

- where the court sanctioned that a number of experts should be instructed, each expert should be expressly required to hold discussions with other experts in the same field and then set out in a joint document before hearing the areas of agreement and disagreement;

- a co-ordinator, normally the guardian ad litem or the local authority, should collate the expert reports and prepare a schedule for the courts setting out the areas of agreement and disagreement;

- where a party proposes to seek leave from the court to instruct an expert, it should give to the court and the other parties a written explanation of the area of expertise of the proposed expert and the reasons why the court should grant leave;

- where a party proposes to seek leave to instruct an expert, the written explanation is required to be lodged at the court at least 10 days before the hearing when the application is due to be heard;

- the party which proposes to instruct the expert should contact the expert to confirm his or her availability to give evidence at the hearing of the substantive issues;

- in the letter instructing the expert to act, the party should indicate that the expert is expected to prepare with the other experts a joint document setting out the areas of agreement and disagreement, and a clear timetable to enable the matter to proceed without unnecessary delay.

Rehabilitation of Offenders Act 1974

The Act allows the introduction in evidence in proceedings under the Children Act details of a persons previous convictions in the following proceedings:

- adoption;

- the marriage of a minor;

- the exercise of the High Court's jurisdiction with respect to minors;

- any question relating to the provision of accommodation, care or schooling for a child or young person;

- any proceedings under the Children Act.

In any of the above proceedings, the fact of the person's conviction can be proved by producing the certificate of conviction of the person involved in the proceedings.

The local authority social services agency can request details of the previous convictions of certain people from the local police. Where a party to proceedings has a criminal record, it is appropriate that details of the convictions are available to the court.

Practice points

Social workers should:

- be aware of the different evidential principles that apply to proceedings under the Children Act 1989;

- remember that the legal burden of proof lies with the party bringing the case;

- be aware that in order to be successful a party is required to prove their case on the balance of probability;

- remember that a child's evidence will be put to the court by the guardian *ad litem*;

- be aware that the tape recording of interviews with children suspected of being victims of abuse are required to have followed the guidelines laid down in the Memorandum of Good Practice;

- do not forget that the general principles of confidentiality and privilege (apart from the lawyer/client relationship) are suspended in proceedings under the Children Act 1989;

- remember that the general rules in relation to hearsay evidence are suspended in proceedings under the Children Act 1989;

- remember the crucial role played by expert evidence;

- be aware of the procedural requirements in relation to expert evidence.

Further reading

Black, J, Bridge, J, and Bond, T, *A Practical Approach to Family Law,* 1997, London: Blackstone Press.

22 Prisoners' rights[*]

This chapter seeks to remind those social workers involved with the criminal process that prisoners have rights. Whilst many probation officers and others might consider the job over after sentencing, social workers might still be called-upon to assist offenders whilst incarcerated, or on remand. Here, we hope to assist those social workers and probation officers to understand the hotchpotch of rules which govern the manner in which British prisons are organised.

The Woolf Report into the state of British prisons in 1992 sought to review the organisation and governance of British prisons. More recently, some British prisons have been privatised. Prisons such as Whitefield, typifying this new 'breed' of contracted-out penal institutions.

Prisons

The current prison population within the UK amounts to some 62,300 prisoners. This figure covers the many categories of both prisoner and prison within the UK penal system. The various categories of prison range from: local prisons (called so because they are located in cities or towns, eg Stafford, Wandsworth); open prisons (for low risk prisoners, less security, eg Leyhill and Sudbury – Category D prisons); special security units (for the purpose of securing likely absconders from prison, eg Durham and Leicester); dispersal prisons (establishments for long-term prisoners, eg Whitemoor, Wakefield, Long Lartin, Frankland, Sutton Full); special unit prisons (units for disruptive, rioting prisoners, eg C Wing at Parkhurst and A Wing at Hull); training prisons (prisons for 'lifers', ie those prisoners serving life sentences, eg Maidstone, Dartmoor, Grendon, Nottingham, Kingston, Garth, Gartree, Albany, Blundeston and Swaleside – Category B prisons); Category C prisons (these make up the largest number of prisons in the UK, culminating over 35 prisons, including Strangeways and Pentonville; women's prisons (eg, Holloway, Durham, Styal, Cookham Wood, Winchester, Drake Hall, Askham Grange); Young Offenders' Institutions (for males between the ages of 15–21, eg Werrington, Aylesbury, Hindley, Swinfen Hall, Stoke Heath, Thorn Cross, Hatfield, Guys Marsh, Feltham, and Dover); remand centres, such as Risley, Low Newton, New Hall

---

[*] The authors would like to thank the Prison Reform Trust and the Home Office for their kind co-operation during the writing of this chapter.

and Pucklechurch; to one experimental 'Boot camp', for young offenders in Warrington, where military marching and training takes place replacing the orthodox prison regime. It was the Mountbatten criteria, instituted since 1976, which categorised prisons from A, the most secure, ie for terrorists and other dangerous offenders, to D, the least secure.

Habeas corpus

For over seven centuries, in fact since Magna Carta 1297, *habeas corpus* has existed in UK law. Now, Order 54 of the Rules of the Supreme Court states that: 'no one shall be falsely imprisoned.' This sets out the rules for obtaining an ancient right establishing the right of a detainee to challenge the lawfulness of their detention by applying for a writ of *habeas corpus*. However, this *ex parte* application, usually made before a High Court judge, gives a fundamental human right to all whether detained temporarily or indefinitely.

The Prison Act 1952

This Act is considered to be the most important piece of prison legislation. Consequently, it has been subject to much amendment over the years. More recently, the Criminal Justice Act 1991 has contained provisions relating to prisoners. The Prison Act's main purpose was to establish who held the requisite power to run and manage British prisons. Such an aim might explain the absence of detailed provisions relating to issues of management and administration, instead vesting powers in office holders. To that end, this statute says very little on prisoner's rights. The very basic provisions contained in the Prison Act 1952 are as follows:

- The Home Secretary holds overall general responsibility for prisons.

- Pursuant to s 4(1) of the Act, the Home Secretary is empowered to 'make contracts and do acts necessary for the maintenance of prisons and prisoners'.

- Subject to s 4(2) of the Act, the Home Secretary is charged with the enforcement of the Prison Act and the adjoining Prison Rules.

- The Act also establishes two bodies: the Chief Inspector of Prisons; and the Board of Visitors, both are to be discussed below, for the purposes of observing the conditions of prisons and the treatment of prisoners.

- Each prison must have a governor, a chaplain, a medical officer and other officer as required, according to s 7 of the Act.

- Section 12 stipulates that a prisoner may lawfully be confined in any prison, whether on remand or convicted. Also, that a prisoner has no right to be held in any particular prison and that prisoners can be transferred from one prison to another.

It is apparent, due to its longitude of some 45 years, that the Prison Act 1952 subsequent to various modifications is perceived as a workable piece of legislation.

The Prison Rules 1964

Section 47 of the Prison Act 1952 allows the Home Secretary 'to make rules and regulations for the management of prisons, remand centres, detention centres and youth custody centres ...'. Subsequently, following the enactment of the Prison Act 1952, in 1964 the Prison Rules were drafted and became law.

In brief these rules cover the areas as listed below:

Rules 1–3:   Set out the aims of the rules and classification of prisoners.

Rules 4–9:   List prison privileges and request and complaints.

Rules 10–16: Govern religion.

Rules 17–19: Provide for medical attention.

Rules 20–28: Concern the physical welfare of prisoners and work.

Rules 29–32: Concern the education of prisoners.

Rules 33–37A: Regard prisoners' letters and visits.

Rules 39–42: Concern prisoners' property, its removal and records.

Rules 43–46: Concern segregation, special control and restraint.

Rules 47–56: List disciplinary offences.

Rules 77–84: Set out the various office-holders in a prison.

Rules 85–87: Regard the rights of those persons who have access to prisons.

Rules 88–97: Concern the role and functions of the Board of Visitors.

Of paramount importance to prisoners is s 47(2) of the Prison Act 1952 which states that under the Prison Rules: '... a person who is charged with any offence under the rules shall be given a proper opportunity of presenting his case.'

Thus, subject to the European Convention of Human Rights, these rules must conform to the requisite standards of natural justice.

In addition, the Prison Act 1952, itself, also gives some indirect rights to prisoners, as follows:

- Right to early release (s 25).

- The discharge of prisoners temporarily on the grounds of ill-health (s 28).

- Discharge of payments to prisoners (s 30).

It is worthy of a mention here, that all social workers and others should remind themselves that following the House of Lords in *R v Deputy Governor of Parkhurst Prison ex p Hague; Weldon v Home Office* [1992] 1 AC 58, the Prison Rules are judicial reviewable and no private law suits for breach of statutory duty are obtainable in respect of these Rules. Though the one, sole exception to this is that prisoners can sue for negligence.

Prison discipline

Like any other institution, prisons have a regulatory framework for acceptable discipline. As discussed above, most of the Prison Rules set out the formal disciplinary procedures and offences already in place within the British Prison system.

Sections 39–42 of the Prison Act 1952 set out some of the common disciplinary offences with which prisoners are charged. These include assisting prisoners to escape from a particular prison; or for bringing alcohol, tobacco or any other unauthorised article into a prison. Pursuant to s 16A of the Prison Act 1952, all prison officer's have the right to administer a mandatory drugs test to any prisoner.

The Young Offenders Institution Rules 1988

Due to the rearrangement of the custody of various types of offenders in 1988 the Home Secretary decided to enact, by way of statutory instrument, similar to the Prison Rules 1964, rules relating to the incarceration of young offenders.

Listed below are the salient rules:

Rule 3:   Set out the aims and principles of Young Offender Institutions.

Rule 4:   Classification of inmates.

Rule 6:   Release rules.

Rule 7:   Privileges.

Rule 8:   Information to inmates.

Rule 9:   Requests and complaints.

Rules 10–14 : Concern inmates' letters and visits.

Rules 15–21: Concern clothing, food and hygiene.

Rule 22:   Female inmates.

Rules 24–26: Regard medical attention.

Rules 27–33: Concern religion.

Rules 34–40: Set out occupation, education and training activities.

Rules 41–49: Set out the disciplinary rules.

Rules 50–52: Concern disciplinary offences and charges.

Rules 53–60: Concern disciplinary punishments.

Rules 61–71: Regard staffing matters.

Rules 71–78: Board of visitors and their duties.

As with the adult prison populous, these rules govern the day-to-day activities of those male young offenders from the age of 15–21 years old.

Parole

The Criminal Justice Act 1991 radically reviewed the 'old' parole system. In legal terms, 'parole' means the early release of prisoners. This concept being first introduced by the Criminal Justice Act 1967. The 1967 Act established a Parole Board under the supervision of the Home Secretary. This Board set up Local Review Committees who would consider prisoner's applications for early release on licence. 'On licence' meaning depending upon their behaviour and not reoffending for a set duration of time.

Since 1 October 1992 this 'new' parole system introduced three categories of prisoners: those with less than 12 months sentences; those with less than four years but more than 12 months; and those with sentences of four years or more. Consequently, a mandatory release scheme allows those prisoners serving less than 12 months and less than four years but more than 12 months to be released after serving half of their requisite sentence. For the remaining prisoners, serving four years or more, a discretionary conditional release scheme exists.

For those prisoners subject to the conditional release scheme, a parole dossier is compiled by the Parole Board and considered and thereafter a recommendation is made to the Home Secretary, who then makes a decision. Prisoners now being allowed to read their own dossier. Should the prisoner be released on licence, then 26 weeks after release a review is undertaken by the Parole Board and again, the Home Secretary is empowered to take the appropriate action, if any arises.

It should also be noted, that apart from parole, compassionate release can be given to prisoners for medical, personal or exceptional circumstances. In addition, the Royal Prerogative of Mercy can be given to those prisoners whom the Home Secretary deems to have been wrongly convicted having spent some long duration in prison. Incidents of this are, but recently one was granted by Her Majesty, on the recommendation of the Home Secretary, posthumously to Dick Bentley.

Prison visitors

Under s 6 of the Prison Act 1952 the Home Secretary is required to establish a Board of Visitors at each prison. Their duties can be summarised as follow:

- To visit the prison and hear prisoner' complaints.

- Authorise the extension of the segregation of a prisoner for further than three days (Prison Rule 43).

- Each visitor holds the right to free access to the prison at any time.

- Each visitor holds the right to free access to see any prisoner at any time.

The Board's disciplinary function was revoked in the 1992, following the recommendation of the Woolf Report.

Prison governors

Section 13 of the Prison Act 1952 deems the prison governor the legal custodian of the prison under her/his control. Following the case of *Leech v Deputy Governor of Parkhurst Prison* [1988] AC 533, the House of Lords, *per* Lord Bridge, held that prison governor's powers were subject to judicial review in their own right. Thus, the rights of prison governors to act arbitrarily were eradicated and subjected to the control of law. See the 'Prison Service and Contracted-Out Prisons' section below for a discussion about Prison Directors. Moreover since 1994 the Prison Service has been headed by a Director General who oversees the day-to-day activities of prisons and also, the prison governors.

The Prisons Ombudsman

A relatively 'new' officeholder, the Prisons Ombudsman was set up in 1994, after the Woolf Report. The term 'Ombudsman' translates from its Scandinavian origin into 'grievance man' or in plain English to complaints body. The first ever Prisons Ombudsman is Sir Peter Woodhead. It is he who is charged with the task of receiving and investigating complaints on the Prison Service and making, non-binding, recommendations to the Home Secretary. Complaints to this new grievance mechanism cover various matters from prison food to issues of prison categorisation and visiting issues. Outside the remit of this ombudsman are complaints about conviction or sentences.

Before complaining to the Prisons Ombudsman the prisoner must first of all exhaust all the internal procedures. The prisoner having exhausted all of these preliminary complaints channels must then write direct to the office of the Ombudsman. Such a letter is classified as 'confidential' and therefore is not read by the Prison Service before reaching the Ombudsman. Had this inaccessible privileged mail system not have been put in place, it was assumed that these complaints would eventually not be received by the Ombudsman. Where the Ombudsman upholds the complaint, a report is sent to the Director General of the Prison Service, who within one month should rectify the matter. Should the Director-General ignore the Ombudsman recommendation, then the prisoner might choose to pursue the matter further, by way of judicial review. In his first public, annual Report in 1995, it emerged that the Ombudsman was an active body and an effective one at expeditiously resolving disputes, once complaints were raised by prisoners.

Prison inspection

Pursuant to s 5A of the Prison Act 1952, the Chief Inspector of Prisons is under a duty to inspect all prisons and report to the Home Secretary on the conditions and treatment in respect of prisoners. He or she must also submit an annual report to Parliament.

In his or her reports on individual prisons, the Chief Inspector can be highly critical and thus, his or her report is often very persuasive when it comes to improving the existing conditions. Therefore, whilst the Chief Inspectors' recommendations contained in his reports are not binding they are usually observed.

The prison service and contracted-out prisons

Since s 7 of the Prison Act 1952 requires 'such officers as may be necessary' to control a prison, the prison service, like the number of those now resident in our prisons, is likely to increase. In fact, the Prison Service is now made up of over 100,000 officers. The Prison Officers Association remains the recognised union.

Following the enactment of the Criminal Justice Act 1991, private security companies, such as Securicor and Group 4, were allowed to operate services to escort prisoners to and from court (under ss 80–83), and the first UK prisons were privatised (see ss 84–88). These measures prompted the Home Secretary to contract-out prisons further in 1992 under the Criminal Justice Act 1991 (Contracted Out Prisons) Order 1992. The remaining prisons being privatised under the framework established under the Criminal Justice and Public Order Act 1994 (more specifically see s 96).

It should be noted that the Prison Act 1952 applies to all prisons, whether contracted-out, or not. Though, where prisons are contracted-out, governors are replaced with directors. With these so-called 'Prison Directors' holding the same powers as traditional prison governors. Except, for the powers to segregate or restrain prisoners, which remain to be powers solely vested in governors.

Immigration detainees

Immigration detainees will be subjected to the same prison regime as normal prisons. Though, they are likely to be detained at three specialist centres – Campsfield House or HMP's Haslsar and Winson Green. Other prisons with immigration detainees are Doncaster, Rochester and Holloway.

The European Convention of Human Rights on prisoners' rights

Clearly, regardless of what UK law says about prisoners' rights, it must adhere to the European Convention of Human Rights 1950 (ECHR).

Articles 2, 3 and 5 of the ECHR set out clearly that 'no one shall be deprived of her or his life intentionally save for the execution of a sentence of a court' and in any event 'shall not be subjected to torture or to inhuman or degrading treatment or punishment'. Furthermore, it is contrary to international human rights law where 'a person is deprived of his or her liberty contrary to any procedure or trail prescribed by law'. These rights have been upheld by the European Court of Human Rights in Strasbourg on may occasions since 1950. Most notably, the court in *Campbell v UK* [1992] 15 EHRR 137 held that privileged correspondence between a detainee and her/his lawyer should not be read by any other, even when their liberty had been lost as prescribed by a court of law. Consequently, Rule 37 of the Prison Rules 1964 was amended to ensure that such a practice, maintaining confidentiality amongst lawyer and client existed at all times.

Practice points

Social workers and probation officers should:

- check the classification of prisoner;

- check the category of prison;

- consult either the Prison Rules 1964 or the Young Offender Rules 1988, depending on the institution where your client is being held;

- contact the relevant Board of Prison Visitors;

- complain to the Prisons Ombudsman;

- telephone the Prison Governor, Probation and the Home Office depending upon the nature of the issue or complaint and its severity;

- consider whether any human rights issue is at stake;

- obtain further advice from a Prison Charity or NACRO.

Further reading

Creighton, S and King, V, *Prisoners and the Law*, 1996, London: Butterworths.

Leech, M, *The Prisons Handbook*, 1997, London: Pluto Press.

'Prison Rules – A Working Guide', 1993, Prison Reform Trust.

Stern, V, *Bricks of Shame*, 1989, London: Penguin.

The Woolf Report, 1992, HMSO.

PART V

SOCIAL WELFARE AND SOCIAL WORK

23 Discrimination law and equal opportunities*

In this penultimate part of the book, we examine the everyday social issues which affect social work practice, such as poverty, discrimination, unemployment and housing and homelessness issues. We also provide up-to-date information on benefits law and the latest developments in immigration law.

The Central Council for the Education and Training of Social Workers' (CCETSW) Equal Opportunity Policy requires that all qualifying candidates have 'a thorough knowledge and understanding of the diversity of individual lifestyles and communities in the UK'. This chapter seeks to enable the student and practitioner alike to recognise and respect the differences in sex, race, disability, religion, culture, sexual orientation and ethnic origin. Moreover, to understand the relevant anti-discriminatory legal framework surrounding these issues, so as to encourage an anti-oppressive environment at work.

Furthermore, the case of Dianne Dietmann *(Dietmann v London Borough of Brent* [1988] IRLR 299, CA), above all others, clearly reminds all social work practitioners that they are frontline officers who, if they should neglect their statutory duties, not only face reprimand, but also could be dismissed. Moreover, the case of Walker *(Walker v Northumberland County Council* [1995] IRLR 35, HC), the social worker who received compensation for stress incurred at work when his employers refused to take seriously his pleas for assistance with an ever increasing workload, illustrates how employment law impacts on social work practice in the 1990s. It is therefore integral to this chapter to not only provide the social worker with some knowledge of the basic tenets of employment law, in order for them to give some advice to their clients should the need arise, but also to give them some 'first aid' type advice for themselves, should they ever need it.

Discrimination

British law makes it illegal for employers, their workers or agents to discriminate against another employee or potential employee on the grounds of sex, race, marital status or disability. In Northern Ireland discrimination on the grounds of religion is also outlawed, when it comes to recruiting and dismissing

* We are grateful for the assistance given by many employment law colleagues in the writing of this chapter, in particular I thank various members of both FRU and the Industrial Law Society.

279

employees (see the Fair Employment (Northern Ireland) Acts 1976 and 1989). Unlike the USA and some European countries, UK law does not yet recognise discrimination in the form of ageism, sizeism, sexual orientation or faceism! All employers should have an Equal Opportunities Policy committing it to: Equality of opportunities irrespective of sex, race, religion, disability and sexual orientation.

Forms of discrimination

Discrimination at work can take three forms:

- **Direct discrimination**: This is overt, and in some cases covert, acts against the individual. This is legally termed 'less favourable treatment'. To establish direct discrimination a person must show a comparison with another person who is treated differently because of their sex or race.

- **Indirect discrimination**: This involves conduct which does not necessarily treat people differently, but it does have the effect of being treatment which amounts to discrimination. Indirect discrimination by its very nature is subtle and often difficult to prove. For example it would involve the setting of a requirement or condition to which a certain group of people can or cannot comply.

- **Victimisation**: This is recognised in law as a separate form of discrimination. It occurs where the complainant suffers less favourable treatment because he has brought proceedings against the discriminator or another person identified in the legislation.

Discrimination and the law

SEX DISCRIMINATION ACT 1975	RACE RELATIONS ACT 1976	DISABILITY DISCRIMINATION ACT 1995
Direct discrimination Treating a person less favourably on grounds of sex or marital status	**Direct discrimination** Treating a person less favourably on grounds of race	**Direct discrimination** Treating a person less favourably on grounds of their disability
Indirect discrimination Applying a condition/ requirement based on grounds of sex or marital status	**Indirect discrimination** Applying a condition/ requirement based on grounds of race	**Indirect discrimination** Not recognised
Victimisation Less favourable treatment because that person taken action under SDA 1975	**Victimisation** Less favourable treatment because that person taken action under RRA 1976	**Victimisation** Less favourable treatment because that person taken action under DDA 1995
Remedy Complaint to IT within three months: where proven – compensation	**Remedy** Complaint to IT within three months: where proven – compensation	**Remedy** Complaint to IT within three months: where proven – compensation and declaration of employee's rights

Racial discrimination

Between the 1950s and early 1970s there was widespread migration of black workers from the new Commonwealth countries to the UK. Evidence slowly became available that this group of workers were racially disadvantaged in employment opportunities, terms, conditions and treatment.

In order to combat this unfair treatment, the Race Relations Act was enacted in 1976. This Act identifies ways in which racial minority groups may be discriminated against in the workplace and makes that discrimination unlawful. The Act provides that at all stages of the employment relationship, from advertising the position, through the selection process, to appointment, the terms and treatment of the employee to dismissal, discrimination on the grounds of race shall be unlawful.

The biggest difficulty in race cases is defining what is meant by 'race' itself. What constitutes a racial group for the purposes of the law can be a difficult question to answer. It can relate to an employee's religion, nationality, origin or racial group. The wide meaning of the word, provides courts and tribunals with a broad discretion to apply to the facts of particular cases. This flexible approach may, in certain circumstances, lead to uncertainty.

For example, it has never been satisfactorily settled whether rastarfarians are a racial group or not. Until recently, the Sikh religion, requiring its followers to wear a 'safa', or turban', were not recognised in law as a racial group. They are now. However, although as a religious group they are given exceptions from wearing a motorcycle helmet or a hard hat on a building site, they are not exempt from adhering to health and safety legislation in other workplaces, other than those already noted. This has given rise to much discussion about the discriminatory implications of such a legal view.

In cases involving discrimination, the employee is often referred to as the complainant. An employee alleging racial discrimination has to satisfy the following tests:

- there has to be an act of racial discrimination which can be a specific act or series of acts;

- but for the act of racial discrimination, he would have been treated differently;

- the discrimination alleged by the complainant must come within the definition of race.

Included in the meaning of race is nationality, origin or racial group.

A claim alleging racial discrimination has to be lodged with an industrial tribunal within three months from the date when the act first took place. Otherwise it will fail, unless it can be shown that continuing acts of discrimination have occurred. Only on those grounds, if reasonable and proven to the tribunal's satisfaction, will the time be extended or when it is 'just and equitable' to do so. Tribunals exercise their discretion to extend the three-month time limit very sparingly.

The successful complainant may receive an award of compensation which includes a sum for the actual losses incurred, usually primarily wages, a sum for injury to feelings and future losses. There is no upper limit to this compensatory award. Aggravated damages might be awarded where the employer has behaved offensively, insultingly or maliciously. Yet no exemplary damages can be awarded in sex or race discrimination cases. We assume that this rule also applies to disability, in the absence of legal guidance on this matter.

A declaration, outlining the complainant's rights, can be made, as can a recommendation, asking the employer to take specific action in the future to eliminate such racial discrimination. The tribunal can also order that a company should implement its equal opportunities policy, or where one does not exist, the tribunal has the power to write the policy for the employer and ensure its implementation.

All social workers should note that all employers hold a primary duty of making the workplace discrimination free. That is why, at the beginning of this chapter, we suggested that all employers should be committed to a clearly stated equal opportunities policy. This will include a positive duty that employers train employees on equal opportunities and that supervisors and line managers actively enforce the policy.

An employer has an opportunity to defend his actions on the basis that the racial discrimination related to a 'genuine occupational qualification', commonly abbreviated to GOQ.

Sex discrimination

The Sex Discrimination Act (SDA) 1975 came into force at the same time as the Equal Pay Act in December 1975. The SDA promotes the equal treatment of men and women in employment and related areas, such as the provision of services. The provisions of the SDA includes protection against discrimination on the grounds of sex or marital status. Like the Race Relations Act it seeks to ensure equal treatment in employment generally from the point of selection, to the availability of opportunities for training and promotion, benefits and facilities, all the way through to dismissal.

The SDA 1975 seeks to eliminate inequality in employment. The tests set out also apply to race discrimination apply equally to sex discrimination. The SDA applies so as protect both sexes. Generally speaking the problems which can arise in defining race, do not arise in defining sex!

The successful complainant may receive an award of compensation which includes a sum for the actual and future losses incurred. There is no upper limit to this compensatory award. Also, a declaration outlining the complainant's rights can be made, as can a recommendation order requiring the employer to take specific action to eliminate future acts of sex discrimination. This may include the activation of an employer's equal opportunities policy or the imposition of a policy where there is not already a policy in existence.

However, the employer has the primary duty to make the workplace discrimination free. At the tribunal hearing, the employer will have an opportunity to defend his or her actions. Employer should always consider whether they have a defence under the genuine occupational qualification clause.

Married or unmarried?

As seen in earlier chapters, co-habitation is common in the UK today. To that end, fortunately, the SDA was forward looking and also outlaws any discrimination based on the marital status of a job applicant or job holder.

Equal pay

The Equal Pay Act was enacted in 1970, and amended by the European Equal Pay Directive 1975 which promotes the principle of Article 119 of the Treaty of Rome. Article 119 provides that *men and women should receive equal pay for equal work*. This Act is concerned with the establishment of equal terms and conditions of employment.

In order to establish an equal value for equal pay claim an applicant must prove the following conditions apply:

- the applicant must be an employee;

- that the issue is one of pay;

- that it is like work which they and their comparator do;

- undertake a job evaluation to prove this.

If equal value can be shown, then the applicant will be successful, unless a *genuine material factor* defence can be raised. However the last requirement means in practice it will be virtually impossible to bring a claim without trade union support, as such studies are very expensive.

Maternity rights

Pregnant workers have the following rights:

- not to be dismissed by reason of pregnancy;

- to time off work for ante-natal care;

- to return to work;

- to statutory maternity pay;

- to medical suspension pay if suspended from work on medical grounds or due to failure to find suitable alternative employment.

Employers should be reminded that pregnant workers are entitled to the same benefits as those employed, otherwise any exclusion might be considered discriminatory.

The statutory rights to maternity leave, the rights to return to work and not to be dismissed, and to maternity pay are very complex. These modified and in part 'new' rights came into force in 1993. Although, it has always been part of dismissal law, that you could not dismiss an employee when she announces she is pregnant. An employee who is absent from work at any time during her maternity leave is entitled to the benefit of the terms and conditions of employment which she is entitled to.

It is a basic right that every pregnant employee has the right to time-off work for antenatal care. The maternity leave period commences with the date which the employee notifies as the date on which she intends to be absent from work, or the day on which the birth occurs. The maternity leave period lasts for 14 weeks. The right to receive maternity leave depends on the employee notifying her employer that she is pregnant and of the date on which she intends to become absent from work. This notice has to be given in writing.

The employee should also inform her employer at least 21 days before her maternity leave is to commence of the expected week of childbirth and provide a certificate from a registered GP or midwife. Before returning to work after the childbirth, the employee should give at least seven days notice of her intention to return. An employer however has the right, not earlier than 21 days before the end of the maternity leave to request confirmation of the employee's desire or otherwise to return to work. Every female employee has the right to maternity leave irrespective of years of service and continuous employment. For two weeks after the childbirth, the employee is compulsorily disallowed from working. This compulsory leave, if not adhered to, renders the employer liable to a fine. If the employer fails to allow the employee to return to work on her notified date of return, the employee is treated as having been unfairly dismissed. Unfair dismissal therefore apply in this situation.

Should an employee be suspended for work on maternity grounds, then the employee is entitled to remuneration at the normal rate, unless she is offered suitable alternative employment. These suspensions normally occur due to health and safety considerations. Subject to national insurance contributions and having been employed for six months or longer, every pregnant employee is entitled to Statutory Maternity Pay (SMP) for a maximum of 18 weeks, payable by employers and recouped by them from the Inland Revenue's national insurance contributions scheme. Where the employee has been employed for less than six months, the employee is entitled to the DSS's maternity allowance.

It is customary practice to engage a temporary maternity leave cover employee whilst the permanent employee is on maternity leave. On the return of the maternity leave employee, employers should give notice to the temporary employee, so as the contract of employment detailed that on the resumption of work by another employee who is on maternity leave, otherwise a notice period should be given. These dismissals are treated as fair dismissals, given the correct notice, under the some other substantial reasons.

Harassment at work

An EC Code of Practice 1993 is voluntarily in force, in order to prevent harassment in the workplace. This code is not legally binding, but is treated a legal guidance by the tribunals and courts, despite it not being a Directive, and a voluntary scheme. Even so, most UK companies have adopted it as it seeks to encourage workers to be aware of offensive behaviour, so as to reduce the harassment in the workplace.

Harassment can involve any unwanted attention, either physical or oral. The display of nude photographs or posters can amount to harassment, as can the unwelcome use of familiar phrases such as 'sweetheart'. Obviously covered are more extreme forms of behaviour such as sexual assault. A person who is the victim of sexual harassment may well be able to bring a claim alleging sexual discrimination in the industrial tribunal.

Disabled worker's rights

There are some 6.5 million disabled people in the UK. As a result of both international and European standards, the UK has recently enacted its Disability Discrimination Act 1995 which was implemented at the end of 1996.

Some social workers might recall that as long ago as 1944, building on the recommendations of the Tomlinson Report, the government recognised the special problems encountered by disabled workers by enacting the Disabled Persons (Employment) Act 1944. The purpose of the Disability Discrimination Act 1995 is to eliminate discrimination against disabled persons in employment.

It covers any discriminatory practices against all employees, including contract workers or trade organisations, which s 13(4) defines as 'an organisation of workers (or) employers'. The Act also applies to the provision of goods, facilities and services; occupational pension schemes, insurance and other financial services; further and higher educational institutions; and public transport. A National Disability Council is established to advise and monitor the Act's implementation. The most significant provisions are described below:

Part I of the Act has provoked controversy. It sets out the meaning of 'disability' and what constitutes a 'disabled person'. The definition is fundamental to the way the legislation operates in that the new statutory framework revolves around of the meaning of disability.

Section 1 defines disability as being where a person has a 'physical or mental impairment which has a substantial and long-term adverse effect on his ability to carry out normal day-to-day activities'.

Schedule 1 to the Act provides further guidance as to what amounts to disability. The two central elements in the definition requires that a disabled employee should suffer an impairment, which is measured in terms of mobility, physical dexterity, continence and perception of the risk of physical danger, affecting day-to-day activities, requiring a history of disability for at least 12 months. Past disabilities are included as well as mild forms of disability or progressive disability, which includes HIV.

Excluded are impairments caused by alcohol, tobacco and any drug addictions; certain personality disorders, such as paedophilia and pyromania; any allergic conditions, like hayfever and allergic rhinitis; and what is termed 'deliberately acquired disfigurements', meaning tattoos and body piercing. Section 3 notes that further guidance on matters to be taken into account in determining disability might be given by the Secretary of State.

Part II of the Act makes it unlawful to discriminate against disabled job applicants or employees. Like the provisions contained in the Sex and Race Discrimination Acts, 1975 and 1976 respectively, ss 4–6 place duties on employers not to dismiss, refuse employment, discriminatorily advertise job vacancies, prevent training or any other benefits on the ground of the employee's, or applicant's disability, subject to the 'ordinarily employed in the UK' qualification. The meaning of discrimination in s 5 applies the same test as for race and sex.

Section 6 also requires employers to make adjustments to any arrangements or physical features of their business premises which, if remained unaltered, would substantially disadvantage the disabled worker. Small businesses, with fewer than 20 employees, are exempted by s 7. The 20 employees liability threshold will be reviewed every five years. Disabled employees have a right to take a claim of discrimination, before an industrial tribunals under ss 8–9 of the Act. Where found to be in breach of their legal obligations, employers can expect to be heavily fined by the courts. Applicants may be assisted in bringing actions by the National Disability Council.

The regulations cover numerous issues arising out of the Act including further clarification on the meaning of disability, the meaning of 'physical features', with regard to employers making reasonable adjustments to their premises requiring them to comply with British buildings standards and allows interest to be paid on awards made by industrial tribunals. The Code of Practice apart from identifying those to whom the Act applies, sets out circumstances in which a substantial reason which could justify discrimination, or as it is described less favourable treatment of a disabled person. It suggests that this must be more than 'minor or trivial'. The Code provides lots of illustrative examples where reasonable adjustments might be made. For instance, taps on sinks, dim lighting and narrow doorways. In response to the examples given, the Code presents some suggested steps which the employer might take in order to comply with their duties.

In respect of recruitment and selection, the Code advises that employers take care in their job specifications and advertisements and reminds employers to be able to justify any health requirements they might impose on applicants. Moreover, it warns about the usage of discriminatory language and assumptions when appointing. Unfortunately, another window of opportunity has been lost, since these regulations and the draft code embellish rather than neutralise the many vague and elusive exceptions which the Act contains. These regulations are in force from July 1996 onwards.

Some general employment rights

The Employment Rights Act 1996 defines an employee as 'an individual who has entered into or works under a contract of service'. For both the employer and employee, this statutory definition does not provide much assistance.

Labels in employment can be misleading and do not always assist in deciding who is or is not an employee. There are various types of workers where the problem of employment status can be misleading:

- **Casual workers**: Staff who work various hours. Often there are no set or promised hours of work. They are generally considered to be self-employed.

- **Homeworkers**: As the name suggest these workers undertake their employment based in the home. These workers can be given employee status if a regular pattern of work is provided.

- **Agency staff**: These are workers sent by an employment agency to work for a separate organisation. The terms and conditions of their employment are governed by the Employment Agencies Act 1973. This means that these workers are employees of the agency, but are self-employed where they exercise the work function. These staff are often referred to as temps.

- **Seasonal workers**: Most commonly included in this category are workers employed for a particular event or period, for instance holiday camp workers, Christmas sales staff, park attendants, stewards at a sporting event.

- **Company directors**: A company director can be an employee, despite the fact that he runs the company. This is because in law the company has a legal personality separate from the individuals employed in it or who manage it. By contracts, most partners, will be self-employed, although care should be taken to distinguish between equitable and salaried partners, the latter of whom will usually be employees.

- **Crown servants**: These are employees of the State, mainly as civil servants. As a consequence of the special nature of government work, they are classified as being neither employees nor self-employed. They are therefore governed by public law which means that for some purposes of employment law they are exempted from the normal statutory protection since they are covered by other unique provisions.

Being an employer has the following effects:

- the benefit employment protection rights, such as unfair dismissal and redundancy;

- the ability to claim social security payments, such as unemployment benefit, statutory sick pay and statutory maternity pay;

- greater protection under health and safety at work legislation;

- the need to pay Schedule E income tax under the Income and Corporation Taxes Act 1970 as opposed to the self-employed's generally more favourable treatment under Schedule D;

- employees do not have to charge and account for VAT, unlike independent contractors and other self-employed workers;

- employees are preferential creditors in the event of an insolvency: the self employed will be considered as independent contractors and are not preferential creditors.

Written statement of terms

Whilst it is desirable for the employment contract to be in writing there is no legal requirement that it should be. Employers are, however, legally bound to issue a written statement containing the most important terms of employment. The statement must be given to the employee within two months of the employment commencing. The right is enjoyed by all employees provided they are engaged for more than one month. Included in the statement must be details relating to:

- the names of the employer and employee;

- the date when the employment began;

- the date when the employee's period of continuous employment began;

- the scale, rate and method of calculating pay;

- the pay intervals;

- the hours of work;

- holiday entitlements;

- sickness and incapacity entitlements;

- pension scheme details;

- notice entitlement;

- job title or brief description of work;

- where the job is not permanent, the expected period of duration;

- the expected place of work and employer's address;

- any collective agreements affecting the employment;

- details of any work abroad lasting longer than one month;

- a note specifying the grievance and disciplinary rules.

Employment dismissals

Employment is terminated by employers for a variety of reasons including misconduct, sickness, retirement, death or redundancy. To help deal with these situations, employers should have prescribed disciplinary procedures, in order to protect their business interests and to establish a system which is fairly operated for employees.

These disciplinary procedures should contain definitions of misconduct, have a clear view of the seriousness of each 'offence', identify of the person(s) entitled to apply the rules, provide for efficient record keeping, ensure proper supervision of the system itself.

Wrongful dismissal

A wrongful dismissal is one where the employee does not give the notice required by the employment contract. Usually an employer will make such a dismissal where there has been serious misconduct. Such misconduct may entitle the employer to dismiss without notice.

If a dismissal is *wrongful* the employee will be entitled to compensation for the period of notice he was entitled to. If he has a contractual right for a certain procedure to be gone through before he is dismissed, he may also receive compensation to cover the period by which that procedure might have delayed his dismissal. This right is enforced through the courts rather than industrial tribunals.

The rights that arise where there is a wrongful dismissal often overlap with but are separate to those that relate to an *unfair* dismissal. these are discussed in detail in the next chapter. In essence an unfair dismissal is one where even though the employee may have been given proper notice it was unfair to deprive him of his employment in all the circumstances. Industrial tribunals have exclusive jurisdiction to deal with unfair dismissal claims.

Constructive dismissal

A constructive dismissal case occurs when an employee resigns. In essence the employee will have to allege that it was the employers conduct that effectively compelled him to resign. the employee must show:

- the resignation was forced on him as 'the last straw';

- the actions of the employer prior to the resignation were of a serious nature and fundamentally breached the contract;

- the employee suffered a detriment as a result.

A constructive dismissal is likely to give an employee claims to both wrongful and unfair dismissal. Almost by definition he will not have been given proper or any notice, and the employer's conduct will have been unfair.

Unfairly dismissed

The right not to be unfairly dismissed was introduced by the Industrial Relations Act 1971. This was partly as an intended 'olive branch' to the trade unions the rights of whom were greatly eradicated by other parts of that Act. The vast majority of cases taken before industrial tribunals are in respect of alleged unfair dismissal.

Has a dismissal taken place? This may appear to be an obvious question but the answer is not always clear. 'Dismissal' can include where the employee resigns and claims constructive dismissal.

- Is the applicant qualified to bring the claim?

- Is the applicant an employee?

- Does the applicants employment fall within an excluded category?

- Has the applicant sufficient continuous service?

- Is the claim within the three-month time limit from the date of dismissal?

Certain categories of workers are excluded from protection against unfair dismissal, including registered dockworkers, the police and armed forces, workers on fixed-term contracts for at least one year who have waived their rights in writing, those who ordinarily work outside the UK and persons excluded for reasons of national security. Those employees who have reached 65 are also an excluded category.

Employees with less than two calender years continuous employment with the employer are also excluded. This requirement is at the time of writing the subject of a decision pending in the Judicial Committee of the House of Lords. There is an argument that this exclusion is discriminatory and conflicts with European law. The qualifying period may as a result of that decision be reduced to 12 months only or a shorter period. Employers and employees should keep a watchful eye on developments.

The central question is: Is the dismissal fair or unfair? When an industrial tribunal considers the fairness of a dismissal there is a two stage test. First, whether the reason for the dismissal was a potentially fair one, and second, whether in all the circumstances of the case it was fair to dismiss that employee for that reason.

The employer must give reasons for dismissal. For instance, reasons that may be fair are:

- ones relating to capability or qualifications;

- ones relating to conduct;

- redundancy;

- the employee could not continue to work without contravention of a statute;

- some other substantial reason justifying dismissal.

Some reasons for a dismissal are regarded as automatically unfair:

- trade union membership and activity, or because of refusal to join a trade union or a particular trade union;

- pregnancy or something connected with pregnancy;

- a conviction which is 'spent' under the Rehabilitation of Offenders Act 1974;

- dismissal connected with the transfer of an undertaking unless there are economic, technical or organisational reasons entailing changes in the work-force.

Where a dismissal is for taking part in a strike or other industrial action where all strikers have been dismissed and there has been no selective re-engagement of those dismissed within a three-month period, the law prevents an industrial tribunal from hearing an unfair dismissal claim on this ground.

The test for fairness of the dismissal as opposed to the reason is whether the dismissal was fair or unfair shall depend on whether:

> ... having regard to in the circumstances (including the size and administrative resources of the employer's undertaking) the employer acted reasonably or unreasonably in treating it as a sufficient reason for dismissing the employee; and that question shall be determined in accordance with equity and the substantial merits of the case.

Procedural fairness is one of the most important factors in this. The ACAS Code of Practice No 1: Disciplinary Practices and Procedures in Employment provides important and helpful guidelines.

Its main requirements are:

- in most cases employees should receive warnings from employers about their conduct, capability or behaviour (para 12);

- allegations about the employee should be carefully investigated by the employer (para 10(I) and 11);

- the employee should be given an opportunity to state his case and be accompanied where requested by a representative (para 10(F)(G) and 11);

- the employee should be given a right of appeal against the employer's decision (para 10(K) and 16).

ACAS supplements this in the form of an advisory handbook 'Discipline At Work'. The handbook incorporates much recent case law and offers sound practical advice. Though the handbook does not have the statutory force of a code, it emphasises the renewed importance being attached to procedural fairness.

An employer is not entitled to rely on information acquired after dismissal and that fairness must be judged in the light of facts known to the employer at the time of the dismissal (though the contents of such information may affect the remedy available to the employee). An employer having grounds to dismiss will normally not have acted reasonably unless he has taken the procedural steps, which are necessary in the circumstances of the case to justify that course of action.

The same emphasis on procedural fairness has been seen in the area of misconduct dismissals. For example, even if a strike is taking place the employer is supposed to give the employee an opportunity to state his case before dismissing him.

In cases of supposed misconduct, employers should not dismiss unless and until they have formed a genuine and reasonable belief in the guilt of the employee. The test of fairness is whether the employer:

- entertained a reasonable belief in the guilt of the employee;

- had reasonable grounds for that belief; and

- had carried out as much investigation into the matter as was reasonable.

Where there is a finding of unfair dismissal three remedies are available:

- An order for *reinstatement*: the old job back.

Reinstatement is chosen where a workable employment relationship still remains following the dismissal.

- An order for *re-engagement*: a requirement that the employer provide a similar job.

Re-engagement is selected in circumstances where it is difficult to obtain another job and that returning to the previous job, would be an embarrassment for the employee or employer, or both. Of course, another job has to be vacant and deemed suitable and appropriate by all concerned.

- An award of *compensation*.

An award for compensation is divided into two parts. There is the basic and the compensatory. The basic award is calculated according to the number of years service, subject to a maximum of 20. This is multiplied depending by a half (for each year in employment the employee was under 22, one (each year from 22 to 41) or one and a half (each year from 42 to 64). The maximum weekly pay allowable for this purpose is £210 per week. The maximum award is thus £6,300 (£210 x 1.5 x 20). Once the employee is 64 the entitlement reduces by one-twelfth for each month after the 64th birthday. The compensatory award is based on what the industrial tribunal considers to be 'just and equitable'. It however is calculated according to established principles to reflect loss of earnings, statutory rights and pensions. The maximum that can be awarded is £11,300.

Both the basic and compensatory awards can be reduced due to the conduct of the employee during the dismissal.

Redundancy situations

Redundancy means that requirements for the work of a particular kind in a place where the employee was employed has ceased.

Section 139 of the Employment Rights Act 1996 states:

(a) the fact that his employment has ceased or intends to cease –

    (i) to carry on the business for the purposes of which the employee was employed ...; or

    (ii) to carry on that business in the place where the employee was so employed; or

(b) the fact that the requirements of that business –

    (i) for employees to carry out work of a particular kind; or

    (ii) for employees to carry out work of a particular kind in the place where the employee was employed by the employer, have ceased or diminished or are expected to cease or diminish.

For the purposes of redundancy, the business of the employer together with the business or businesses of associated employers are treated as one. Employers are required not to dismiss workers unfairly when they make redundancies. In order to act lawfully, employers must either follow agreed procedures in selecting employees for redundancy or adopt a procedure which would be regarded as objectively fair.

When making workers redundant, an employer should:

• announce their intention to the workforce as a whole;

• inform the individual employees and any recognised trade union or the elected worker representatives of the selection criteria to be used;

• attempt to agree the selection criteria with the trade union;

• individual employees should then be given an opportunity to discuss the criteria judged against their overall score, as to whether they should be made redundant or not.

This consultation process is essential to all redundancy situations. Consultation should always take place – unless the employer can show that consultation would be irrelevant and not make any difference to the overall outcome. Unless the employer has exceptionally firm grounds for making this contention, they would be very ill-advised not to follow the procedure outlined above.

Once an employer has completed the consultation process, the redundancy notices can be issued and the Department of Trade and Industry informed. An employee dismissed for redundancy may be entitled to a redundancy payment. The conditions for a redundancy payment are:

- that he was in fact an employee;

- two years' continuous service;

- dismissal;

- the dismissal was by reason of redundancy.

The amount of a redundancy payment is calculated according to years of service and age.

Data Protection Act 1984

An employee's right of access to the file containing his personal details would be open to him to inspect if it were contained on a computer or some other form of automatic processing equipment. The Data Protection Act allows employees to access personal data held by their employers including work sheets, training, schedules and pension schemes. It also permits employees, if they discover an inaccuracy in the information, the right to challenge the employer about the information and require it to be deleted or amended. If an employer suffers damage through a serious inaccuracy he can claim compensation in the courts. Unauthorised disclosure of such information by an employer can be a criminal offence.

Medical reports

The Access to Medical Reports Act 1988 allows employers to request a medical report on employees, prospective employees and even those engaged as independent contractors subject to the following conditions:

- the report must be connected with their employment, either as an employee or a self-employed contractor;

- the employee must give his consent;

- the employer must inform the employee that his consent is required and the employee notifies the employer that consent is given;

- it must be a report, not records (and can cover physical and mental matters);

- the employee has the right to see the report and to challenge its contents;

- the employer remains under a duty of confidentiality not to disclose the report or any information contained in the report;

- the report cannot be used as a reason to dismiss the employee, transfer or demote him.

Where an employer fails to comply with the Act, the employee's only remedy is to go the county court to seek an order which requires the employer to comply with the provisions of the Act. There is no right to award damages against the employer. Included in the Act are reports compiled by the employee's general practitioner or an independent doctor who has been consulted by the employee on a number of occasions.

Excluded from the Act are examinations of existing employees by the company doctor or an independent doctor being consulted on a specific issue. Also excluded are reports of the medical examination of new employees. The Access to Health Records Act 1990 also entitles employees to have access to their health records kept in manual form in the employer's records. Failure to comply with the Act entitles the employee to seek a county court order requiring the employer to comply with the Act. Damages are not available.

Proceedings and appeals

Industrial Tribunals (ITs) are the usually the first port of call for an aggrieved employee (see Appendix 1, Application to an Industrial Tribunal). ITs were established in 1964. They are composed of a lawyer chair and two lay members, one from the employers' side of industry, the other from trade unions. Decisions are taken by a simple majority and the lay members can out vote the chair even on matters of law.

In recent years, tribunals' workloads have increased considerably. Between March 1993 and April 1994, 69,612 cases were dealt with, an increase of 30% on the previous year. In the following years this upward trend has continued. Most commonly, tribunals will hear claims involving unfair dismissal, which make up the vast majority of the workload, as well as cases involving redundancy, sex, race and disability discrimination and unauthorised deductions from employee's wages. The party bringing the case, usually the employee, is called the applicant and the party defending the case, usually the employer, is called the respondent. Whilst the procedure tends to be more informal than court proceedings, and there is no requirement that representation should be by a lawyer, there is a growing tendency in tribunals towards legalism. Statistics indicate that parties represented by a lawyer have twice as much chance of success than a party which is unrepresented.

Should an employer or an employee lose their case, they can appeal, on legal grounds, to the Employment Appeal Tribunal, within 42 days of receiving the decision of the IT. There is a filter process, where the grounds of each appeal are considered, ex parte, and a tribunal will consider whether or not the appeal should be heard.

More often than not, once a case is initiated before an IT the Advisory, Conciliation and Arbitration Service (ACAS) is involved. As its name suggests, ACAS's main function is assisting in the settlement of industrial disputes. It provides written and oral advice to employers and employees on a wide range of employment law matters; provides a conciliation service by bringing the parties to an industrial dispute together in an attempt to achieve a settlement. Where the parties agree to do so, a dispute can be referred to ACAS for arbitration. The arbitrator will decide between the competing claims and make a decision, which is not enforceable in a court. ACAS may conduct enquiries into any industry and issues codes of practice.

In discrimination cases, again it is likely that one of the relevant statutory bodies will be involved. For instance, it may be either the Equal Opportunities Commission (EOC) or the Commission for Racial Equality (CRE). The EOC seeks to eliminate discrimination in the workplace on grounds of sex or marital status. The EOC actively supports applicants who take tribunal proceedings in respect of sex or marital discrimination. The EOC also provides research information, advice and publishes codes of practice. The CRE performs a similar function to that of the EOC in matters of race discrimination.

In disability matters, the National Council for Disability (NDC) might be consulted, thought they will not become involved, since they are distinct from both the EOC and CRE, whose remit includes litigation involvement. In contrast, the NDC does not have such a remit, it's role is to advise on disability issues in employment, and provide advice to employers and employees about their responsibilities and rights under the legislation. In any event, any of these bodies are a useful resource in any of the matters discussed above. Social workers are advised to use them.

Children at work

Even long before the industrial revolution, as depicted in the novels of Charles Dickens, children have worked, and this has certainly not changed in the 1990s. In fact it is a reflection of our modern society that children need or want to earn their pocket money, or often have to work to contribute to the family income. Yet this situation gives rise to two important questions: what are children's rights to work; and, what basic health and safety provisions ought to be secured in the workplace.

Under English law, a contract of employment entered into by a minor, a person under the age of 18, is regarded by the law as a valid agreement provided that it is for the child's benefit. Otherwise, it will be deemed void. In employment terms, minors are children below the school leaving age of 16. Although, children aged 13 or over may engage in part-time work, provided this does not amount to more than two hours per day on school-days; and they do not work before 7am or after 7pm on school-days, or during school hours.

In fact, local authorities have supervisory powers over child labour under the Employment of Children Act 1973 and may impose byelaws restricting their employment. Although, children are categorically excluded from working in industrial undertakings or on a sea-going vessel, unless accompanied by a fellow employee who is also a relative. Most importantly, a child may not be employed in a factory subject to s 14 of Education Act 1918, nor be employed underground in a mine pursuant to s 124 of the Mines and Quarries Act 1918. Also, there are special provisions relating to the employment of child entertainers in the Young Persons (Employment) Act 1938. Children are, however, permitted to be employed for work experience under the Education (Work Experience) Act 1973. The law surrounding the employment of children is therefore clearly statutorily controlled.

However, the most important factor surrounding the employment of young persons is health and safety. Again, this area is massively regulated by statute. Under the Health and Safety at Work Act 1974, which should be displayed in every workplace, every employer shall 'ensure, so far as reasonably practicable, the health, safety and welfare at work of all employees'. To ensure this, a written safety policy must be established and safety representatives and a Safety Committee appointed. Most importantly, an employee is entitled not to be subjected to any detriment by any act or failure by an employer to secure safety. Each employee who believes that he or she has suffered a detriment may bring a complaint before an IT. Moreover, a dismissal of an employee because of a refusal to work due to a reasonable belief of serious and imminent danger will automatically be deemed unfair. Employers, even self-employed, owe a duty to any person who lawfully enters their premises. Likewise, employees are under a duty at work to take reasonable care for the health and safety of others and to cooperate with employers with safety provisions.

Health and safety at work is also now governed by European law. Under the Treaty of Rome, as amended, a number of Directives have been adopted. In particular, the 1989 Framework Directive establishing new standards for employers on safety training and mandatory risk evaluations in the workplace. Other European provisions include the usage of VDU equipment and the personal Protective Equipment at Work Directives. Essentially these European provisions tighten up safety laws and provide wider protection at work.

However, this EU governance of child labour has been widened in recent years. Under an EU initiative in this area has consolidated the law relating to the employment of children. Since the Young Persons Directive (Council Directive 94/33/EC on the protection of Young People at Work) seeks to place health and safety at the top of the agenda when employers employ children. The impetus for such legislation can be found in both the EU Social Charter of 1986 and Article 17 of the UN Convention on the Rights of the Child of 1989. The main provisions of the Directive are:

- Children aged 14 or above can be engaged in 'light work' ('light work' is defined as 'not likely to be harmful to the safety, health or development of children, and ... to their attendance at school').

- Before the young person commences work an employer holds a duty to assess whether or not the work is likely to present a risk to the young person's safety.

- During term time, a young person can only work for two hours per school-day or 12 hours per week.

- Outside term time, a young person can only work for seven hours per day or 35 hours per week.

- It is illegal for young persons to undertake any night work.

These provisions only apply to those below compulsory school leaving age (in the UK that means 16, whereas elsewhere in the EU it can mean those 15 or older). It should also be noted that no minimum wage is set for children at work. Thus, child labour remains historically low paid employment and the law does not prevent this.

Rehabilitation of offenders

For some social workers the Rehabilitation of Offenders Act 1974 is a significant piece of legislation, since whilst it is supposed to assist some of their clients it often hinders their opportunities. This is simply because although the Act aims to ensure no unauthorised disclosure of a client's previous convictions, rehabilitation is viewed by many employers as unachievable. The Act itself, however, is a useful tool for enforcing rights, as set out below:

- Where an individual has been convicted of any offences which are not excluded under the Act (sentences for life imprisonment, preventative detention, court martials and persons sentenced to 30 months or more under s 53 of the Children and Young Persons Act 1933) and he or she has not been

reconvicted, then on the expiry of their conviction they are treated as rehabilitated in law (s 1).

- Once deemed rehabilitated, then the person's conviction is treated as having
  not been committed (s 4).

- Any unauthorised disclosure of spent convictions will result in a fine (s 9).

Within the Act are various tables which set out the complex requisite rehabilitation periods for the relevant offence(s) concerned (see s 6).

Moreover, an important feature of this statute is that according to s 4(3)(b)
failure to disclose any spent convictions is not itself sufficient grounds for dismissing or excluding a person from any employment. Though, subject to the
statutory powers contained within the 1974 Act, statutory instruments have
been enacted which allow for the non-applicability of this Act to the medical
and legal professions, as well as accountants, dentists, opticians, nurses, the
police, veterinary surgeons and social workers (see the Rehabilitation of
Offenders Act 1974 (Exceptions) Orders 1975 and 1986). In a social work context, CCETSW has laid down clear guidelines, when it comes to both enroling
on a social work qualifying course and being employed in social work practice,
about spent convictions. These must be disclosed and could prevent a person
from becoming a social worker. CCETSW's Registrar is the ultimate person
responsible for these matters, as are individual approved course providers for
undertaking the relevant police checks on all enrolled students.

Social workers should remind themselves that the whole ethos underlying
this Act is to protect those persons who have made a genuine effort to rehabili-
tate themselves into society after serving a conviction.

Reform

At the time of writing the new government has recently announced its intentions
to opt-in to the EU Social Chapter. This will mean that at last UK employers will
have to enforce all EU social measures, rather than adopt them voluntarily.

Practice points

In employment matters, social workers should:

- check employment status/age of the person – employer, employee, self-
  employed, or unemployed;

- consider facts of complaint – ie, discrimination or dismissal, etc;

- consult relevant legislation;

- seek assistance from local CABx, Law Centre, Welfare rights organisation, union, CRE or EOC, Solicitor, or other specialists;

- assist client in writing a letter to employer or in completing an IT1 form to initiate proceedings before an Industrial Tribunal;

- send client to Unemployment Office to sign on or GP/counselling for assistance with distress.

Further reading

Butterworth's Employment Law Handbook, 3rd edn, 1997, London: Butterworths.

Hannibal, M and Hardy, S, *Employment Law Handbook*, 1996, London: Fitzwarren Publishing Ltd.

Jefferson, M, *Employment Law*, 1997, 3rd edn, London: Cavendish Publishing.

Tolley's Discrimination Law, 1996, London: Longman.

24 Immigration law*

'Immigration' in general terms defines the laws in which a nation decides who should and should not belong to it. It is for this reason alone that immigration and nationality law remain the most controversial laws in the UK, due to their highly politicised nature. However, in legal terms, they are controversial for two very different reasons: their complex nature, causing confusion to the many people who seek to interpret them, and the human rights dimension presented by any question of nationality.

In this chapter we most ambitiously seek to provide a very rudimentary coverage of the latest law in this highly politicised and volatile subject area. With that cautious warning given, we will examine the issues of nationality, the most current legislation, and the impact of both international law and the EU on British immigration laws.

Nationality

Simply defined, the legal term 'nationality', which is carelessly bounded about in immigration matters, means: *the country in which the person concerned of is a citizen*. This is usually confirmed by the fact that their passport bears that country's name and it was that state which issued them with a passport in the first instance. Nationality law therefore informs people about the ways in which they can become citizens of a particular country. For instance, according to the British Nationality Act 1981, four classifications of nationality exist: British citizenship; British Dependent Territories citizen; British Overseas citizen; and British subject and since 1 January 1983 these are acquired in four different ways:

- by birth or adoption;

- by descent;

- by registration;

- or by naturalisation.

---

* We have received much assistance in this chapter from many immigration advice workers and various immigration advisory services. We are thankful to them all.

The legislative framework

The amount of both primary and delegated legislation covering immigration control amounts to the most extensive coverage of any area of law in the UK. Whilst we cannot cover all the various statutory instruments, we will detail below the salient pieces of legislation this century, some of which have been amended or even repealed by the latest legislation, which will be discussed in some detail throughout the remainder of this chapter:

• The Aliens Act 1905

This Act began British immigration control.

• British Nationality Act 1948

The first piece of major nationality law in the UK, governing the categories of British subjects and dividing them into three classes: citizens of the UK and Commonwealth; citizens of independent Commonwealth; and, British subjects without citizenship.

• Commonwealth Immigrants Acts 1962 and 1968

Immigration control was placed on certain British citizens in former colonies.

• Immigration Act 1971

This Act is concerned with the travel rights to and from the UK and the settlement rights of persons within the UK. This Act sought to control entry into and stay in the UK. The concepts of patriality and the right of abode were established in this Act.

• British Nationality Act 1981

Four new categories of citizenship were created, as listed above.

• Immigration Act 1988

Under this Act further restrictions were placed on the rights of Commonwealth citizens.

• British Nationality (Hong Kong) Act 1990

This statute sought to set up a registration scheme by which Hong Kong families and persons could register as British citizens before the island was handed back to the Chinese government in June 1997.

- Asylum and Immigration Appeals Act 1993

This Act came into force on 26 July 1993 making provision for refugees, by giving effect to the UN Convention, and granting the right of appeal to asylum seekers.

- Asylum and Immigration Act 1996

As will be discussed below, this statute seeks to reduce the current high numbers of UK asylum seekers, as well as modify the current immigration appeals process, as amended by the 1993 Act.

It should be noted that pursuant to s 3(2) of the Immigration Act 1971, giving the Home Secretary powers to make relevant statutory instruments, that since then there has been a succession of Immigration Rules enacted to supplement all of the above mentioned statutes. The latest rules under the 1996 Act, effectively replace the 1971, 1993 and 1994 pre-existing rules.

EU citizenship and EEA nationals' rights

By virtue of Article 8 of the Treaty on European Union (formerly the Treaty of Rome 1957) and since 1 November 1993, all UK subjects have been EU citizens. Whilst this at first glance might seem esoteric, it does grant specific rights to free movement within the EU. In fact, the rights associated with EU citizenship as spelt out in Article 8 of the Treaty are four fold: the right to move freely in the EU; to vote and stand as a candidate in both local and European elections in the Member State of residence; to apply for diplomatic and Consular protection of any Member State when outside the EU; and the right to petition the European Parliament and make complaints to the European Ombudsman. These provisions merely apply the commonplace principles of equal treatment and non-discrimination throughout the EU. These rights are also extended beyond the EU and into the European Economic Area (termed the EEA) which in effect means that the rights listed above are applicable to citizens in all of the following countries: Austria, Belgium, Denmark, Finland, France, Germany, Greece, Iceland, Ireland, Italy, Luxembourg, Netherlands, Norway, Portugal, Spain, Sweden and the UK.

For further details see the Immigration (European Economic Area) Order 1994 SI 1994/1895. The key issue is the right 'to move freely within the territory of the Member States, subject to the limitations and conditions laid down in the Treaty'.

Unlike the UK, other EU Member States have faced increasing pressure from their nationals to remove frontier controls on their common borders. Many people cross those borders on a daily basis, without the psychological and time factors of having to cross the sea. People have become exasperated by the immigration bureaucracy that has become attached to going to work. Consequently, the Schengen Accord came into force on 26 March 1995, when seven out of the 15 Member States abolished their respective immigration controls, passport checks and internal frontiers. The Accord was signed initially between France, Germany and the Benelux States. However, this group expanded to 10 members, and the Nordic states, Denmark, Finland and Sweden, are considering membership. This removal of internal borders marks greater cooperation between EU Member States on immigration issues. However, the two States which are neither signatories nor seeking admission, UK and Ireland, remain steadfast in their opposition to Schengen.

Prior to Schengen, a passport was needed to give effect to any right to leave or enter an EU Member State. However, with the creation of EU citizenship and the abolition of internal frontiers under the Schengen Accord, free movement rights allow mobility without a passport or any proof of identity at least between some Member States of the EU.

'Family' immigration rights

'Family' immigration rights, *per se*, do not exist in English law. Notably, it is a common misconception to believe that marriage to a British citizen entitles a spouse to either enter or remain in the UK. Under UK immigration law no such automatic rights are given.

It needs to be clarified that spouses married under UK law and have entry clearance to enter the UK and are married to a person settled in the UK and intend to live together permanently as 'husband and wife' are likely to be given the rights to enter and remain. These rights will also be granted to fiances and fiancees who intend to marry and live together permanently. In both cases what each party must overcome is the 'primary purpose' rule. Namely that: 'they have not married primarily to obtain settlement in the UK.' This rule affects those persons who are already in the UK, normally as visitors or students, who meet and become engaged and/or married. These persons need to apply to the Home Office to remain because they are married to a British citizen or a person settled in the UK. Social workers should note that non-marital relationships, ie cohabitation, and gay and lesbian relationships are not provided for in the Immigration Rules. The case law on the 'primary purpose' rule alone is massive.

As for children, those under 18 years of age with entry clearance and are supported and accommodated by their parents, are free to settle with their parents. As identified above at the beginning of this chapter, this excludes adopted children, who obtain nationality in that process.

Under EC law, 'relative in the ascending line', including spouses, cohabitees, children and other dependants, to an EU citizen have the right to join an EEA citizen who has travelled to another EEA country to work. This is part of the EU's movement of workers freedom. Though, in a recent decision the Court of Appeal ruled that a person who was not a citizen of a Member State of the EU but was married to an EU national was not entitled to the same residence rights as those of her or his spouse when they returned to live and work in an EU Member State (see *Sahota v Secretary of State for the Home Department* (1997) *The Times*, 30 April. Such confuses the purpose of EC law, but also the current rights of EU citizens. Yet when ambiguities arise, those affected are directed to return to the Treaty for assistance and since Articles 8 and 48–52 grant rights to EU, now EEA, citizens then these most obviously prevail over domestic laws.

Refugees and asylum seekers

The former Home Secretary, Michael Howard, introducing the Asylum and Immigration Act 1996 stated that the Act had three aims: 'first, to strengthen our asylum procedures ...; secondly, to combat immigration racketeering ...; and thirdly, to reduce economic incentives which attract people to [the UK] ...' (see HC Hansard, 11.12.95, col 699).

In keeping with the EU Dublin Convention, an asylum seeker should apply for asylum in the first safe country which she or he reaches. To make a successful asylum claim, the seeker must in accordance with the 1951 UN Convention Relating to the Status of Refugees establish a reason for his intention to seek asylum or refugee status.

Article 1 (2) of the 1951 UN Convention defines a 'refugee' as:

> ... a person who owing to well-founded fear of persecution for reasons of race, religion, nationality, membership of a particular social group or political opinion, is outside the country of his or her nationality and ... is unwilling to avail himself or herself of the protection of that country ..., or ... is unable or ... unwilling to return to it.

The burden of proof therefore lies on the asylum seeker to show that she or he has well-founded fear of persecution. The legal test is set out in *R v Secretary of State for the Home Department ex p Sivakumaran* [1988] 1 All ER 193, HL. Though this test has been modified to include the 'likelihood' of persecution following the court's ruling in *Ex p Sandralingham* (1995) *The Times*, 30 October.

Clearly the Asylum and Immigration Act 1996 does very little to change the rules regarding 'asylum status', but does more in terms of reforming the appeal procedures. For instance, once a case has been considered by the Home Office it will be rendered either: 'a claim with foundation' and asylum will be granted automatically; or, 'a claim without foundation'. Further to s 5(3) of the 1996 Act, the later cases will be heard by the Special Adjudicator, instead of an Immigration Appeals Tribunal (these will be discussed below).

It is worth noting that most asylum claims post-1996 will be found to be 'without foundation', since the new Act categorises cases according to the so-called 'White List'. This list of countries is those whom the Home Secretary designates as 'safe' countries. Thus, those countries not on this list are deemed to be unsafe. However, to date the Home Secretary has not entered any countries on the 'unsafe' list. Therefore, asylum seekers will find it difficult under English law to claim 'persecution', in order to sustain a case 'with foundation' to be granted asylum.

Moreover, social workers ought to be aware that an asylum seeker will be treated as 'dubious' by the Home Office authorities, if they do not present either a valid passport or offer an explanation for their failure on arrival in the UK. Schedule 2 to the 1996 Act presumes that successful asylum seekers will be those who arrive at a UK port of entry and declare themselves asylum seekers immediately.

In accordance with Schedule 2 to the Act, late claimants (ie those persons who make a claim for asylum when they are informed that they are to be deported, rather than those who do not apply at the point of entry for whatever reasons) no appeal will be heard by an Immigration Appeal Tribunal, unless it can be shown that the claimant will be subjected to torture, or be in danger of torture; or, where the Special Adjudicator considers the deportation certificate to have been erroneously issued.

In any event, proof of persecution or evidence of the likelihood of persecution is required. Furthermore, social workers should be aware at the outset when interviewing an asylum seeker that s 2 of the 1996 Act permits the removal of an asylum seeker from the UK, if the Home Secretary certifies that the following conditions are met:

- the person is not a national or citizen of the country or territory to which he or she is to be sent;

- that the person's life and liberty would not be threatened in that country or territory by reason of his race, religion, nationality, or membership of a particular social group or political opinion;

- that the government of that country or territory would not send the person to another country or territory in circumstances contrary to the UN Convention (see Article 33 of the Convention).

Subject to the 1996 Asylum Appeals (Procedure) Rules (SI 1996/2070) an appeal against the removal of an asylum claimant to a safe third country does lie to the Special Adjudicator on the grounds that such a certificate should not have been granted. However, the Home Secretary's reasons for the issuing of such a certificate do not have to be disclosed, thus the asylum appellant more often than not challenging a decision in the dark and is likely to lose. Though, she or he might be successful if they can contend that one of the conditions, as set out above, is not met, or alternatively, the decision to deport them is unreasonable in all the circumstances of their case. Should an appellant be successful, then the certificate will be set aside.

The 'new' immigration offences

Section 24 of the Immigration Act 1971 establishes the following 'immigration offences':

- illegal entry;

- entry in breach of a deportation order or without leave;

- overstaying or breach of condition of leave;

- overstaying after lawful entry;

- leaving the UK contrary to a court order;

- harbouring illegal entrants;

- assisting illegal entry;

- failure to provide information or documents;

- failure to submit to a medical examination by the immigration authorities;

- alteration of, and possession of altered passports or visas;

- acts of terrorism.

Sections 4 and 5 of the Asylum and Immigration Act 1996 add to this list by including the offences of:

- seeking to obtain leave to enter or remain in the UK by deception;

- assisting the seeking of leave to enter or remain in the UK by deception.

These offences are both punishable by way of a high fine (over £2,000) or by not more than six months imprisonment. Note that, in Chapter 9, a list of specialist detention centres and prisons housing immigration detainees was given.

Social workers should note that the power of arrest without a warrant is available to both police and immigration officers in respect of the offences of:

- illegal entry;

- obtaining leave or remain by deception;

- overstaying beyond the time given by leave;

- failing to observe a condition of entry.

Moreover, a JP – or in Scotland a sheriff – may grant a warrant authorising a police officer to enter premises, by force if necessary, to search for and arrest persons suspected of committing any of the offences listed above.

Accommodating immigrants

This area is more often than not the commonest point of contact between immigrants and social services within the UK. Yet this is not too surprising a factor, when s 9 of the 1996 Act seeks to ensure that local authorities, known as 'housing authorities', do not house or find accommodation for those persons subject to immigration control, unless the Home Secretary has authorised such. This order includes assistance under the homelessness statutory measures of the UK. However, the exceptions to the rule and those to whom housing is available and given Home Office authorisation are categorised in the Housing Accommodation and Homelessness (Persons subject to Immigration Control) Order 1996 (see SI 1996/1982), as set out below:

- Class A – recorded as a 'refugee';

- Class B – a person given exceptional leave to remain without conditions and is able to fund him- or herself and his or her family/dependants;

- Class C – a person who has unconditional leave to enter or remain;

- Class D – an overseas student who lets property for the purpose of student accommodation during his or her education overseas;

- Class E – an asylum seeker who declares him- or herself on arrival or not more than three months after their arrival into the UK;

- Class F – an asylum seeker before 4 February 1996 who is entitled to Housing Benefit.

Social workers should note that despite this rigid rule and the exceptions listed above, this is an area where the courts have sought to widen the law. For example, in *R v Hammersmith & Fulham LBC ex p M* (1996) *The Times*, 10 October, the High Court held that an asylum seeker who lacked a means to support himself or herself was deemed to be in need of care and attention under s 21 of the National

Assistance Act 1948. Thus, the asylum seeker held a right to be housed under that legislation. This case therefore indirectly imposed a duty on a local authority to house an immigrant, against the spirit of the existing legislation. Such should be borne in mind when considering the merits of the application made by an immigrant for housing.

Immigration and employment rights

The first principle with regard to immigrants working is that they must hold a valid work permit. Where a person employs a person subject to immigration control without a requisite work permit, then that employer will be fined by magistrates. To reacquaint yourself with employment law generally, see Chapter 23 above.

Immigration and social security

It was clear law prior to the 1996 Act, as contained in the well-known Social Security (Persons From Abroad) Miscellaneous Amendments Regulations (see SI 1996/30), that most immigrants were excluded from welfare benefits. To that end, the Joint Council for the Welfare of Immigrants (JCWI) sought to challenge these Regulations with some success (see *R v Secretary of State for Social Security ex p JCWI* (1996) *The Times*, 27 June). A partial success which was removed by s 11 and Schedule 1 to the 1996 Act which provides for regulations to be enacted to exclude immigrants from obtaining: Jobseekers, Attendance, Disability Living, Disability Working, Invalid Care and Severe Disablement Allowances and Housing and Council Tax benefits and Family Credit.

The only exception to this rule, is where the Home Secretary either declares a country from where the immigrant has abandoned as 'unsafe', as discussed earlier, or declares the person eligible for benefits. Lastly, as discussed above, any asylum seeker who sought asylum before 4 February 1996 is entitled to Housing Benefit. For a further discussion of the relevant general social security measures, see Chapter 25.

The appeals process

Any unsuccessful party in an immigration claim can appeal in the first instance to the Special Adjudicator within seven days following the receipt of their decision. Though, this time limit is reduced to two days, where the decision relates to a refusal to allow the claimant to enter the UK. In contrast, where the matter is one concerning the applicant's removal to a safe third country, as detailed above, then the time limit is extended to 28 days. In certain circumstances, where an appeal is lodged out of time, it may be deemed 'just and equitable' by the Home Secretary or the appropriate immigration officers as within the time limit for the purposes of an appeal hearing (see s 8 of the 1993 Asylum and Immigration Appeals Act). Following the commencement of a notice of appeal, the Home Secretary has 42 days in which to provide documents relating to the case to the Special Adjudicator. These documents include the notice of appeal; interview notes; and the original application documents. It is expected that a hearing will be convened within 42 days of the Special Adjudicator receiving the appeal papers for consideration. After the hearing, all the parties are expected to receive written notice of the decision within 10 days.

Social workers should note that the above mentioned procedure is expedited to 10 days instead of 42, and five days instead of 10 for the result, where the case concerns a claimant outside the UK.

Should the appeal before a special adjudicator be unsuccessful, then each party has a further appeal lies to an Immigration Appeal Tribunal on certain grounds. Such an appeal must be lodged with the Tribunal within five days from the receipt of the Special Adjudicator's decision. These appeals are usually commenced by requesting leave to appeal from the Tribunal, stipulating the grounds on which the appeal ought to be heard. Such applications for leave are completed on a standard form, known as the A2 form, which is accompanied by a copy of the original decision given by the Special Adjudicator. Grounds for appeal, include:

- error of law;

- Secretary of State and the Home Department have not discharged their burden of proof (ie the conditions are not met);

- unreasonable decision on the facts of the case.

Again within 10 days of a receipt of an appeal, the Tribunal has to decide whether or not to grant leave in the instant case. Should leave be granted, then, a hearing must be convened as soon as is practicable, but usually not later than 42 days after the tribunal has reached its decision to proceed. Though, all parties to an appeal will be notified at least five days in advance of a fixed date for such a hearing. Where leave is refused, then the Tribunal must give its reasons for such a decision.

According to Rule 35 of the Asylum Appeals (Procedure) Rules 1996 some cases may be determined without a hearing. Otherwise, subject to the discretion of the requisite appellate authority the conduct of such appeals is commonly as follows:

- The Home Office Presenting Officer or other representative sets out the case for the Crown.

- Witnesses for the Crown may be called and examined and cross-examined by the claimant/appellant.

- The claimant/appellant or his or her representative sets out the case for the claimant/appellant.

- Witnesses for the claimant/appellant may be called and examined and cross-examined by the Crown.

- The claimant/appellant sums up his or her case.

- The Crown concludes their case.

Appeals may be heard in the absence of either party. Yet the decision reached in absentia of either party might be later overturned.

No rules regulate discovery or the disclosure of documents or the presentation of bundles of evidence to be put to the Tribunal. A party to an appeal may act in person or obtain representation. Social workers should already be aware of who is available and able to represent clients on immigration matters before these tribunals in their locality. If not, at this point, they should consult the useful addresses part of this text and consult the various major charities in this area for advice or consult local solicitors or local immigration agencies.

Where an appeal is lost in the Immigration Appeal Tribunal, a further appeal lies to the Court of Appeal, within 10 days of receiving the Tribunal's decision. Once more leave must be granted and a Form A3 completed, similar to the A2 form. Scottish social workers, in particular, should note that here an appeal lies to the Court of Session, where the same rules as above apply.

Unlike the other, much stricter rules of evidence discussed in the earlier chapters of this text, in immigration proceedings the admissibility rule, as regards is evidence, is based solely on what is or is not relevant. No other rules of evidence apply.

Lastly, two further remedies for aggrieved immigration claimants exist:

- judicial review (see RSC Order 53), where the Home Secretary's actions may be challengeable on grounds of illegality, irrationality or procedural impropriety;

- *habeas corpus* (see RSC Order 54), where the immigrant is unlawfully detained (see Chapter 9 for further elaboration of the principle in question).

Bail applications in immigration matters

Chapter 10 on criminal justice explained the rigorous rules regarding bail. However, when applied to illegal entrants or any type of immigration claimant bail becomes more complex. An immigration claimant seeking bail should address their application to an immigration officer or the police. It should be made either in writing or orally (though it is customary practice that it is in writing). If in writing it should state:

- the applicant's name;

- the present address of the applicant (ie where he or she is currently detained);

- whether or not an appeal is pending at time of the bail application;

- the address where the applicant will reside should bail be granted;

- the amount of bail monies the applicant has available;

- the names, addresses and occupations of two persons who would act as sureties should bail be granted; and

- the grounds on which bail is sought.

For further particulars, see r 25 of the Asylum Appeals (Procedure) Rules 1996.

Future reform

With a change of government, comes a change in law. The new government has recently announced its intentions to publish a new Bill: the Immigration Appeals (Amendment) Bill (granting a new right of appeal against deportation on national security grounds). Moreover, the Home secretary has announced his intention to revoke the 'primary purpose' rule, as outlined above (see (1997) *Guardian*, 28 May). The ending of this notorious immigration rule would mean that a person wanting to marry a British citizen and settle in the UK could do so without the permission of the immigration authorities. Repealing this law, in practice, should mean that genuine couples will no longer have to hide the fact that they are coming to the UK to get married. Moreover, removing this rule will no longer impose hardship on some families, who despite being married were forced to reside miles apart due to the imposition of the primary purpose rule. The likely change in law is that the burden of proof will be shifted onto the immigration officer to show that the marriage is bogus.

Final comment

Whilst this chapter has been fairly extensive, social workers should consult more widely for a more thorough answer to their queries, since this is very much a basic guide and not one covering all facts and circumstances. Moreover, practitioners are reminded constantly that immigration law is forever changing, so consideration ought to be had for any potential changes in this controversial are of social policy.

Practice points

In immigration matters, social workers should:

- check the client's passport or birth certificate;

- ascertain the client's nationality;

- obtain the facts of the circumstances;

- consult law and/or legal advice/assistance;

- arrange for legal representation;

- where possible seek emergency financial support (hardship monies/benefits) and accommodation for the claimant and his family;

- consult relevant community support groups.

Further reading

Asylum and Immigration Act 1996, London: HMSO.

Immigration: The Law and Practice, 1996, London: Longman

JCWI Immigration and Nationality Law Handbook, 1997, London: Joint Council for the Welfare of Immigrants.

Rosenblatt, J, and Lewis, I, *Children and Immigration*, 1997, London: Cavendish Publishing.

Social Services Inspectorate, *Unaccompanied Asylum-Seeking Children – Training Pack*, June 1995, CI(95)17, HMSO.

25 Housing, money advice and social security*

This chapter covers a vast area which forms the final part of the social welfare section of law with which social workers are likely to confront in practice. Unfortunately, whilst the areas covered here form what used to be called the 'common sense' part of social work law, in recent years the courts have shown this no longer to be the case. Furthermore, Parliament has been very active in this area, at least in terms of welfare benefits and so, this area like all others is covered by a patchwork quilt of legislation.

In the first part of this chapter, housing law is discussed, covering the salient areas of homelessness and eviction, which social work practitioners are likely to encounter. Next comes money advice, which seeks to examine income and that is followed, perhaps more accidentally than by design, as well as being symbolic of the times, by a cursory look at the current welfare benefits system and its adjudication system.

Basic housing law

The statutory framework surrounding housing law in the UK is immense. Let's take a brief look through the minefield. However, before doing so, we must acquaint ourselves with the common law's classification of residence:

- owner occupier;

- trespasser;

- licensee; and

- tenancy.

The various classifications can be sub-divided into a combination of circumstances, as listed below:

- joint-tenancy;

- sub-tenancy;

* The authors express their gratitude to numerous CABx workers and welfare rights' advisers who have indirectly contributed to this chapter over the years. Also, our thanks go to the Independent Tribunals Service for providing up-to-date information on the adjudication system.

- mortgages – mortgagees/mortgagors; and

- tied accommodation.

The housing legislation

The first pieces of statutory intervention were:

- **Prescription Act 1832** – The right to claim common and other profits a prendre and easements.

- **Married Womens Property Acts 1882 and 1891** – Gave married women their first ever entitlement to property rights.

- **The Law of Property Act 1925** – Following the Settled Land and Trustee Acts of the same year, the LPA statutorily established the legal estates of property, equitable interests and powers. Section 1 defines them. The birth of conveyancing, mortgages and land registration and registration of interests in land.

- **The Public Health Act 1936** – Local authority power for slum clearance to continue and placed on duties to maintain properties in fit state of repair.

- **The Landlord and Tenant Act 1954** – This established the statutory relationship between landlords and tenants.

- **The Housing Acts 1957, 1961** – Local Authority powers and duties increased.

- **The Rent Act 1974** – The first rent protection was introduced, temporarily in 1915. Extended rent protection to tenants of furnished accommodation. Established the jurisdiction of the Rent Tribunal.

- **The Rent Act 1977** – Established the rights of the protected tenant to security of tenure and to the regulation of rent paid. The Rent Officer emerges and the registration of rents can now take place. Right not to be unlawfully evicted.

Housing Law in the 1980s

Since the beginning of this century, housing law has increased in importance, especially during the 1980s, and so further enactments were made, these were:

- **The Housing Act 1980** – The right to buy (public sector) and the protected shorthold tenancy emerged.

- **The Housing Act 1985** – Restates 1980 and gives further security of tenure.

- **The Housing Association Act 1985** – This established Housing associations for the purposes of collective housing and estate management.

- **The Landlord and Tenant Act 1985** – This sets out further rights of tenants against their landlords, should their landlord not meet the minimum standards.

- **The Housing Grants Construction and Regeneration Act 1996** – Provides for home repair assistance. A whole ream of Regulations implement this statutory regime.

- **The Leasehold Reform, Housing Grants and Urban Development Act 1996** – A code on residential property management has been issued under this legislation.

- **The Housing Act 1996** – This the latest piece of legislation covering a vast array of areas and controversial issues, such as the allocation of housing accommodation, homelessness and tenancies' categorisation. Again numerous regulations and orders bring this Act into force. In particular, a new Code of Guidance replaced DoE Circular 7/96 from October 1996.

Categories of ownership

With so much legislative change over three decades, new categories of occupation emerged:

- **Owner occupiers** – Owner occupiers have a lot of rights. The two main types are freeholders – that is those who own the land and building in which they live and secondly leaseholders who buy a lease on their accommodation, for example people who have a leasehold flat or maisonette.

- **Secure public sector tenancies** – Most ordinary 'council' and housing association tenancies beginning before 15th January 1989 will be secure. Secure tenants can only be evicted for special reasons.

- **Protected tenancies** – These are tenancies from private landlords created before 15th January 1989. If your client has a private landlord and the tenancy:

  (a) started *before* 15 January 1989; *and*

  (b) there is no landlord living on the premises; *and*

  (c) you have exclusive occupation of at least one room.

- **Assured tenancies** – These are tenancies with private non-resident landlords, and housing association tenancies created after 14 January 1989 (some are called assured shorthold tenancies). Assured shorthold tenants have little real security, but do have a right to an independently assessed rent.

- **Unprotected tenants and licensees** – Includes people in bed and breakfast hostels, people with resident landlords, etc. Their rights are minimal, eg right to some notice before they have to leave.

- **Unprotected public sector tenants/licensee**s – This covers tenancies such as service tenancies (eg caretakers) and homeless persons temporary accommodation.

Rights and responsibilities

Those given by Parliament – these are called statutory rights and those given by contract – these are called contractual rights.

Statutory rights

The main statutory rights and obligations that are covered by legislation concern:

- To keep the exterior structure of the home in good repair as well as drains, pipes, fuel supplies, fixed fires and water heaters and bathroom fittings, etc.

- Security of tenure – the right of the tenant to remain so that the landlord can only repossess in certain specified circumstances.

- Payment of rent – how to get a fair or reasonable rent set and how to challenge rent increases.

- Passing on the tenancy after death to surviving family who live there.

- Protection from harassment and illegal eviction.

Contractual

Any agreement (contract) between a landlord and tenant will usually have two types of contractual terms:

- express terms; and

- implied terms

Express terms
The most common of these are:

- the length of time of the letting, eg fixed term or for an indefinite period;

- the length of notice to end the tenancy, whether it includes fuel, etc;

- the amount of rent and whether it is paid in advance or in arrears and when and how often;

- the frequency with which rent must be paid and the day(s) on which it is due.

Implied terms

Terms may be implied by:

- custom and practice;

- common law; and

- statute.

Terms implied by common law

The most important terms always implied by common law include:

- the right of the tenant to live peacefully and without interference in his or her accommodation;

- the tenant's obligation not to damage the accommodation;

- the tenant's obligation to take proper care of the accommodation. This includes reporting faults;

- the landlord's obligation not to reduce the size or the amenities of the accommodation and not to do anything which would detract from the tenant's right to use the accommodation according to the original tenancy agreement.

Landlords' and tenants' rights

The tenant's obligations are:

- to keep the interior of the accommodation in a good state of repair and decoration;

- not to damage the furniture (if any);

- to allow the landlord reasonable access to inspect the accommodation and to carry out repairs;

- not to cause a nuisance or annoyance to the neighbours;

- not to use the premises for trade or business purposes.;

- not to keep pets.

In contrast, the landlord's obligations are:

- to keep the common areas in good condition;

- to provide any services agreed in the contract;

- to determine whether the tenant may alter or improve the accommodation. If this is allowed, under what circumstances the landlord's permission must be sought;

- to determine whether the tenant may pass on (assign) and/or sub-let the tenancy to someone else. If this is allowed to decide under what circumstances the landlord may refuse his or her permission.

Council tenants and the law

Tenancy agreements should set out fully the council's responsibilities. This should avoid any confusion or misunderstanding. The Landlord and Tenant Act 1985 requires the council to keep their properties in good repair, in terms of the structure, exterior, drains, gutters, downpipes, water pipes, taps, gas pipes and appliances (if any), electric wiring, sockets and switches, basins, bath, toilet, sinks, fixed heaters – such as back boilers, storage heaters, underfloor heating, water heaters and radiators.

The council should also maintain any common parts of property which they own, eg stair cases, rubbish chutes, hall lighting and roofs. A common law duty to keep these premises safe also exists (see *Liverpool City Council v Irwin* [1977] AC 239). Any disrepair which is prejudicial to health (eg condensation, dampness) is likely to be a statutory nuisance.

Like private tenants, the rent stop to pay for repairs can be exercised. Except, unlike private tenants, the repair must be reported to the repairs section of the requisite housing department, The Inspector must then visit and an order for the works, then be passed onto the local depot. A maximum wait of 10 weeks is the national guidance. Both the local authority landlord or the tenant can take legal action to enforce any statutory or contractual rights they have, but remember without security of tenure the tenants may risk losing their home if they follow this course of action.

Statutory nuisance

Where the landlord leaves his property in a state of disrepair, then the tenant can claim 'statutory nuisance'. This mean that the tenant will:

- report the disrepair to his or her landlord;

- call in Environmental Health Officer (EHO) from council;

- EHO will visit and may serve an abatement notice with a time limit or even apply to magistrate' court for nuisance order with time limit

- the landlord might even get fined.

Statutory nuisance procedure does not offer more than a sticking plaster solution to stop the risk to your health, so you may only end up with a patched roof, unstopped drains, but the roof may leak again and drain block up again because they have not sorted out the real cause, a completely new roof is needed, the drain needs relaying.

If a home is 'unfit for habitation' the council has to take action. The council first has to decide it is 'unfit'. They consider a whole range of things. State of repair of windows, doors, floors, roof, stairs, subsidence, dampness (including condensation), lay out (eg toilet straight off a kitchen and openable windows amongst other things.

Where the disrepair is 'prejudicial to health', it must either have caused or is likely to cause ill health to those in your home, eg bronchitis, asthma from dampness. In these circumstances:

- Serve a 21 day notice on the landlord stating that you intend to start an action in the magistrates' court for statutory nuisance and what the statutory nuisance is (the cause – a hole in the roof, and the effects, water in the bedroom and electric shocks from the light switch).

- Then 'lay' the information before the magistrates' court. You can get green form legal help up to this stage. There is a hearing: if there is a statutory nuisance you get a compensation order for your expenses (eg the cost of a surveyor's report) a nuisance order with a time limit.

- The landlord may be fined and you also may get a compensation order for damages of up to £2,000. You could later sue for more compensation in the county courts.

If there is no written agreement it will be harder to convince the court of what the landlord agreed to regarding repairs. However, fortunately most tenants can rely on the statutorily implied terms of the Landlord and Tenant Act 1988 where it is the landlord's job to keep in repair the structure and exterior (walls, floors, roof, windows, drains, gutters and external pipes, water, gas pipes, wiring, taps, sockets, basins, sinks, baths, toilets, fixed heaters such as gas fires, storage heaters and water heaters. Cooker are not included).

Alternatively, lots of tenants stop-paying rent as a way of pressuring the landlord to do repairs. This is risky (eg persistent arrears or arrears of over 13 weeks can lead to eviction for assured tenants). However, for minor repairs, where the tenant does not want to use the council or take legal action, a rent stop can be a useful way of paying for the repairs.

In houses where several people live together who are not a single household, eg bedsits, hostels, houses shared by students or others are known as Houses or Multiple Occupation. There are special powers for the Council to make sure there are enough baths, toilets and basins and proper fire escapes and that they are not overcrowded and are properly run.

Eviction and grounds for possession

Where a tenant does not keep up rent or breaches the contract or commits a crime, the landlord might wish to reclaim the property. Such an action is called seeking 'repossession'. Possession proceeding are based upon what are known as the 'discretionary grounds' for possession in order to distinguish them from the 'mandatory grounds'. It is important always to bear in mind that this requirement is additional, and must be considered in every case (*Peachey Property Corporation v Robinson* [1966] 2 WLR 1386).

The purpose of this overriding requirement of reasonableness is to ensure that a tenant does not lose his home because of some trivial breach, or perhaps because the landlord has written into the tenancy unduly onerous terms. The parties' conduct (*Yelland v Taylor* [1957] 1 WLR 459), and other factors affecting the parties and the public generally (*Cresswell v Hodgson* [1951] 2 KB 92) may be taken into account under this heading.

The mandatory ground for possession are known as 'grounds', under the Housing Act 1985). In comparison, the discretionary grounds are termed Case I, which are situations where either the tenant is in arrears with his rent, or the tenant has broken a term of the tenancy. Conviction for immoral, or illegal, user is also a ground for possession, as is nuisance and annoyance to adjoining occupiers. Immoral user will normally lead to an order for possession, though not invariably (*Yates v Morris* [1950] 2 All ER 577, CA). Illegal user only applies when the use of the premises has something to do with the criminal conviction, even if the offence was not one which necessarily involved use of premises, but the use of the premises must have been part of the facts leading to the conviction, rather than incidentally being the site of the commission of the offence (*Schneider & Sons v Abrahams* [1925] 1 KB 301, CA). The final 'ground for possession', in relation to which reasonableness must still, and additionally, be shown, does not appear in the schedule of discretionary grounds. It is that the landlord can provide or obtain suitable alternative accommodation for the tenant. The landlord may be able to establish his claim by producing a certificate from the local authority that the tenant will be rehoused by them. In the alternative, a landlord can himself provide another private tenancy or obtain one for the tenant from another landlord.

In cases where there is occupancy without security, such as trespassers or licensees, then Orders 24 (county court) or Order 113 (High Court) can be used to dispose of the proceedings speedily and remove the occupant. Yet violent eviction is not permissible – see s 12 of the Criminal Law Act 1977.

Harassment and illegal eviction can be pursued in both the criminal courts, triable by magistrates, or in the civil courts, if seeking damages or an injunction.

Homelessness

Since 1977, local authorities have had a duty to house those persons who are deemed homeless. This duty was first established under the Housing (Homeless Persons) Act 1977. Latterly, the 1985 Housing Act replaced the 1977 Homeless Persons Act, which sought to protect homeless persons. Though, it would be wrong to assume that all homeless persons have a right to be accommodated, since they do not.

Primarily, due to the controversy surrounding the homeless UK Governments have either chose to neglect these persons or legislate, either sympathetically or harshly. It therefore comes of no surprise that recent legislation, enacted under the Housing Act 1996, seeks yet again to overturn the good work done by the courts in assisting and protecting homeless persons.

The new regime is therefore as follows:

- Every local housing authority shall register those persons whom qualify for housing accommodation.

- Asylum seekers, as discussed above already, are not eligible for housing accommodation, unless the Home Secretary permits such provision (see Part VII of the Housing Act 1996, *R v Southwark LBC ex p Bediako* (1997) *The Times*, 19 February and *R v Kensington & Chelsea ex p Korneva* (1997) *The Times*, 1 January).

- Each local housing authority must have a scheme for determining priorities amongst the various applicants.

- Local housing authorities can opt-out of and thus, contract-out their functions for housing generally and those for homeless persons

Whatever laws are in place, it remains a basic principle of law with regard to homelessness, that intentional homelessness grants no rights to housing at all in any circumstances (see *R v Brent LBC ex p Baruwa* (1997) *The Times*, 12 February, CA).

Moreover, to successfully claim a right to housing as a homeless person, it must be shown that:

- the applicant is in priority need (ie pregnant, ill, has children, or otherwise);

- the applicant has sufficient local connections to deserve housing by the local housing authority; or

- the applicant is unintentionally homeless.

All of the above listed key concepts need to be satisfactorily met before any local authority will house the individual applicant for housing.

It should be noted that any applicant temporarily housed in a refuge or the like is likely to be considered as not homeless (see *R v Ealing LBC ex p Sidhu* [1982] LGR 534, HC). Moreover, 'priority need' refers to:

- has dependent children who reside, or will be residing, with the applicant;

- is homeless as the result of an emergency, such as flood, fire or another disaster;

- the applicant or another residing with them, or likely to reside with them, is vulnerable due to old age, mental illness, disability, or some other relevant condition;

- the applicant is pregnant, or resides with a pregnant woman.

Furthermore, a person becomes intentionally homeless if they deliberately do anything or fail to do something which causes her or his occupation of accommodation to be ceased. Lastly, the concept of 'local connections' refers to normal residence, either by actual residence or family associations, in the area for which the applicant has sought accommodation.

In addition, homelessness, local authorities must make enquiries following an application from a homeless or threatened with homelessness person about the facts and potential accommodation, should the applicant succeed. Local authorities therefore have duties to make accommodation available where relevant and legally required to do so and to provide homeless applicants with advice and assistance. Most notably, this is imperative under s 20 of the Children Act 1989, where children are also involved. More recently, the government has announced its plans to enact a new measure to assist the homeless in its Local Authority (Capital Receipts) Bill which will amend the Housing Act 1989.

Money advice

This area of social welfare requires the deployment of the everyday social work skills of interviewing, negotiation and case management, in a different context of finance. In 1996, some 860,000 or more of enquirers at various advice agencies were concerned with debt. Moreover, the Council of Mortgage Lenders has reported that a 6% increase on repossessions in the UK suggested that poverty and debt problems were spreading far and wide across the UK still. Obviously, social workers will encounter debt problems and money advice problems in their day-to-day practice, as a consequence of these trends. Whilst their clients might have problems with benefits, eviction/repossession, or even obtaining employment, others will have their water, gas or electricity connected, or find themselves borrowing and getting deeper and deeper into debt resulting in harassment from many creditors. To deal with these everyday issue, the legally competent social worker ought to be aware of various rights and remedies available to those who need some money and/or debt advice.

Primarily, all social workers ought to know that any harassment by creditors of their debtors is illegal. Under s 40 of the Administration of Justice Act 1970 'harassment' is defined as: '... attempting to coerce a person to pay a contract debt by making demands which alarm, distress or humiliate, by the nature of their frequency or public manner.' For the purposes of this Act, harassment can be both oral or in writing. Such harassment can be punishable by a fine or imprisonment by a court.

The social worker should also know that various agencies can assist them in their work. For instance, the Office of Fair Trading and local trading standards departments; the regulatory bodies, such as OFFER, OFGAS, OFTEL and OFWAT can often assist with problems and complaints with the utilities; councillors, MPs and MEPs can help; as can the various ombudsmen, as already described in Chapter 2.

Furthermore, with regard to bailiffs, either court based and other public or private bailiffs, or in High Court matters they are called 'sheriffs' officers, they must have a warrant of execution or possession in order to seize goods or evict occupants from their homes, or in a High Court context, a *fierri facias* writ.

Bailiffs are used to:

- repossess houses;

- to recover sums/goods to the value to pay off county court judgments against them (ie orders by the court to pay sums owed);

- to recover goods which cover unpaid taxes;

- to recover sums to cover unpaid fines or compensation orders awarded by a magistrates' court;

- to enforce local authorities' orders (often referred to as 'distress warrants') to recover unpaid business rates or council tax (formerly community charge, or the 'Poll Tax' as it was nicknamed) or rent arrears.

However, in terms of bailiff's powers, most bailiffs do not have the right to enter persons property with force, unless they have already gained entry peacefully. Bailiffs can only seize goods, upon entry, to the value specified and levied by themselves as meeting that value; though, s 89 of the County Court Act 1984 exempts certain goods from bailiff action, such as tools, vehicles and other goods required for employment purposes and clothing, furniture, bedding, household equipment required for basic domestic needs. Obviously on obtaining the goods, the bailiff holds the right to sell to recover the sums sought. Whatever, the dispute or warrant, all bailiffs have a duty of care for all goods in their possession, but for acts of God. Moreover, complaints about bailiffs can be made to the relevant court which either controls or orders them, should they have 'acted improperly' in the execution of their duty. Actually, a bailiff's certificate can be withdrawn, by way of punishment, or fined.

Clearly, most money advice matters and/or debts are interlinked with poverty, generally. Whether it be a consumer credit debt (ie one regulated by the Consumer Credit Act 1974), business debt or personal debt, clearly some cause lies behind the debt related to either greed, or more often than not, by poverty of some description. Obviously, the social worker cannot do miracles with client's personal financial circumstances, but they can give advice about income and expenditure and prioritise the debts. Thus, making the debt situation a manageable one. Debt management can be undertaken in two ways; first, separate the debts into two categories, by separating those under a court order or liable to be so (as these are priority debts), from those which are not, nor are likely to be so (as these are *non-priority* debts), or may be written off (usually very small sums). Once this is done, then the social worker can write letters to all debtors explaining the situation offering to pay a nominal sum to each one, or requesting those which are not subject, or likely to be, to a court order to be written off or withholding payment for six months whilst your client seeks to regain control over their finances and hopefully improve the situation. This simple arrangement will allow your client to use the little resources they have to subsist, whilst keeping all the creditors in abeyance under law.

Future social justice

Having discussed the issue of poverty, it is worth noting here that prior to the last General Election, the new Labour government established a Social Commission which considered a range of social problems, including poverty and unemployment. This Commission made several wide-ranging recommendations which the Labour government pledged to honour and implement.

Should that be the case, then new measures relating to some of the issues related to money, in particular debts management, will be forthcoming and could formalise some of the matters discussed above which are already informally in place in the UK. Overall, a serious debate about poverty and its causes would be much welcomed.

The UK's benefits system

It is a fact of modern society that more and more people have become dependant on social security benefits for daily living. This is not an indictment upon those individuals and families, but more a question which the government needs to address, in terms of employment, skills and education, as well as finance. Yet this needs to be balanced against those who are found to be cheating the so-called 'system'. Some 312,000 cases were found in 1994. It is partly due to this statistic, rather than the former why so many changes have been witnessed in this area of social welfare during the 1980s and early 1990s.

Since the advent of the Welfare State, following the Beveridge Commission, a State benefits system has developed at a rapid pace. This guaranteed, minimum level of subsistence evolved from two sources: national insurance and a National Health Service. The difficulty with this basis for a welfare system in 1990 is that it was based on full employment and also could predict the demographic changes experienced in the UK today. Subsequently, in the 1990s the social security benefits have undergone radical reform and a change in emphasis. In particular, with the increase in private health and pension provision and mass unemployment, the Treasury's disposable national insurance bank has decreased. Also, the introduction of the Jobseeker's Allowance, replacing both unemployment benefit and Income Support, now brings alongside a name change a greater need to make the state and benefit claimant relationship more contractual and one where the claimant has to prove his effort, in order to receive benefit. In response to these circumstances, state benefits were divided into two distinct categories: income-related (once called 'means-tested') and 'non-means-tested', now termed 'contributory' and 'non-contributory' benefits:

- **Contributory benefits** – These are only payable to those persons who have paid sufficient national insurance contributions, by way of deductions from their salaries. Examples are: retirement pension, widow's benefit, Jobseeker's Allowance (formerly unemployment benefit) and long-term incapacity benefit.

- **Non-contributory benefits** – To the contrary, these do not require a contribution and therefore, the claimant does not have to satisfy any national insurance or other contributions. Any entitlement to these benefits is determined by the claimant's personal circumstances. Examples are: child benefit, disability living allowance, family credit and Jobseeker's Allowance.

Readers should note that the Jobseeker's Allowance (JSA) is both a contributory and non-contributory benefit. Thus, the JSA is a hybrid benefit with two routes. The reason for this is that this particular benefit replaces both a former contributory (ie unemployment benefit) benefit, and a non-contributory one (ie income support). The only other method of distinguishing or categorising benefits, is by their duration. Whilst some are given for life, for example retirement benefit upon retirement, and those for a specified period, such as family credit.

Moreover, social workers should be aware that ascertaining whether their client is employed or self-employed at the outset of the interview is crucial, when considering their entitlements to benefits due to their clear association with contributions. For some self-employed persons proof of contributions might be difficult. In any event, they might be asked to prove it. So, readers ought to be alerted to it to understand the basis of UK benefits law.

Some common principles and rules

Even with over 60 benefits existing within the UK social security system, what binds all these together are some common principle and rules:

- **Capital limits** – No person will qualify for benefits usually if he or she has over £8,000 in capital (or £16,000 in the case of Housing Benefit). In addition £1 is deducted for capital over £3,000. This increases incrementally with an increase in capital.

- **Income limits** – Earnings limits vary from benefit to benefit (so consult each as applicable). However, it is a common principle that persons will not be entitled to benefits if their weekly earnings exceed any prescribed figure set by the Statute. However, another common principle to all benefits is that certain disregards can arise in the assessment of income. For example, some other benefits received are disregarded, as are some debts.

- **Dependants** – It is common to most benefits that additional payments can be made where the claimant has a dependant. Dependants can be both adults and children.

It should be noted that another common rule is that should a claimant be hospitalised for up to six or more weeks, then their benefit might be affected, even reduced.

Apart from these common rules and principles, each benefit is regulated as prescribed by the Act and any other guidance or Regulations given by the Secretary of State. However, certain other special generic rules exist for special cases, as set out below:

- **'Habitual residence'** – To claim all benefits the claimant has to be 'habitually resident', at least present in, or have a connection with the UK. The exceptions to this rule being: airmen, mariners, offshore workers, armed forces members or former members and EEA nationals and others prescribed by the Secretary of State as satisfying the Act.

- **Prisoners** – A prisoner or person otherwise detained is disqualified from claiming any benefits.

- **Children** – Whilst benefits may be given to parents, guardians or carers for children, children are only restricted to claiming benefits themselves if they are disabled (see DLA) or suffering from vaccine damage.

- **Students** – Students are generally disentitled to claim any benefits whilst studying full-time. However, special rules permit the claiming of some benefits.

- **Pensioners, disabled persons, widows and married couples** – These are the last groups of persons affected by special benefits rules, usually relating to their contributions, living arrangements, needs, or other benefits.

Benefits guide

Below, in their various groupings, are the salient benefits currently available. Readers are reminded that the rates of benefit are changed and reviewed on an annual basis. Those given in the tables below are from the 7 April 1997 (see Social Security Uprating Order 1997 SI 1997/543 for further details):

Contributory benefits

BENEFIT	AMOUNT PER WEEK	LAW/CONDITIONS/ TRIBUNAL
INCAPACITY Short term 　Lower rate 　Higher rate Long term Age related 　Lower rate (35–44)	 £47.10 £55.70 £62.45 Plus £6.60	Social Security Contributions and Benefits Act (SSCBA) 1992 & Social Security (Incapacity for Work) (General) Regs 1995 /(Misc Amendment) Regs 1996

BENEFIT	AMOUNT PER WEEK	LAW/CONDITIONS/ TRIBUNAL
INCAPACITY Higher rate (under 35)	Plus £13.16	• Under 65 or no more than 70 years old • Incapable of work before retirement • Satisfy the 'all work' test and be deemed incapable of work SSAT – IB Tribunal
JOBSEEKER'S ALLOWANCE Under 18 18–24 Over 25	 £29.60 £38.90 £49.15	Jobseekers Act 1995/ Jobseekers Act Regs 1996 • Be available for work • Be actively seeking work • Have a Jobseeker's agreement SSAT
STATUTORY SICK PAY (SSP)	£55.70	Statutory Sick Pay Act 1994 • Be an employee • Be aged under 65 years of age • Earn over £65 pw SSAT

BENEFIT	AMOUNT PER WEEK	LAW/CONDITIONS/ TRIBUNAL
WIDOW'S **PAYMENT** (Lump Sum) Widowed Mother's Allowance Pension	£1,000.00 £62.45 £62.45	SSCBA 1992/Claims and Payments Regs 1987 • Under 65 years of age at time of spouse's death • Dead spouse paid sufficient contributions • Not living with another partner as spouse SSAT
RETIREMENT PENSION Category A B C D C (without contribution) Aged over 80 years old+	£62.45 £37.35 £37.35 £37.35 £22.35 £0.25	Pensions Act 1995/SSCBA 1992 • Have reached pensionable age (65+) • Have made sufficient contributions SSAT PENSIONS OMBUDSMAN

Non-contributory benefits

BENEFIT	AMOUNT PER WEEK	LAW/CONDITIONS/ TRIBUNAL
CHILD Eldest or only child Couple Lone Parent Other children	 £11.05 £17.10 £9.00	SSCBA 1992/Child Benefit Regs 1991 • Have a child who is under 16 or in full-time education post-16 and not 19 • Claimant is responsible for the child's upbringing SSAT
DISABILITY LIVING ALLOWANCE Care component 　Higher rate 　Middle rate 　Lower rate Mobility component 　Higher rate 　Lower rate	 £49.50 £33.10 £13.15 £34.60 £13.15	Disability Living Allowance Act 1991/SSCBA 1992/DLA Regs 1991 **Care** • Needs assistance (day and/or night) from another on a day to day basis **Mobility** • Unable or virtually unable to walk from physical disablement, or mental impairment DAT
ATTENDANCE ALLOWANCE Higher rate Lower rate	 £49.50 £33.10	SSCBA 1992/AA Regs 1991/ DLA Regs 1991 • Require frequent attention throughout the day or night DAT

BENEFIT	AMOUNT PER WEEK	LAW/CONDITIONS/ TRIBUNAL
GUARDIAN'S ALLOWANCE	£11.20	SSCBA 1992/GA Regs 1976 • Claimant receives child benefit • Not the child's parent • Contributes to the child's maintenance • Either both or one of the child's parents are dead and/or cannot be traced • Claimant has adopted the child SSAT
INVALID CARE ALLOWANCE	£37.35	SSCBA 1992/SS(ICA) Regs 1976 • Person engaged in caring for a severely disabled person • Claimant is over 16 years of age DAT
SEVERE DISABLEMENT ALLOWANCE Age-related additions under 40 40–49 50–59	£37.75 £13.15 £8.30 £4.15	Health and Social Security Act 1984/SS9 (Incapacity for Work) Act 1994 • Be incapable of work • Have been absent from work for a continuous 196 days or more • At least 16 but not over 65 years of age • Must satisfy the degree of disablement test DAT

Maternity benefits

maternity allowance is . . . .£48.35 pw

statutory maternity pay is . . . .£55.70 pw

social fund maternity payment is (lump sum) £100.00

Dependants allowances

These are divided into adult and child dependants:

Adult (applicable to spouse or person)
Looking after a child, where claimant is receiving

- long-term incapacity benefit, or
  - retirement pension . . . .£37.35 pw

- short-term incapacity benefit
  - over pension age . . . .£35.90 pw

- short-term incapacity benefit
  - under pension age . . . .£29.15 pw
  - severe disablement allowance . . . .£22.40 pw
  - invalid care allowance . . . .£22.35 pw

Child (applicable claimant)
Receiving –

- incapacity benefit, or
- retirement pension, or
- widowed mother's allowance
- widow's benefit
- severe disablement allowance
- invalid care allowance

The applicable amount is . . . .£11.20 pw

Family credit

The applicable amount is . . . .£77.15 pw

Maximum family credit limits are:

Adult . . . .£47.65 pw

Child

  0–10 . . . .£12.05 pw

  11–15 . . . .£19.95 pw

  16–17 . . . .£24.80 pw

  18 . . . .£34.70 pw

Capital limits are:

  cut-off £8,000.00

  disregard £3,000.00

Disability working allowance

The applicable amounts are:

  single person . . . .£57.85 pw

  couple or lone parent . . . .£77.15 pw

Maximum disability working allowance limits are:

  single person . . . .£49.55 pw

  couple or lone parent . . . .£77.55 pw

The capital limits are:

  cut-off £16,000.00

  disregard £3,000.00

Income based allowances, premiums and housing costs

The applicable amounts are:

Single person

  under 18 . . . .£29.60 pw

  under 18 (higher rate) . . . .£38.90 pw

  18–24 . . . .£38.90 pw

  Over 25 . . . .£49.15 pw

Lone parent

under 18 . . . .£29.60 pw

under 18 (higher rate) . . . .£38.90 pw

over 18 . . . .£49.15 pw

Couple

both under 18 . . . .£58.70 pw

one over 18 . . . .£77.15 pw

Child

0–11 . . . .£16.90 pw

11–16 . . . .£24.75 pw

16–18 . . . .£29.60 pw

Premiums

family . . . .£10.80 pw

lone parent . . . .£15.75 pw

disabled child . . . .£20.95 pw

care premium . . . .£13.35 pw

Other premiums exist for persons with a disability or a severe disability, and pensioners.

A capital cut-off of £8,000 and disregard of £3,000 applies. Moreover, deductions for non-dependants for housing costs apply.

Housing and council tax benefits

Personal allowances

Single person

under 25 . . . .£38.90

over 25 . . . .£49.15

Lone parent

under 18 (housing benefit only) £38.90

over 18 . . . .£49.15

Couple

both under 18 (housing benefit only) £58.70

one over 18 . . . .£77.15

A capital cut-off of £16,000 and disregard of £3,000 applies to these benefits. In addition, the same premiums as for those listed in income based allowances above applies, with the exception of a lone parent which is £22.05. Also, deductions for non-dependants for both benefits apply.

Other benefits

Irrespective of those principal benefits already listed, below are some other benefits, grants and state assistance which exist:

- funeral expenses;

- Christmas bonus;

- independent living fund;

- motability;

- prescriptions;

- vaccine damage payments;

- sight tests/dental treatment;

- work injuries and diseases.

Readers should note that since this chapter has not provided an exhaustive list of all the social security benefits available, nor the minutiae in terms of regulations and rules which surround them, then social workers should know that most welfare rights organisation, such as a CABx or advice centre should be able to give you up-to-date advice on the benefits available and the pre-conditions for entitlement. Furthermore, the Benefits Agency itself offers a very helpful enquiry, helpline on 0800 882200.

The benefits adjudication and independent appeals system

Surrounding UK benefits law is a huge appeals and adjudication framework. In this part of the chapter we seek to illuminate upon this public process.

Often social workers only encounter with social security benefits will be when either a client's benefit has stopped, or a claim has been rejected. In these circumstances the claimant can:

- make a fresh claim; or

- appeal.

Should the client decide to appeal, then first and foremost the client should request a Benefits Agency Adjudication Officer (AO) to review their decision. The AO will then decide whether to uphold the Benefits Agency's previous decision or overturn it and grant the benefit applied for by the claimant. Pursuant to s 20 of the SSCBA 1992, once a claim form is received by the benefits Agency, it is processed and referred to an AO to make a decision as to whether or not the claimant qualifies for the benefit which she or he is making a claim for. These reviews are made on grounds of mistake or a relevant change in circumstances.

However, should a review be unsuccessful, then the claimant can appeal to an appeal tribunal. Several types of appeal tribunal exist within the benefits system.

Social Security Appeal Tribunal (SSAT)

An SSAT decides whether or not a claimant should receive benefit, assess a claimant's credits for National Insurance purposes, as well as claims for maternity, cold weather payments, funeral expenses, statutory maternity pay, statutory sick pay and incapacity from work. The tribunal consists of two lay persons and a chairwoman/man who is a lawyer. Except, where the benefit is incapacity benefit, sin these cases the tribunal is assisted by a Medical Assessor (MA), who is a local GP, who does not take part in the deliberations of the tribunal, but advises the tribunal on medical matters. In fact the MA behaves like a 'medical dictionary' to the tribunal. It should be noted that all applicants for Incapacity Benefit undergo a medical examination, a so-called 'assessment' by the Benefits Agency Medical Services (BAMS) doctor. In all Incapacity Benefit cases the report of the BAMS doctor is referred to.

Medical Appeal Tribunals (MAT)

Medical questions are determined by two or more medical practitioners, often one is a GP and the other is a consultant. For example, a dispute may arise between a benefit claimant and the Benefits Agency in respect of whether pneumoconiosis is a disease or not. An MAT will adjudicate on such matters. Again, here the tribunal will be chaired by a lawyer. Part of the hearing in these cases involves a medical examination of the appellant by the medical practitioners. The benefits often determined by this tribunal are: severe disablement allowance and industrial disablement benefit.

Disability Appeal Tribunals (DAT)

From 1991, DATs hear appeals relating to disability living allowance and attendance allowance. As with SSATs this tribunal consists of a chairperson and two lay persons, though one of the lay member should be disabled. Also, these tribunals have two panels: the first is a medical one (chair, plus two doctors); and the second, is the tribunal panel (chair, plus two lay persons, one of which is disabled). No medical examinations are undertaken by this tribunal.

Child Support Appeal Tribunals (CSAT)

Since 1991, the law relating to child support, briefly dealt with in Chapter 8, has evolved. Alongside its enactment came another appeal tribunal, the CSAT. This tribunal adjudicates on the system of calculating maintenance for children from parents who are no longer living together. Consequently, CSATs differ from the other tribunals in that both parties, ie both parents, are both present at the hearing. Again, this tribunal is serviced by a chair and two lay persons, but all cannot be of the same sex.

Social Fund Officer

All claims concerning the Social Fund are determined by the Social Fund Officer, against whom there is no further appeal. Although, judicial review proceedings can be initiated.

Reviews and appeals relating to housing benefit, council tax benefit or rent are not subject to tribunals, but special review boards, organised by the appropriate local authorities concerned. Furthermore, war pensions appeals are governed by the War pensions Agency and a special Pensions Appeal Tribunal, established in 1943 and 1949, and under the jurisdiction of the Lord Chancellor, or Lord President in Scotland, or Lord Chief Justice in Northern Ireland.

All of these tribunals exist under one umbrella, which is coordinated by the Independent Tribunal Service (ITS) and each locality is served by its own tribunal. There are about 275 centres in the UK organised by Regional Chairmen/women, who administer local tribunals. As the title 'ITS' suggests, all of the people involved in these Tribunals, either the chairman/women (lawyers), members (local, lay people) or medical assessors (GPs, Consultants) are strictly independent and have no connections with the Department of Social Security, or the Benefits Agency. The Chairperson provides the legal expert and takes control of proceedings, determining the rules and procedures to be followed. Each tribunal is assisted by a clerk who administers the proceedings, whilst taking no part in them. In addition, appeals before all of these tribunals are heard on matters of law. Namely, that the appellants are claiming that the Adjudication Officer has made a decision which is wrong in law.

These tribunals therefore hear cases on the entitlements of claimants to benefits which have been denied or stopped; about late claims and 'good cause' claims (late claims which merit acceptance); and also about people's incapacity for work; and day-to-day disability, and/or poverty and needs. There is no right of appeal, *per se*, on the Jobseeker's Agreement. The job seeker must first of all have sought a review by the AO.

Hearings are informal and strict rules of evidence are used. In fact, no swearing on oath, as in courts of law and Industrial Tribunals, occurs. Usually, the Chairperson introduces the people present in the tribunal room and explains why the hearing is taking place. Then, a benefits agency AO or presenting officer will put the Department of Social Security's case, after which the appellant (formerly the claimant) or his representative or friend will put the case. Each will be able to ask each other questions and the Tribunal will ask questions. Normally, all the parties will be asked to leave and only those who will be determining the case will remain in the room to confidentially discuss the case and reach a decision. The parties will then either be informed orally on the day or by latter after the proceedings of the outcome of the appeal. More recently, attempts have been made to expedite appeal and as a result, appellants are given the choice as to whether they wish to attend and out their case orally, or have it dealt with *ex parte*. That is, in the absence of all the parties. Hence, paper hearings have become increasingly commonplace In these proceedings, the appeal tribunal meets in private and determines the case on the basis of the papers only. Afterwards, all the parties concerned receive a written decision from the tribunal.

Commissioners

Whatever type of hearing is convened, a further appeal to the Social Security Commissioners from an SSAT, MAT or DAT; or the Child Support Commissioners from an CSAT, is available to both the DSS and the appellant after the appeal tribunal's hearing. This lies on a point of law. Leave to appeal must be obtained, from either a Commissioner or the Chairwoman/man of a tribunal and must be lodged within 42 days from the date of the tribunal's decision. Again, these appeals can either be on paper, written submissions only, or orally. As with the abovementioned tribunals, all the parties will be represented before the Commissioner.

Appeals from the Commissioners' lie to any appropriate court of law with leave from the Commissioner or the court. Again a 42 days time limit applies.

Note: Recently, the government has published its Social Security Bill which seeks to simplify procedures and the appeals adjudications system surrounding benefits.

Practice points

In housing matters, social workers should check:

- status of occupier – owner or tenant;
- security of tenure;
- type of landlord;
- urgency and seriousness;
- options available.

In money advice issues, social workers should check:

- the income of the client;
- the expenditure of the client;
- prioritise the debts;
- advise about bailiff's rights;
- consider bankruptcy, if applicable;
- avoid repossession and eviction;
- attend court or write a report for court or arrange legal representation, or further advice from a financial specialist or legal practitioner.

With regard to benefits, social workers should check:

- whether the client is employed or self-employed;
- what needs do they have;
- what benefits cover their needs;
- what benefits are they entitled to;
- what claim form should they fill in;
- if their claim is rejected what action should they take – reapply or appeal;
- if they need to appeal (want to appeal) who can assist them and/or represent at the tribunal;
- what solicitors/voluntary organisations with welfare rights experience exist in your area.

Further reading

Arden, A, *Manual of Housing Law*, 1995, London: Sweet and Maxwell.

Burnet, D, *Introduction to Housing Law*, 1996, London: Cavendish Publishing.

CCETSW, *Welfare Rights*, Paper 16, February 1993.

Child Support Handbook, 1996, London: Child Poverty Action Group.

Disability Rights Handbook, 1996, London: Disability Alliance.

National Welfare Benefits Handbook, 1997, London: Child Poverty Action Group.

Wolfe, M, *Debt Advice Handbook*, 2nd edn, 1995, London: Child Poverty Action Group.

PART VI

THE MODERN SOCIAL WORKER: LEGAL ADVICE AND ACTION

26 Advice work and legal aid[*]

In this final part of the book, we examine the skills required by a social worker in a legal context; the availability of legal aid; and evaluate the legal competence of the modern social worker in the 1990s.

The High Court gave a startling decision recently about the rights of access to courts which most clearly has ramifications on the cost of law and also the assistance to which any citizen is entitled. In the *Witham* case, the highest judicial office in the UK, the Lord Chancellor, was challenged for the raising of court fees. An action which resulted in an increase in fees which according to Mr Witham prevented him from bringing his case to court. Both Rose LJ and Laws J agreed that access to the courts was a constitutional right and that the raising of fees causing hardship to those persons on benefits or low incomes income, in fact denied those persons of their constitutional right of access to the courts (see *R v Lord Chancellor ex p Witham* (1997) *The Times*, 13 March).

The legal aid system

According to 'Striking the balance' (Report on Legal Aid (1996)): 'Legal aid will, in principle, be capable of providing any help – not just from lawyers – that can either (1) prevent court proceedings ..., or (2) promote their settlement or other, ...'

The Legal Aid Scheme in the UK, since its inception in 1972 under the so-called 'Green Form' scheme, has been divided between: criminal, family and civil, legal aid (see Appendix 1, Green Form Application). All legal aid, however, is granted according to the merits of the case and the individual person's financial means.

Eligibility for legal aid

From 7 April 1997 the following financial eligibility limits were enacted:

---

* The authors thank the Legal Aid Board for their co-operation with the writing of this chapter

'Green Form' (Advice/Assistance) Legal Aid

Capital limits

0 dependants	£1,000.00
1 dependant	£1,335.00
2 dependants	£1,535.00

Income limit .... £77.00 pw

Civil Legal Aid

Capital limits

lower limit	£3,000.00
upper limit	£6,750.00

Income limits

lower limit	£2,563.00
upper limit	£7,595.00

Criminal Legal Aid

Capital limit £3,000.00

Income limit .... £50.00 pw

'ABWOR' (Advice/Assistance) Legal Aid

Capital limits

0 dependants	£3,000.00
1 dependant	£3,335.00
2 dependants	£3,535.00

Income limits

lower limit	£69.00 pw
upper limit	£166.00 pw

Due to these thresholds it is common nowadays for litigants to contribute to their legal costs.

The Legal Aid Board

Legal aid is governed by the Legal Aid Board (LAB). The duty of LAB is to ensure that the best price for quality services to met people's requirements, in terms of advice and assistance, is achieved. The LAB also produces and enforces a code of practice, containing directions and guidance on legal aid advice and assistance.

Legal aid franchising

Since 1994, some legal aid services have been provided under contracts, known as franchises, between the LAB and various providers, from either the private or voluntary sectors. Under this franchising, the LAB has devolved its powers to solicitors, law centres and other advice agencies. Franchising has become widespread, particularly in personal injury, family matters and welfare benefits.

Advising your clients and non-clients in civil legal aid matters

Whilst this book has already dealt with criminal litigation legal aid in some detail in Chapter 13 above, we now focus briefly on civil legal aid.

As has already been established, when we talk of civil legal aid, we mean both family and civil, in more general terms. In any event, both civil and family legal aid, ie giving advice and assistance, is subject to a simple means-test undertaken by the provider. Benefits claimants receive free advice and assistance. others may be asked to contribute towards some of the cost. A minimum contribution is payable by all assisted persons, except benefits claimants. See the tables in Chapter 22.

Where you can get advice from

A wide variety of organisations and statutory bodies provide information and advice on rights. These include government departments, voluntary organisations, charities and welfare rights organisations. Below are some of the most common ones:

Citizens' Advice Bureaux (CABx)

A generalist, national organisation of advice agencies. CABx are largely funded by local authorities and are run by management committees who are made up of representatives of the local community. Most of a CABx's staff are volunteers. Each are listed in your local telephone directory. They provide advice and information on almost anything and are free, independent and confidential. Providing a non–judgmental service, local CABx are provided with information and support from NACAB (the National Association of CABx, the HQ of agencies in London), who arrange for the training of all the volunteers. Often, some CABx will provide representation in both the courts and various tribunals.

Law centres

Law centres, usually found in large urban areas, are staffed by qualified lawyers. They will largely advise on a variety of legal issues and represent clients for free in court and elsewhere.

Local authority advice centres

Formerly known as 'council welfare rights units', these advice centres which are open to the public, very often are usually a support organisation for the staff of a local authority. However, many in 1997 mainly provide information and advice on welfare rights' issues, housing and consumer affairs. Details of these are usually in the local press and/or libraries.

Neighbourhood/community centres

An emerging force in the 1990s, neighbourhood and community centres, if not run by the local authority, CAB, church or a charity, are largely a base for self–help, such as tenants, women, lone parents and pensioners.

Advice for young people

Young persons' advice centres, typically provide information and advice on drugs, contraception, unemployment, education, training and other welfare/legal issues.

Specialist advice

For any specialist advice on specific issues, such as housing, consumer affairs, counselling, disability and many others. See your local telephone directory or contact a local charity or agency for further assistance.

For further information can be retrieved from either the Social Services Yearbook, the Charities Digest, or Whittakers Alamanc.

Legal aid review

Lord Irvine of Lairg, the Labour government's newly–installed Lord Chancellor, has recently announced that legal aid provision will be reviewed. The last reforms were recommended by the Royal Commission on legal services, chaired by Lord Benson, in 1979. This new review, however, is to be undertaken by Sir Peter Middleton, deputy chairman of Barclays Bank. It is the intention of this review to see what legal aid, society can afford and what people are willing to pay within the overall context of public expenditure demands. The Report of this review is expected sometime during this forthcoming September.

Practice points

When giving advice, social workers should:

- ensure that it is accurate;

- maintain their professional ethics at all times;

- think practically and legally, utilising their professionalism and common sense;

- know when to seek specialist advice;

- know where to seek further advice from and who is most appropriate within their locality .

In terms of legal aid provision, social workers ought to:

- understand the framework and rationale underlying the UK legal aid system;

- know the differences between criminal, civil and ABWOR legal aid;

- be fully conversant with the latest legal aid eligibility thresholds, relevant to each type of legal aid;

- recognise the relevance of legal aid franchising and how this might affect the local provision of legal aid amongst local legal practitioners.

Overall, social workers should be:

- fact-finders;

- objective;

- realistic;

- honest, accurate and professional at all times.

Further reading

Legal Aid Board, *Guidance*, 1997, London: HMSO.

Morby, G, *Know How to Find Out Your Rights*, 1982, London: Pluto Press

Social Services Year Book – 1996, London: Pitman Publishing.

27 The modern social worker[*]

Many social work practitioners argue that the face of social work has dramatically changed over the last decade. Some social workers believe that the traditional skills of the social worker, based largely on good interpersonal skills, have become second place to business efficiency and costs. From a legal perspective, both need to exist and be exercised in order to ensure that the statutory duties are fulfilled and that the job is done successfully in the best interests of the client. As the contents of this text have demonstrated to be able to both communicate effectively, seek accurate advice from the right people and to ensure that you understand your client's case and that your client understands your role and advice are the hallmarks of a professional social work practitioner. Above all, this text has sought to clearly show that a full and thorough understanding of the law, or at very least a knowledge of where to find the law or from whom to seek advice, makes for responsible social work practice and reduces the prospects of litigation against you and your employer.

The legal context and legal competence

CCETSW quite regularly sets out the qualities and competences required of the social worker in practice. In a legal context, it becomes clear from this text and guidance given by CCETSW and practitioners in social work and law, that modern social workers need:

- to be competent advocates for their clients;

- to be clear communicators;

- to be effective negotiators;

- to have good interpersonal skills;

- to practice in an anti-oppressive manner;

- to recognise the theoretical and value bases in which they work;

- to respect other professionals, both in social work and related fields;

---

[*] Lastly we must thank the many social workers who have spoken to us about their need for further legal training in social work. We hope that this text has contributed somewhere towards filling the gap they desire to be filled.

- to be realistic at all times in their practice;

- to be knowledgeable in their specialism;

- to recognise the importance of research in improving their practice or in challenging practices;

- to understand, implement and apply the law.

All of these qualities are recognised by the law in the statutory framework which surrounds social work practice. To that end, modern social workers need to be more legally aware and competent when tackling legal issues.

Continuing education and the perennial student

Clearly social work students and practitioners alike must keep up with legal developments. To that end, anyone involved in social work is a perennial student. It is hoped that the chapters of this book have assisted all readers on where to find the relevant and up-to-date information.

Legal reform

Following the election of a new Labour government legal reform and reform of the legal profession will most certainly be on the agenda. It is likely that the legal profession, for instance, will be referred to the Monopolies and Mergers Commission and many of the issues discussed and others will be placed under review and future reform will be enacted. As above, in response to this students and practitioners alike must follow closely any proposed developments. The simplest way to do this, is to read daily newspapers, who often take note of any substantial changes. Otherwise, consult the government department concerned.

Guidance on employment

CCETSW's existing guidance on employment clearly explains where the major sources of employment for social workers lies and the training required, setting out the experience and qualities required for social work. In 1997, the qualities which a social worker needs are:

- tact and diplomacy;

- knowledge;

- commonsense;

- social awareness;

- anti-oppressive/discriminatory person;

- conscientious; and

- cope with pressure/pressurised situations.

Ready for action!

Having reached the final page of this book, you should now be equipped to deal with the many complex legal decisions that you will have to make in your professional life, if not first and foremost your professional and other examinations. Hopefully you will take this book with you, beyond your studies and into practice, continuing to use it as a reliable friend and confidant. Good luck and be vigilant of the law and its consequences always!

Further reading

'Guidance on Employment', Paper 19, CCETSW, July 1996.

Appendix 1 – specimen forms

The following forms are intended to familiarise students and practitioners with the most common processes and paperwork for:

- a s 8 order (Children Act order);
- a domestic violence injunction;
- an application for ancillary relief;
- a legal aid (Green Form) application;
- an application to commence proceedings before an Industrial Tribunal.

By studying these, readers ought to understand further their importance in social work practice.

Application for an order

Form C1

Children Act 1989

The court

To be completed by the court

Date issued

Case number

The full name(s) of the child(ren)

Child(ren)'s number(s)

1 About you (the applicant)

State • *your title, full name, address, telephone number, date of birth and*
relationship to each child above
• *your solicitor's name, address, reference, telephone, FAX and DX numbers.*

2 The child(ren) and the order(s) you are applying for

For each child state • *the full name, date of birth and sex*
• *the type of order(s) you are applying for (for example, residence order,*
contact order, supervision order).

C1

Tel: 0161-745 8222   Meredith Fournat

1

3 Other cases which concern the child(ren)

If there have ever been, or there are pending, any court cases which concern
- *a child whose name you have put in paragraph 2*
- *a full, half or step brother or sister of a child whose name you have put in paragraph 2*
- *a person in this case who is or has been, involved in caring for a child whose name you have put in paragraph 2*

attach a copy of the relevant order and give
- *the name of the court*
- *the name and **panel** address (if known) of the guardian ad litem, if appointed*
- *the name and contact address (if known) of the court welfare officer, if appointed*
- *the name and contact address (if known) of the solicitor appointed for the child(ren).*

4 The respondent(s)

Appendix 3 Family Proceedings Rules 1991; Schedule 2 Family Proceedings Courts (Children Act 1989) Rules 1991

For each respondent state
- *the title, full name and address*
- *the date of birth (if known) or the age*
- *the relationship to each child.*

C1

5 Others to whom notice is to be given

Appendix 3 Family Proceedings Rules 1991; Schedule 2 Family Proceedings Courts (Children Act 1989) Rules 1991
For each person state • *the title, full name and address*
• *the date of birth (if known) or age*
• *the relationship to each child*

6 The care of the child(ren)

For each child in paragraph 2 state
• *the child's current address and how long the child has lived there*
• *whether it is the child's usual address and who cares for the child there*
• *the child's relationship to the other children (if any).*

7 Social Services

For each child in paragraph 2 state
• *whether the child is known to the Social Services.*
  If so, give the name of the social worker and the address of the Social Services department.
• *whether the child is, or has been, on the Child Protection Register. If so, give the date of registration.*

C1

8 The education and health of the child(ren)

For each child state
- *the name of the school, college or place of training which the child attends*
- *whether the child is in good health. Give details of any serious disabilities or ill health.*
- *whether the child has any special needs.*

9 The parents of the child(ren)

For each child state
- *the full name of the child's mother and father*
- *whether the parents are, or have been, married to each other*
- *whether the parents live together. If so, where.*
- *whether, to your knowledge, either of the parents have been involved in a court case concerning a child. If so, give the date and the name of the court.*

10 The family of the child(ren) (other children)

For any other child not already mentioned in the family (for example, a brother or a half sister) state
- *the full name and address*
- *the date of birth (if known) or age*
- *the relationship of the child to you.*

C1

361

11 Other adults

State • *the full name of any other adults (for example, lodgers) who live at the same address as any child named in paragraph 2*
 • *whether they live there all the time*
 • *whether, to your knowledge, the adult has been involved in a court case concerning a child. If so, give the date and the name of the court.*

12 Your reason(s) for applying and any plans for the child(ren)

State briefly your reasons for applying and what you want the court to order.
 • ***Do not*** *give a full statement if you are applying for an order under Section 8 of Children Act 1989. You may be asked to provide a full statement later.*
 • ***Do not*** *complete this section if this form is accompanied by a prescribed supplement.*

13 At the court

State • *whether you will need an interpreter at court (parties are responsible for providing their own). If so, specify the language.*
 • *whether disabled facilities will be needed at court.*

Signed   Date
(Applicant)

C1

Application for Injunction

(General Form)

Between

_____

and

_____

☐ Plaintiff
☐ Applicant
☐ Petitioner
(Tick whichever applies)

☐ Defendant
☐ Respondent

In the

County Court

Case No *Always quote this*

Plaintiff's Ref

Defendant's Ref

Seal

Notes on completion

Tick whichever box applies

(1) Enter the full name of the person making the application

(2) Enter the full name of the person the injunction is to be directed to

(3) Set out here the proposed restraining orders (if the defendant is a limited company delete the wording in brackets and insert 'Whether by its servants, agents, officers or otherwise')

(4) Set out here any proposed mandatory orders requiring acts to be done

(5) Set out here any further terms asked for including provision for costs

(6) Enter the names of all persons who have sworn affidavits in support of this application

(7) Enter the names and addresses of all persons upon whom it is intended to serve this application

(8) Enter the full name and address for service and delete as required

☐ By application in pending proceedings
☐ In the matter of the Domestic Violence and Matrimonial Proceedings Act 1976

The Plaintiff (Applicant/Petitioner)[1]

applies to the court for an injunction order in the following terms:
That the Defendant (Respondent)[2]

be forbidden (whether by himself or by instructing or encouraging any other person)[3]

And that the Defendant (Respondent)[4]

And that[5]

The grounds of this application are set out in the sworn statement(s) of[6]

This (these) sworn statement(s) is (are) served with this application.
This application is to be served upon[7]

This application is filed by[8]
(the Solicitors for) the Plaintiff (Applicant/Petitioner)
whose address for service is

Signed   Dated

This section to be completed by the court

* *Name and address of the person application is directed to*

To *
of
This application will be heard by the (District) Judge
at
on   the   day of   199   at   o'clock
If you do not attend at the time shown the court may make an injunction order in your absence.
If you do not fully understand this application, you should go to a Solicitor, Legal Advice Centre or a Citizens' Advice Bureau

The Court Office at
is open from 10 am to 4 pm. When corresponding with the court, address all forms and letters to the Chief Clerk and quote the case number.

Form F 1172 (N16A) General form of application for injunction (O.13, r 6(3); O. 47, r.8(2).
This edition © 1991 Meredith Fourmat

Meredith Fourmat
Tel: 0161-745 8222

† Amend if the proceedings are pending in the High Court

In the

County Court †
[Principal Registry]
No of matter:

(Seal)

Between _____ Petitioner

and _____ Respondent

[and _____ Co- Respondent]

Notice of application for ancillary relief

TAKE NOTICE THAT the petitioner [*or* respondent] intends to apply to the Court for

* Here set out the ancillary relief claimed, stating the terms of any agreement as to the order which the court is to be asked to make and, in the case of an application for a property adjustment order or an avoidance of disposition order, stating briefly the nature of the adjustment proposed or the disposition to be set aside. If the application is to *vary* periodical payments or secured periodical payments for *children*, state here whether there are or have been any proceedings in the Child Support Agency relating to their maintenance.

*

If you are applying for any periodical payments or secured periodical payments for children, please say whether you are applying for payment:

☐　for a step child or step children

☐　in addition to child support maintenance already paid under a Child Support Agency assessment

☐　to meet expenses arising from a child's disability

☐　to meet expenses incurred by a child in being educated or training for work

☐　when either • the child OR • the person with care of the child OR • the absent parent of the child is not habitually resident in the United Kingdom

☐　other (please specify)

Notice of application
for ancillary relief

Form F916 (M11)
© Fourmat Publishing
133 Upper Street
London N1 1QP
April 1993

PTO

Notice will be given to you of the place and time fixed for the hearing of the
application [*or* The application will be heard by the district judge in chambers at

on _____the _____ day of _____ 19 _____
at _____ o' clock.]

The probable length of the hearing of this application is

[*Unless the parties are agreed upon the terms of the proposed order, or the
application is for a variation order, add:*

TAKE NOTICE ALSO THAT you must send to the district judge, so as to reach him
within twenty-eight days after you receive a copy of the affidavit of the petitioner
[*or* respondent], an affidavit giving full particulars of your property and income. You
must at the same time send a copy of your affidavit to [the solicitor for] the
applicant. **A standard form of affidavit may be obtained from the court office.**
    If you wish to allege that the petitioner [*or* respondent] has property or income,
you should say so in your affidavit.]

Dated this _____ day of _____ 19 _____

Signed _____ [Solicitor for the] Petitioner
                                                                                    [*or* Respondent]

Green Form

To be used ONLY by solicitors with a
franchise contract which covers the
category of work into which this
green form falls

GF 7 [Key Card]

LEGAL AID BOARD LEGAL AID ACT 1988

Legal aid
account no:

Ref:

(Copy from extension / authority before sending claim)

➤ If you do not have a franchise contract covering the category of work into which this claim falls, complete form GF1.

➤ If you give advice and assistance about making a will you must submit form GF4 with your claim.

➤ You should keep a copy of the entire green form.

Client's details
*Please use block capitals *Delete the one which does not apply* Male/Female*

Surname: _____ First names: _____

Address: _____

Postcode: _____

National
Insurance No: ☐☐☐☐☐ Date of birth: _____ [A]

Capital details
(give these details even if the client gets income support, family credit or disability working allowance)

How many dependants (partner, children or other relatives of his/her household) does the client have? _____

Give the total savings and other capital which the client has (and if relevant his or her partner)

Client: £ _____

Spouse (or person living as if a spouse of the client): £ _____

Total: £ _____

Income details [B]

Does the client get Income Support, Family Credit or Disability Working Allowance?

☐ Yes: ignore the rest of this section   ☐ No: give the total gross weekly income of

The client: £ _____

The client's spouse (or person living as if a spouse of the client): £ _____

Total: £ _____

Calculate the total allowable deductions: Income tax: £ _____ [C]

National Insurance contributions: £ _____ [D]

Spouse (or person living as if a spouse of the client): £ _____ [E]

Attendance allowance, disability living allowance, constant
attendance allowance and any payment made out of the Social Fund: £ _____ [F]

Dependent children and other dependants: Age   Number

Under 11 _____   £ _____

11 to 15 _____   £ _____

16 to 17 _____   £ _____ [G]

18 and over _____   £ _____

Less total deductions: £ _____

Total weekly disposable income: £ _____

Client's declaration

I confirm that:
➤ I am over the compulsory school-leaving age (or, if not, the solicitor is advising me under Regulation 14(2A) Legal Advice & Assistance Regulations 1989);

➤ I have/have not *(delete whichever one is not correct)* previously received help from a solicitor on this matter under the green form; and

➤ I understand that I might have to pay my solicitor's costs out of any property or money which is recovered or preserved for me.

As far as I am aware, the information on this page is correct. I understand that if I give false information I could be prosecuted.

Signed: _____   Date: ___/___/___

95/4/18

Attach a completed Form GF3 as proof of every financial extension (including any granted under devolved powers)

Category of problem *Please tick the relevant box*

☐ Personal injury ☐ Debt ☐ Housing ☐ Welfare benefits ☐ Crime ☐ Immigration ☐ Employment

☐ Consumer/general contract

☐ Matrimonial/family: *please also tick one of the following boxes:*

☐ Petitioner in divorce or judicial separation ☐ Child support assessment

☐ Other *specify in the summary* ☐ Respondent in divorce or judicial separation ☐ Other family matters *(please specify in the summary)*

Solicitor charge

Has any money or property been recovered for the client? ☐ No: go on to the next section ☐ Yes: please give details:

_____

_____

Devolved powers

Was an extension granted under devolved powers? ☐ No: go on to the next section ☐ Yes: please give date devolved powers were first exercised and complete and attach form GF3 with this form   /   /

Have you exercised devolved powers by accepting an application from a child/patient? ☐ No ☐ Yes: please give details in the summary below

Have you exercised devolved powers by accepting an application from a client resident outside England or Wales? ☐ No ☐ Yes: please give details in the summary below

Have you exercised devolved powers by accepting an application where advice has been given by a previous solicitor? ☐ No ☐ Yes: please give details in the summary below

Was telephone advice given before the Green Form was signed? ☐ No ☐ Yes: please explain why in the summary below & include the amount claimed in the attendances time

Did you attend the client away from the office before the Green Form was signed *(you can claim outward travel costs but not time)*? ☐ No ☐ Yes: please explain why in the summary below & include your outward travel costs in the disbursements section

Was this a postal application? ☐ No ☐ Yes: please explain why in the summary below

Summary of work

Has a legal aid certificate or order been granted or applied for? ☐ No ☐ Yes: give the reference _____

Please give below a brief summary of the work done *(if necessary continue on a separate piece of paper and attach it to this claim):*

	Preparation	Attendance	Travel
Total time			
old rate:			
current rate:			
Total costs			
old rate:	£	£	£
current rate:	£	£	£

Details of disbursements	£	VAT
Counsel's fees:		
Mileage:		
Other disbursements:		
Totals		

Letters and Telephone Calls *(not telephone advice calls)*	Number	£
Letters written old rate:		
current rate:		
Telephone calls old rate:		
current rate:		
Totals		

	Claimed	Area office use only Assessed
Profit costs: £	£	£
VAT on profit costs: £	£	£
Total disbursements: £	£	£
VAT on disbursements: £	£	£
Total claim: £	£	£

I certify that all the information given in this claim is correct: I have not claimed and will not otherwise claim for the same items from the Legal Aid Fund and I have held a valid practising certificate throughout the conduct of this matter.

Solicitor's personal signature:_____ Date:___/___/___ Sol ref:_____

Name & address of firm/office:_____

May 1995

Application to an Industrial Tribunal

Notes for Guidance

Before filling in this form please read:
- **these guidance notes**
- **Leaflet ITL1 which you were given with this form**
- **the correct booklet for your type of case**

Information
There are many things you can complain to a Tribunal about. Leaflet ITL1 tells you what they are, which law (an Act of Parliament) covers your complaint and which booklet you should get. Each of the booklets explains the law in simple terms. You can get the booklets free from any employment office, Jobcentre or Unemployment Benefit Office. If you are in doubt, your Trade Union or a Citizens' Advice Bureau may be able to give you further advice or information.

Time Limits
You must send in your application form so that it arrives at the Central Office of the Industrial Tribunals within the time limit. The time limit depends on which complaint you are making; for example, for unfair dismissal complaints it is three months beginning with the date of dismissal. So if you were dismissed on 10th January, the form must arrive by 9th April.

Qualifying periods
There are rules about how long you have to work for an employer before you can bring a case to a Tribunal. These rules are explained in the booklets.

If you are in any doubt about the time limits or qualifying periods, please contact your local employment office, Jobcentre or Unemployment Benefit Office; or get in touch with the Advisory Conciliation and Arbitration Service (ACAS) - see leaflet ITL1 for addresses and telephone numbers.

Representatives
You can present your own case at the Tribunal. If you want someone else to present your case, try to consult him or her before you complete your application form, but remember your form must arrive within the **time limit. If you name a representative, all future dealings will be with him or her and not with you.** If you name a representative, you should ask him or her any questions you have about the progress of your case and when the Tribunal hearing will be.

If your complaint concerns equal pay or sex discrimination, you may wish to contact the Equal Opportunities Commission for advice or representation. If your complaint is about racial discrimination, you may wish to contact the Commission for Racial Equality for advice or representation.

Help for people with disabilities
If you, or anyone who needs to visit a Tribunal, are disabled and may have difficulty getting in or out of the office, or using normal seating or toilets, please inform our staff at the office where your case is being handled. They will do all they can to help.

Data Protection Act 1984

We may put some of the information you give in this form on to a computer. This helps us to monitor progress and produce statistics. We may also give information :

- to the other party in the case;
- for the same purposes, to other parts of the Employment Department Group and organisations such as the Advisory, Conciliation and Arbitration Service (ACAS), the Equal Opportunities Commission or the Commission for Racial Equality.

Filling in the form

Help
Your Trade Union or local Citizens' Advice Bureau may be able to help you fill in the form if you have any problems, but make sure your form arrives within the **time limit.**

Questions to answer
Try to complete all the boxes that apply in your case. You must answer the questions in boxes 1, 2, 4, 8 and 10.

Be clear
This form has to be photocopied, so please use black ink, or type your answers, and use **CAPITAL LETTERS** for names and addresses. Where boxes appear in this form which give you a choice of answer(s), please tick those that apply. If there is not enough space for your answer, please continue on a separate sheet of paper and attach it to this form.

Box 1
Put here the type of complaint you want the Tribunal to decide (for example, unfair dismissal, redundancy payment, equal pay etc). A full list of types of complaint is given in leaflet ITL 1. If there is more than one complaint you want the Tribunal to decide, please say so. Give the details of your complaints in Box 10.

Box 2
Give your name and address and date of birth, and if possible a telephone number where the Tribunal or ACAS can contact you during the day about your application.

Box 4
Give details of the employer, body or person (the "respondent") you wish to complain about. In the second box, give the place where you worked or applied for work, if different from that of the respondent you have named. (For example, complete both boxes if you have named a liquidator, the Secretary of State for Employment, or your employer's Head Office as the respondent).

Box 10
Give full details of your complaint. If there is not enough room on the form, continue on a separate sheet and attach it to the form. Do NOT send any other documents or evidence in support of your complaint at this stage. Your answer may be used in an initial assessment of your case, so make it as complete and accurate as you can. (See **Help** above).

When you have finished:
- **sign and date the form**
- **keep these guidance notes and a copy of your answers**
- **send the form to:**

ENGLAND AND WALES
The Secretary of the Tribunals,
Central Office of the Industrial Tribunals,
Southgate Street,
Bury St Edmunds,
Suffolk,
IP33 2AQ.
Telephone 0284 762300

SCOTLAND
The Secretary of the Tribunals,
Central Office of the Industrial Tribunals (Scotland),
St Andrew House,
141 West Nile Street,
Glasgow,
G1 2RU.
Telephone 041 331 1601

FOR COIT USE ONLY

Received at COIT	Case Number	Code
	Initials	ROIT

Application to an Industrial Tribunal

Please read the notes opposite before filling in this form

1. Say what type of complaint(s) you want the tribunal to decide *(see note opposite)*.

2. Please give your name and address in CAPITALS

Mr ☐   Mrs ☐   Miss ☐   Ms ☐

Surname

First name(s)

Address

Postcode

Telephone

Date of birth

3. Please give the name and address of your representative, if you have one.

Name

Address

Postcode

Telephone

4. Please give the details of the employer or body (the respondent) you are complaining about *(see note opposite)*.

Name

Address

Postcode

Telephone

Please give the place where you worked or applied for work, if different from above.

Name

Address

Postcode

Telephone

5. Please say what job you did for the employer (or what job you applied for). If this does not apply, please say what your connection was with the employer.

IT 1 and IT 1(Scot) (Revised Feb 1991) ———————————————— Over ▶

6. Please give the number of normal basic hours you worked per week.

Hours [ ] per week

8. Please give the dates of your employment. *(if applicable)*

Began on [ ]

Ended on [ ]

7. Basic wage/ salary £ [ ] per [ ]

Average take home pay £ [ ] per [ ]

Other bonuses or benefits £ [ ] per [ ]

9. If your complaint is not about dismissal, please give the date when the action you are complaining about took place (or the date when you first knew about it).

Date [ ]

10. Please give full details of your complaint *(see notes attached)*:

11. **Unfair dismissal claimants only** *(Please tick a box to show what you would want if you win your case)*

[ ] **Reinstatement:** to carry on working in your old job as before. ──────

[ ] **Re-engagement:** to start another job, or a new contract, with your old employer. ──────

→ Orders for re-instatement or re-engagement normally include an award of compensation for loss of earnings.

[ ] **Compensation only:** to get an award of money.

You can change your change your mind later. The Tribunal will take your preference into account, but will not be bound by it.

12. Have you already sent us a copy of this application by facsimile transmission (fax)?

Yes [ ]   No [ ]

Signed [ ]   Date [ ]

508 / 91 ¹ ¹

Appendix 2 – useful addresses

Age Concern
1268 London Road
London SW16 4ER
Tel: 0181 679 8000 Fax: 0181 679 6069

Arbitration, Conciliation and Conciliation Service (ACAS)
27 Wilton Street
London SW1X 7AZ
Tel: 0171 210 3000 Fax: 0171 210 3708

Association of Directors of Social Services
c/o Devon County Council
County Hall
Topsham Road
Exeter
Devon EX2 4QR
Tel: 01392 384947 Fax: 01392 384984

Association of Residential Care
ARC House
Marsden Street
Chesterfield
Derbyshire S40 1JY
Tel: 01246 555043 Fax: 01246 555045

Barnados
Tanners Lane
Barkingside
Ilford
Essex IG6 1QC
Tel: 0181 550 8822 Fax: 0181 551 6870

British Association of Social Workers
16 Kent Street
Birmingham B5 6RD
Tel: 0121 622 3911 Fax: 0121 622 4860

Carers National Association
20–25 Glasshouse Yard
London EC1A 4JS
Tel: 0171 490 8818 Fax: 0171 490 5824

Central Council for the Education & Training of Social Workers (CCETSW)
Derbyshire House
St Chad's Street
London WC1H 8AD
Tel: 0171 278 2455 Fax: 0171 278 2934

Central Office of the Industrial Tribunals (England and Wales) (COIT)
100 Southgate Street
Bury St Edmunds
Suffolk IP33 2AQ
Tel: 01284 762300 Fax: 01284 766334

Children's Legal Centre
20 Compton Terrace
London N1 2UN
Tel: 0171 359 9392 Fax: 0171 354 9963

Commission for Racial Equality (CRE)
Elliot House
10–12 Allington Street
London SW1E 5EH
Tel: 0171 828 7022 Fax: 0171 630 7605

Crown Prosecution Service (CPS)
50 Ludgate Hill
London EC4M 7EX
Tel: 0171 273 8152

Equal Opportunities Commission (EOC)
Overseas House
Quay Street
Manchester M3 3HN
Tel: 0161 8339244 Fax: 0161 8351657

EU Commission (London Office)
8 Storey's Gate
London SW1P 3AT
Tel: 0171 973 1992 Fax: 0171 973 1900

European Commission and Court of Human Rights (ECHR)
67006 Strasbourg
Cedex
France
Tel: 001 33 88 41 20 0692

European Parliament (London Office)
Queen Anne's Gate
London SW1P
Tel: 0171 227 4300 Fax: 0171 227 4302

Free Representation Unit (FRU)
Room 140
First Floor
49–51 Bedford Row
London WC1R 4LR
Tel/Fax: 0171 831 0692 Fax: 0171 831 2398

Health and Safety Executive (HSE)
Baynard's House
1 Chepstow Place
London W2 4TE
Tel/fax: 0171 221 0870

Home Office – Immigration and Nationality Department
Lunar House
Wellesley Road
Croydon CR9 2BY
Tel: 0181 686 0688 Fax: 0181 760 1181

Home Office – Asylum Division
Quest House
11 Cross Road
Croydon CR9 2BY
Tel: 0181 686 0688 Fax: 0181 760 1181

House of Commons (for MPs)
House of Commons
Westminster
London SW1A 0AA
Tel: 0171 219 3000

House of Lords
House of Lords
Westminster
London SW1A 0PW
Tel: 0171 219 3000

Human Rights Watch
33 Islington High Street
London N1 9LH
Tel: 0171 713 1995 Fax: 0171 713 1800

Joint Council for the Welfare of Immigrants (JCWI)
115 Old Street
London EC1V 9JR
Tel: 0171 251 8706 Fax: 0171 251 5110

JUSTICE
59 Carter Lane
London EC4V 5AQ
Tel: 0171 329 5100 Fax: 0171 329 5055

Law Centres Federation (LCF)
Duchess House
18 Warren Street
London W1P 5DP
Tel/Fax: 0171 387 8570

Law Commission
Conquest House
37–38 John Street
Theobalds Road
London WC1N 2BQ
Tel: 0171 453 1220 Fax: 0171 453 1297

Law Society
Duchess House
113 Chancery Lane
London WC2A 1PL
Tel: 0171 242 1222

Legal Action Group (LAG)
242–244 Pentonville Road
London N1 9UN
Tel: 0171 833 2931 Fax: 0171 833 6094

Liberty
21 Tabard Street
London SE1 4LA
Tel: 0171 403 3888 Fax: 0171 407 5354

Lord Chancellor's Department
Selbourne House
54–60 Victoria Street
London SW1E 6QW
Tel: 0171 210 8500

MIND
Granta House
15–19 Broadway
Stratford
London E15 4BQ
Tel: 0181 519 2122

Minority Rights Group
379 Brixton Road
London SW9 7DE
Tel: 0171 978 9498 Fax: 0171 978 6265

Money Advice Association
First Floor
Gresham House
24 Holborn Viaduct
London EC1A 2BN
Tel: 0171 236 3566

National Association of Citizens Advice Bureaux (NACAB)
Muddleton House
115–123 Pentonville Road
London N1 9LZ
Tel: 0171 833 2181 Fax: 0171 833 4371
(Nb – See local press or telephone directory for your local CAB or Law centre).

National Association of Racial Equality Councils
8–16 Coronet Street
London N1 6HD
Tel: 0171 739 6658 Fax: 0171 739 1528

National Council for Voluntary Organisations
Regent's Wharf
8 All Saints Street
London N1 9RL
Tel: 0171 713 6161 Fax: 0171 713 6300

National Disability Council (NDC)
The Adelphi
1–11 John Adams Place
London WC2N 6HT

National Institute for Social Work
5 Tavistock Place
London WC1H 9SN

Office of Fair Trading
Field House
15–25 Breams Building
London EC4A 1PR
Tel: 0171 242 2858 Fax: 0171 269 8800

Refugee Council
Bondway House
3–9 Bondway
London SW8 1SJ
Tel: 0171 582 6922 Fax: 0171 582 9929

Relate
Herbert Grey College
Little Church Street
Rugby
Tel: 01788 573241 Fax: 01788 535007

Solicitors Complaints Bureau
Victoria Court
8 Dormer Place
Leamington Spa
Warwickshire CV32 5AE
Tel: 01926 820082

Social Services Inspectorate (SSI)
Richmond house
70 Whitehall
London SW1A 2NS

Trade Union Congress (TUC)
Congress House
Great Russell Street
London WC1 3LW
Tel: 0171 636 4030 Fax: 0171 636 0632

UN High Commission for Refugees
7 Westminster Palace Gardens
Artillery Row
London SW1P 1RL
Tel: 0171 222 3065 Fax: 0171 222 4813

The authors are contactable at:

Dr Stephen Hardy
Department of Social Work
University of Salford
Frederick Road
Salford M6 6PU
Tel/Voicemail: 0161 295 2386 Fax: 0161 295 2378
Email: S.Hardy@social-work.salford.ac.uk

Martin Hannibal
Law School
Staffordshire University
Leek Road
Stoke on Trent ST4 2DE
Tel: 01782 294684 Fax: 01782 294335
Email: M.C.Hannibal@staffs.ac.uk

Index